AF478189

Above sea

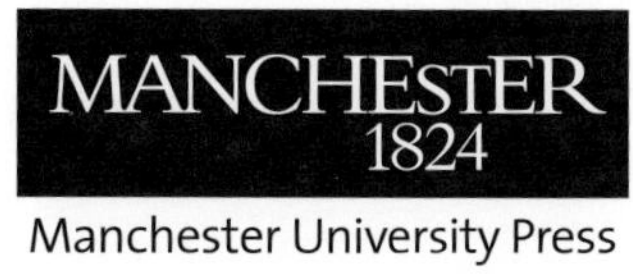

Manchester University Press

rethinking
art's histories

SERIES EDITORS
Amelia G. Jones, Marsha Meskimmon

Rethinking Art's Histories aims to open out art history from its most basic structures by foregrounding work that challenges the conventional periodisation and geographical subfields of traditional art history, and addressing a wide range of visual cultural forms from the early modern period to the present.

These books will acknowledge the impact of recent scholarship on our understanding of the complex temporalities and cartographies that have emerged through centuries of world-wide trade, political colonisation and the diasporic movement of people and ideas across national and continental borders.

Also available in the series

Colouring the Caribbean: Race and the art of Agostino Brunias   Mia L. Bagneris

Performance art in Eastern Europe since 1960   Amy Bryzgel

Art, museums and touch   Fiona Candlin

Travelling images: Looking across the borderlands of art, media and visual culture   Anna Dahlgren

The 'do-it-yourself' artwork: Participation from fluxus to relational aesthetics   Anna Dezeuze (ed.)

Fleshing out surfaces: Skin in French art and medicine, 1650–1850   Mechthild Fend

The political aesthetics of the Armenian avant-garde: The journey of the 'painterly real', 1987–2004   Angela Harutyunyan

The matter of miracles: Neapolitan baroque sanctity and architecture   Helen Hills

The face of medicine: Visualising medical masculinities in late nineteenth-century Paris   Mary Hunter

Glorious catastrophe: Jack Smith, performance and visual culture   Dominic Johnson

Otherwise: Imagining queer feminist art histories   Amelia Jones and Erin Silver (eds)

Addressing the other woman: Textual correspondences in feminist art and writing   Kimberly Lamm

Photography and documentary film in the making of modern Brazil   Luciana Martins

After the event: New perspectives in art history   Charles Merewether and John Potts (eds)

Women, the arts and globalization: Eccentric experience   Marsha Meskimmon and Dorothy C. Rowe (eds)

Flesh cinema: The corporeal turn in American avant-garde film   Ara Osterweil

Migration into art: Transcultural identities and art-making in a globalised world   Anne Ring Petersen

After-affects|after-images: Trauma and aesthetic transformation in the virtual Feminist museum   Griselda Pollock

Vertiginous mirrors: The animation of the visual image and early modern travel   Rose Marie San Juan

The synthetic proposition: Conceptualism and the political referent in contemporary art   Nizan Shaked

The paradox of body, building and motion in seventeenth-century England   Kimberley Skelton

The newspaper clipping: A modern paper object   Anke Te Heesen, translated by Lori Lantz

Screen/space: The projected image in contemporary art   Tamara Trodd (ed.)

Art and human rights: Contemporary Asian contexts   Caroline Turner and Jen Webb

Timed out: Art and the transnational Caribbean   Leon Wainwright

Performative monuments: Performance, photography, and the rematerialisation of public art   Mechtild Widrich

Above sea

Contemporary art, urban culture, and
the fashioning of global Shanghai

Jenny Lin

Manchester University Press

Published by Manchester University Press
Altrincham Street, Manchester M1 7JA

www.manchesteruniversitypress.co.uk

British Library Cataloguing-in-Publication Data
A catalogue record for this book is available from the British Library

ISBN 978 1 5261 3260 4 hardback

First published 2019

Typeset by
Deanta Global Publishing Services, Chennai, India
Printed in Great Britain by Bell and Bain Ltd, Glasgow

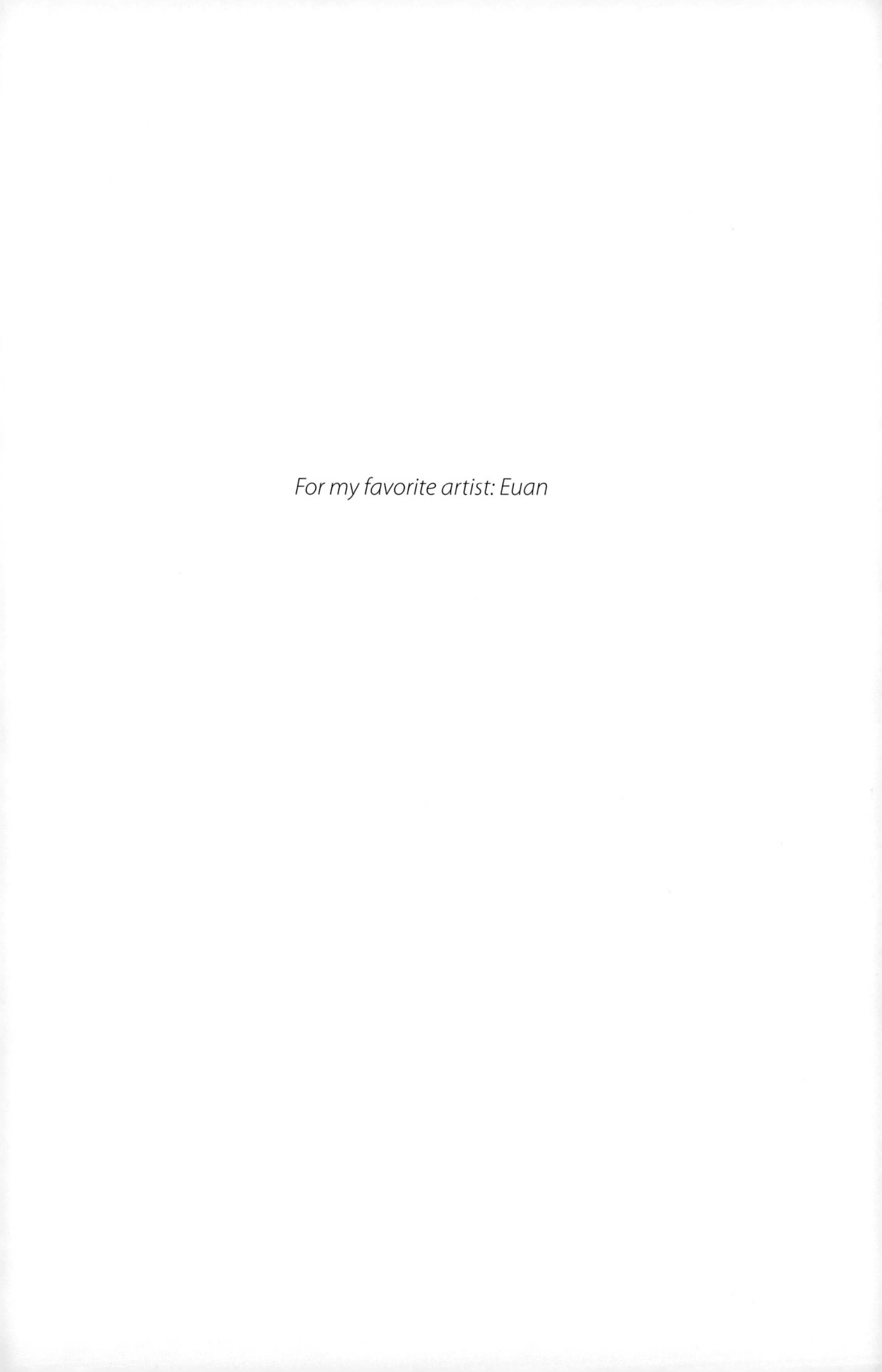

For my favorite artist: Euan

Contents

Illustrations

Figures

Every effort has been made to obtain permission to reproduce
copyright material, and the publisher will be pleased to be informed of
any errors and omissions for correction in future editions.

Preface: On naming

I think of *Shanghai* (上海) in its literal sense, as a city *above sea* (上/*shang* translates into English as *above*; 海/*hai* as *sea*). For me, this name has evoked the promise of transcending cultural divides ever since my grandfather, Yeye, spoke of the metropolis he travelled to as a youth before the 1949 founding of the People's Republic of China. "Shanghai was the most modern city in the whole Republic … full of foreign fashions, architecture, movies, police, and dancehalls … terrifying and enthralling!" The *above sea* translation took on new meaning when I visited Shanghai as a teenager—the sky in those days was full of brightly colored construction cranes. "All German cranes," proclaimed my Shanghainese aunts, uncles, and cousins, as they whisked us to the freshly constructed Oriental Pearl TV Tower of the Pudong New Economic Zone, Shanghai Museum in People's Square, and Nanjing Road with its flashing neon—sparkling signs announcing Shanghai's re-emergence as a global capital. Living in Shanghai in ensuing years, I observed those cranes swiftly being replaced by towering high-rises and increasing emphases placed on Shanghai's cultural industries amidst the Chinese Communist Party's widespread promotion of soft power.

The name *Shanghai* originated during the Northern Song Dynasty and referred to "a land on the sea."[1] Over the many years I've worked on this book, I have received multiple comments about my title, *Above Sea*. "So poetic," according to a classical Chinese painting specialist. "Awful," said an historian of modern Western European art. A reader of my manuscript wrote, "She puts too much meaning into Shanghai's name. It is after all only a name." Amidst such divided opinion, I would like to state that I am deliberately (and in a Derridean gesture) playing with the Chinese name for Shanghai and my own literal reading of its English translation. My translation of the name of Shanghai undoubtedly influences my interpretations of the city and its culture and will likely influence my English readers' interpretations as well.

When I began research for this book, I received another comment about a name, this time my own in Chinese, Zhenni (珍妮), given to me at birth by my father, Pei-teh Lin. He had migrated first from mainland China to Taiwan and then to the United States, where he adopted the English name Peter (so foreigners could pronounce it, he's prone to explain). Zhenni means *Precious Pearl* and is partially transliterated from my English name, Jenny. As such, it was deemed unsophisticated and too Americanized by a scholar of Chinese literati painting. "You should think about adopting a different Chinese name," the expert told me, as I began my fieldwork in Shanghai. At first, I considered the suggestion. I even asked the ink painter Wang Dongling, whom I interviewed at Hangzhou's Zhejiang Academy of Fine Arts, to help me devise a new name; as a result, I have one of his books signed *To Zhenyin* (珍寅). Soon after, a Chinese curator friend in Shanghai and I were talking. "Zhenni is your name!" he exclaimed, "It was given to you. Why would you want to change it?" I considered some of the figures who would appear in my book, such as the modern revolutionary writer Lu Xun, born Zhou Zhangshou, who adopted numerous pennames for fear of being found, persecuted, and prevented from writing. I was reminded of the privilege of maintaining one's name, however inauthentic it may seem. I decided to remain Zhenni not only to my Chinese family and friends but also to all those colleagues and artists in Shanghai who generously opened their homes and studios to me. This book is dedicated to them.

Note

1 Niu Ruchen, 中国地名由来词典/*Zhongguo diming youlai cidian*/*Chinese Placenames Original Dictionary* (Beijing: Central People's University Press, 1999), 106.

Acknowledgments

My dad loves telling the Chinese fable of old man Sai who lost his horse (塞翁失马/*Sai weng shi ma*). The fable illustrates how perceived loss can bring good fortune, as when Sai's horse runs away only to return with a beautiful mare. I have taken many twists and turns while writing this book, and I am full of gratitude for all those who helped transform apparent dead ends and runaway horses into unexplored paths and new modes of transport.

Firstly, I would like to thank the series editors, Amelia Jones and Marsha Meskimmon, for radically re-thinking art's histories. Amelia provided instrumental encouragement and expert counsel as I framed this project. Marsha offered insightful comments throughout the review process. I also want to thank Emma Brennan and Alun Richards for their invaluable editorial skills, and the entire staff at Manchester University Press for tireless assistance. I am very grateful to the anonymous peer reviewers who helped me write a better book, and for the institutional support that made my research possible: a University of California Pacific Rim Research Fellowship; a United States Department of Education's Foreign Language and Area Studies Fellowship; a University of California, Los Angeles (UCLA) Graduate School Dissertation Year Fellowship; Confucius Institute fellowships and grants; and University of Oregon Center for Asian and Pacific Studies grants.

My deepest gratitude goes to my PhD advisor, Miwon Kwon, for her keen intellectual guidance. I received critical input from Hui-shu Lee, an art historian hip to art, and Simon Leung, an artist hip to art history. I am further indebted to the wise teachings of George Baker, Dell Upton, Saloni Mathur, Steven Nelson, Cindy Fan, Yvonne Rainer, Theodore Huters, and the late Denis Cosgrove. Willem Henri Lucas was a dream collaborator on the related *Picturing Global China* project and is my model designer and thinker. I was surrounded by exceptionally bright classmates and collaborators at UCLA, including, amongst many, Siddarth Puri, Jennifer Flores-Sternrad, Tobias Wofford, Legier Biederman, Tom Folland, Mika Yoshitake, Ying-chen Peng, Natilee Harren, Christine Robinson, Sarah-Neel Smith, Chinghsin Wu, and Lesley Ma.

I want to thank Ann Goldstein for hiring me as her curatorial assistant at the Museum of Contemporary Art, Los Angeles, a vibrant hub for art practice and creative research, and Lisa Gabrielle Mark for gifting me her *2000 Shanghai Biennial* catalogue. I will remain forever inspired by my former mentors at Brown University: Dietrich Neumann, who gave me my first teaching assistantship in *Film Architecture*, and Massimo Riva, who introduced me to *Chung Kuo Cina*. I have learned so very much from my inimitable collegiate peers, especially Elizabeth Christensen, Margarita Almada Gutierrez, Adah Chan, Arthur Nguyen, Aiko Wakao, and Julia Otis; and from my first drawing mate, Marrikka Trotter.

I would not have been able to complete this book were it not for the support of my wonderful colleagues at the University of Oregon, and I sincerely thank Charles Lachman, Keith Eggener, Akiko Walley, Joyce Cheng, James Harper, Maile Hutterer, Kris Seaman, Nina Amstutz, Derek Burdette, Jeffrey Hurwit, Ocean Howell, Albert Narath, Charlene Liu, Rick Silva, Christopher Michlig, Dan Powell, Tannaz Farsi, Anya Kivarkis, Laura Vandenburgh, Christoph Lindner, and the late Kartz Ucci. I am especially thankful to Kate Mondloch, who has offered steadfast support at critical junctures. Anne Rose Kitagawa at the Jordan Schnitzer Museum and Xiaotong Wang at the Knight Library have provided indispensable access to artworks, resources, and ideas. I am also deeply indebted to the brilliant Jerome Silbergeld, Maud Lavin, Jiayun Zhuang, and Aynne Kokas for their sage feedback on various chapters and manuscript drafts, and for stimulating conversations at College Art Association and Association for Asian Studies conferences.

Amongst my many interlocutors within China, I would like to especially thank Gu Zheng, whose guidance brightly illuminated my research paths; Pang Tao, artist and daughter of Pang Xunqin, for her grace and generosity; Tang Sheng, who has long supported me with key connections and inspired ideas on art; Er Dongqiang and Tess Johnston, whose historical thinking added new dimensions to my research; Yang Peiming and Liu Debao, for opening their incredible collections to me; and Gu Wenda, Zhou Tiehai, Yang Fudong, Liu Jianhua, Ding Yi, Xu Bing, Cai Guo-Qiang, Victoria Lu, Li Lei, David Nieh, Benjamin Wood, Liu Tao, and Liu Jiajia, for their active presence in Shanghai's contemporary art and design developments and for helping me grasp the stakes of these fields. I am very grateful to those who connected me to the artists and artworks featured in this book: Lorenz Helbling, Helen Zhu, and Sequin Ou at ShanghART Gallery; Rose Lord, Yunsung Hong, and Junette Teng at Marian Goodman Gallery; Emily De Wolfe Pettit at Atkins & Ai Gallery; Zhang Fan, Linda Tang, and Rio He at Gu Wenda's studio; Caoyan Chen at Xu Bing's studio; Stephanie Ni at Liu Jianhua's studio; Yvonne Zhao at Cai Guo-Qiang's studio; Sydnee Wang at Minsheng Museum; Phoebe Wong at Asia Art Archive; Wu Wenxiong at Changshu Museum; Yin Jinan at the

Central Academy of Fine Arts; Qiu Ruimin at the Shanghai Oil Painting and Sculpture Institute; and Zheng Shengtian at the China Academy of Art. I also extend my heartfelt thanks to Jocelyn Liu Delgado and Jacky and Tony Liu, who first brought me to Shanghai; Adah, Tom Birbeck, Auntie Stephanie and Uncle Frank, for so kindly hosting me in their Hong Kong, Shanghai, and Beijing homes; and Echo Guan, Wang Jun, Joy Lu, Song Tao, Ji Weiyu, Lee Kit, Liu Nunu, and Liu Dudu, for all the late-night conversations and adventures.

I am so lucky to have family members who cared for me in Shanghai, Ningbo, and Wenzhou: Mingzhi, Loonwah, Xiao Ni, Jing Jian, Li Qilu, Wenzhou Aiyi, Wenzhou Shushu, Wenzhou Nini, Wenzhou Yeye, Shanghai Nini, Xiao Yeye, Ningbo Yeye, Ningbo Aiyi, Ningbo Shushu, Da Bao, and Xiao Bao. I also want to say a very special *xiexie* to my Yeye and Nini, who inspired me to learn Chinese so I could understand their stories. And to my dearest ones—Euan Macdonald, my heart and light; Heron Delin Macdonald, *wo zui hao de xiao pengyou*; Jean and Peter Pei-teh Lin, for their groundbreaking cross-cultural love; Jamie Atherton, for reminding me to wander and wonder; and Jeremy Atherton Lin, for his enduring editorial support and making me find my voice—any accomplishment would be meaningless without being able to toast it with all of you!

Notes on Chinese-to-English translations

I introduce Chinese terms through simplified Chinese characters/pinyin Romanization of Mandarin Chinese, except in some cases when I use the Chinese term or title throughout the book (e.g., *Xintiandi*). In cases when English translations are the same as pinyin (e.g., Shanghai), I omit pinyin.

In cases where cited authors use a system other than pinyin (e.g., Wade-Giles), spellings in footnotes, quotes, and main text might differ (e.g., Mao Tse-tung versus Mao Zedong).

I write most Chinese names in pinyin following mainland Chinese conventions, with surnames before given names (e.g., Ai Weiwei). When I discuss people from outside mainland China (e.g., Hong Kong, Taiwan), I employ their own local conventions and/or the names they usually use (e.g., Wong Kar-wai, David Tang, Ang Lee).

See glossary for translations of personal names and titles.

Glossary

Personal names and selected titles of artworks/films/exhibitions/texts

Ai Weiwei	艾未未
"Fuck Off"	不合作方式/*Bu hezuo fangshi*
River Crab Feast	河蟹宴/*Hexie yan*
Sunflower Seeds	葵花籽/*Kuihua zi*
Antonioni, Michelangelo	安东尼奥尼/*Andongniaoni*
Chung Kuo Cina	中国/*Zhongguo*
Cai Guo-Qiang	蔡国强
APEC Cityscape Fireworks	APEC大型景觀焰火表演/*APEC daxing jingguan yanhuo biaoyan*
"Peasant Da Vincis"	农民达芬奇/*Nongmin dafenqi*
Cai Ruohong	蔡若虹
Avenue Joffre	霞飞路/*Xiafei lu*
Ding Yi	丁乙
Appearance of Crosses	十示/*Shi shi*
Cross Bridge	十字桥/*Shizi qiao*
Fang Zengxian	方增先
"2000 Shanghai Biennale"	2000上海双年展/*Shanghai shuang nian zhan*
Feng Boyi	馮博一
"Fuck Off"	不合作方式/ *Bu hezuo fangshi*
Fu Lei	傅雷
"Xunqin's Dream"	薰琴的梦/*Xunqin de meng*

Gu Wenda 谷文达
Heavenly Lantern 天堂红灯/*Tiantang hongdeng*

Gu Zheng 顾铮
Expressions of the City 城市表情/*Chengshi biaoqing*

Hou Hanru 侯瀚如
"2000 Shanghai Biennale" 2000上海双年展/*Shanghai shuang nian zhan*

Hu Yichuan 胡一川
To the Front! 到前线去/*Dao qianxian qu!*

Hua Tianxue 華天雪
"Fuck Off" 不合作方式/ *Bu hezuo fangshi*

Li Hua 李桦
Roar, China! 怒吼吧, 中国!/*Nuhou ba, Zhongguo!*

Li Xu 李旭
"2000 Shanghai Biennale" 2000上海双年展/*Shanghai shuang nian zhan*

Liu Jiajia 刘佳佳
*The Forgotten Corner of the 城市被遗忘的角落最后的宁静/Chengshi bei
City was Quiet at Last*   *yiwang de jiao zuihou de ningjing*

Liu Jianhua 刘建华
Export—Cargo Transit 艺术出口－货物转运/*Yishu chukou—
    huowu zhanyun*

Regular/Fragile: Starlight 日常• 易碎－星光/*Richang • yisui－xingguang*
Transformation of Memories 记忆的转换/*Jiyi de zhuanhuan*
Obsessive Memories 迷恋的记忆/*Milian de jiyi*
Merriment 嬉戏/*Xixi*
Yiwu Survey 义乌调查/*Yiyu diaocha*
The Virtual Scene 虚幻的场景/*Xuhuan de changjing*

Liu Tao 刘涛
A Weak Road 脆弱的路/*Cuiruo de lu*

Liu Yuanyuan 刘媛媛
*Girl's Mind You 女孩的心事你别猜/Nuhai de xinshi bu bei cai
Do Not Guess*

Lu Xun   鲁迅
"Beijing Style and   京派与海派/*Jingpai yu Haipai*
    Shanghai Style"

Ni Yide   倪贻德
"Storm Society Manifesto"   决澜社宣言/*Juelanshe xuanyan*

Pang Xunqin   庞薰琹
Such is Shanghai   如此上海, 人生的哑谜/*Ruci Shanghai,*
    The Riddle of Life   *Rensheng de yami*
Chinese Traditional Patterns   中国传统图案/*Zhongguo chuantong tuan*

Xu Bing   徐冰
Tobacco Project   烟草计划/*Yancao jihua*

Yang Fudong   杨福东
The First Intellectual   第一个知识分子/*Di yi ge zhishi fenzi*
Seven Intellectuals   竹林七贤/*Zhulin qi xian*
    in a Bamboo Forest

Yu Youhan   余友涵
Waving to the World   向世界招手/*Xiang shijie zhaoshou*

Zhang Ailing   張愛玲
Lust, Caution   色, 戒/*Se, jie*

Zhang Huan   张洹
HeHe and XieXie   和和谐谐/*Hehe Xiexie*

Zhang Qing   張晴
"2000 Shanghai Biennale"   2000上海双年展/*Shanghai shuang nian zhan*

Zhang Zeduan   张择端
Along the River During   清明上河图/*Qingming shanghe tu*
    the Qingming Festival

Zhou Tiehai   周铁海
Will   必须/*Bixu*
Press Conference   新闻发布会/*Xinwen fabu hui*

Introduction: Locating global contemporary art in global China

At the turn of the twenty-first century, issues of globalism dominated contemporary art discourse. High-profile exhibitions like Swiss curator Harald Szeemann's "dAPERTutto/APERTO over ALL" (1999), the first group show at the Italian Venice Biennial to prominently feature artists from a multitude of nations including the People's Republic of China (PRC), South Korea, Iran, Egypt, and Cuba, charted a geographically expansive terrain. While successfully introducing previously marginalized artists into the Western European and North American-dominated canons of modern and contemporary art, such projects risked enforcing neocolonialist binaries and cultural stereotypes. Consider the watershed 1989 exhibition "Magicians of the Earth," curated by Jean-Hubert Martin at the Centre Pompidou in Paris, which framed the drastically diverse traditions of non-Western artists, such as Lamu Baiga (a shaman from the forests of Madhya Pradesh, India) and Huang Yongping (founder of urbane Chinese neo-avant-garde collective Xiamen Dada), as if all imbued with magic.[1] By contrast, the Western artists referenced in "Magicians of the Earth" (e.g., Joseph Beuys, Barbara Kruger, John Baldessari) appeared to merely play with the trope of artist-as-shaman in *civilized* postmodern jest. Not unlike large-scale international exhibitions, global contemporary art histories, such as Terry Smith's ambitious *Contemporary Art: World Currents*, group together dozens of artists from disparate backgrounds on the ambiguous bases of being contemporary (loosely defined by "qualities of freshness, recentness, uniqueness, and surprise") and popular: on the biennial circuit, featured in art magazines, represented by blue-chip galleries, fetching high auction prices—markers of art star status that feed into each other.[2] Confronted with dizzyingly crowded global contemporary art surveys, we should heed the advice of film director Wong Kar-wai, delivered to the curator of "China: Through the Looking Glass," a recent Metropolitan Museum of Art exhibition on Chinese-influenced fashions: "Try not to make the show too busy, because seeing too much is seeing nothing."[3]

As global contemporary art became an increasingly popular category, intimating art's traversal of national identifications, the term *global* simultaneously appeared within nationalist rhetoric. In relation to the PRC, *global China* (全球中国/*quanqiu Zhongguo*) has in recent years widely circulated as a patriotic rallying cry for Chinese Communist Party (CCP) cadres, a subject heading of academic conferences, and a concept proliferated in Chinese and foreign news media, generating both excitement and suspicion. The notion of a global China heralds the PRC's rise as an international power. While emphasizing external economic, sociopolitical, and cultural relations, the global China label also presumes the expansion of a singular, unified state. Like global contemporary art surveys, the global China label promises the impossible: to neatly package an immensely diverse terrain undergoing nearly unfathomable phenomena, including unprecedented urbanization and the CCP's adaptations of capitalism under a system called "socialism with Chinese characteristics." The 1989 fall of the Berlin Wall supposedly signaled the widespread victory of capitalism over communism and the end of decades of Cold War tensions. Months before that momentous event, China's Communist Party vehemently enforced its reigning power, as leaders quelled pro-democracy protests in Beijing and moved full speed ahead to develop the nation's capitalist economy. Communist/capitalist hybrids, perplexing to outsiders, abound in the PRC and are experienced to an extreme degree in the city of Shanghai, where consumers sip Starbucks lattes and shop at upscale international fashion boutiques beside a museum honoring the origins of Chinese communism.

Above sea: Contemporary art, urban culture, and the fashioning of global Shanghai intervenes into discourses of global contemporary art and global China by investigating art and design created in Shanghai and in dialogue with the city's twentieth and twenty-first-century identity as the PRC's most cosmopolitan metropolis. This book should be read as a counter-touristic guide to one of the world's fastest developing megacities, one that penetrates the contradictions and buried layers of specific locales and artifacts of visual culture. Informed by years of in-situ fieldwork, including interviews with Shanghai-based artists, designers, and curators, my research looks beyond global hype, revealing how sociopolitical tensions linked to legacies of colonialism and Maoism inform art, design, and exhibitions produced in and about Shanghai during the 1990s–2000s—the decades of the city's most rapid post-socialist development. I consider the contradictions underlying Shanghai's declaredly global cultural projects, such as *Xintiandi*, a shopping mall surrounding the site of China's first communist congress; Shanghai Tang, a company promoting contemporary Chinese art/fashion hybrids; CCP-sponsored exhibitions, namely the 2000 Shanghai Biennial and 2010 World Expo; and spectacular art installations by transnational art stars Gu Wenda and Cai Quo-Qiang. I argue that these projects erect glamorizing artifices that obfuscate Shanghai's local histories and concerns while branding the city as an international economic and cultural capital. I further look to counter-models, including avant-garde painting, subversive sculpture, curatorial interventions, and experimental video and film by Pang Xunqin, Liu Jianhua, Ai Weiwei, Zhou Tiehai, and Yang Fudong, which represent what Shanghai's glamorizing artifices mask: conflicts rooted in vying early twentieth-century notions of foreign-influenced modernity versus anti-colonialist nationalism and social anxieties associated with the city's repressed Maoist past and consumerist present. The case studies I explore all support and/or critique Shanghai's own mythologized global status, sometimes subverting dynamics of globalization (e.g., by utilizing artisanal craftsmanship) to challenge the PRC's current reputation as "the world's factory" or primary producer of foreign-designed goods (e.g., Apple iPhones, famously designed in Silicon Valley, California, and assembled in China).

While focusing on Shanghai's visual culture at the dawn of the twenty-first century, I also discuss related cultural histories of the Republican (1911–49) and Mao (1949–76) eras. My attention to these formative developments, and to exemplary design projects, serves as a mode of rethinking art's histories. Refusing to present artworks as precious autonomous objects or solely in relation to Western aesthetic traditions and theories, I situate Shanghai-based paintings, sculptures, films, and installations, many of which are explicitly tied to architecture and fashion, within the sociopolitical, economic, and mass-cultural contexts from which they emerge. My Shanghai focus stands not as a total rejection of the global turn in art history; I believe wider geographic coverage is essential in order for the field to maintain relevance. Rather, in foregrounding some of art's largely ignored histories through the kaleidoscopic lens of Shanghai, I posit an interdisciplinary mode of diversification that considers a particular segment of contemporary Chinese art in relation to its own urban legacies, however transnationally informed.

On and across seas

In English, the name of Shanghai (上海) literally translates as *above sea*, suggesting a place above borders and cultural divides. To occupy a position, *above sea*, despite implications of freedom, requires a precarious balancing act evident in Shanghai's conflicted strata—colonial architecture covered by nationalist slogans, failed negotiations between experimental modernism and state-sponsored propaganda, and dual identification as the site of China's first communist congress and a present-day shopping mecca. Within the context of colonialism, the sea has long served as a geopolitical territory and strategic passageway to foreign lands to be conquered. In light of colonial conditions, and considering recent accounts of corpses of refugees deposited onto shores, humans trafficked in shipping-cargo containers, nationalist troops guarding disputed islands, and coral reefs crumbling, the sea betrays the brutalities of mankind and the fragility of our existence.

Often employed as a metaphor for explorations of the unknown, the sea also holds a storied place in artistic and literary imaginaries. The first book translated by famed modern Chinese writer and founder of the 1930s Shanghai-based revolutionary woodcut movement, Lu Xun, was Jules Verne's 1870 French novel *Twenty Thousand Leagues under the Sea* (*Vingt mille lieues sous les mers*). Translating the novel from a Japanese version into Chinese in 1903, Lu Xun prefaced the text as his way of "introducing modern science by the back door, in the guise of entertainment."[4] A year earlier, Lu Xun had travelled from Qing Dynasty–ruled China to Japan to study Japanese language and later Western medicine. Amid Japan's rising nationalism and Pan-Asian imperialist expansions, Lu Xun found himself sitting in a Sendai Medical School class, in which students were shown images of mutilated Chinese bodies. That none of his classmates cried out reportedly sparked Lu Xun's decision to devote his life to writing, translating, and promoting anti-imperialist woodcuts inspired by politically charged European and Japanese prints. In crossing the sea between China and Japan, to this day an intensely contested and highly militarized terrain, Lu Xun witnessed the cruelties of colonial expansion while embracing artistic resistance forged through cultural exchange.

As I explore contemporary art and design in Shanghai, I integrate not only critical theories generated by present-day Shanghai-based intellectuals but also those of influential early twentieth-century figures like Lu Xun. My analyses account for the transnational experiences, production methods, and motivations of locally and foreign-trained Chinese (and, in relevant cases, non-Chinese) artists, filmmakers, curators, and designers who have fashioned, reflected, and/or critiqued Shanghai's urbanization and capitalist development.[5] Here, I myself draw inspiration across seas, from Caribbean philosopher and poet Édouard Glissant's notion of an urban-oriented "Relation Identity" as "linked not to a creation of the world but to the conscious and contradictory experience of contacts among cultures."[6] In describing the dislocation of slaves from Africa to the Americas, Glissant referred to the "depths of the sea" as an "abyss" of immense suffering, while simultaneously identifying in this abyss potential for sharing, cultural relations, and "our cry of poetry."[7] Studying Shanghai's design and art, including critical "cries of poetry," promises to resist global constructs premised on national and/or corporate agendas and the exertion of cultural, political, and economic dominance.

Mapping art's many centers

Global or world art histories written in English, even while purporting to expand the discipline's geographic limits, tend to rely on theoretical tropes rooted in Western European philosophy and art history. Read, for instance, the title of David Summers' tome *Real Spaces: World Art History and the Rise of Western Modernism*, and the book's introduction, which cites Vasari, Kubler, Panofsky, Gombrich, Hegel, Kant, Heidegger, Schiller, Lukacs, Lefebvre, Steinberg, and so on, without one mention of a non-Western writer.[8] Seeking a common lexicon that can be applied to all the world's art, Summers theorizes "real" and "virtual spaces" and poses this fundamental definition: "Architecture is the art of social spaces because it both encloses and includes institutions. … This definition embraces suburban American houses as well as Maya ritual centres or Chinese imperial capital cities."[9] Summers' examples not only register diverse cultures and spaces; they attach entirely different epochs to each culture and space, from post-Second World War US suburbs to ancient Mesoamerican centers to pre-1911 Chinese imperial cities. Such statements, while aiming to unify distant cultures, enforce the pesky binary of the modern West, or what is today called the Global North, versus the ancient and pre-modern non-West, or Global South.[10] Readers in the United States may delight in the ability to explore "real" and "virtual spaces" both in their own familiar suburban surrounds and in imperial cities as remote as those in China. Here, readers imagine the far-flung context of China as full of palatial architecture, when in reality the PRC has its own sprawling suburban developments, some of them modeled on their Orange County counterparts, not to mention ultra-modern cities filled with soaring towers, cutting-edge technologies, and thriving contemporary art scenes. World art histories proclaiming to collectively analyze diverse cultures threaten to perpetuate the colonialist model of West as center/non-West as periphery by neglecting to account for multiple contemporaneities and the differences not only *between* but *within* cultures.[11]

More rapidly than art-historical texts, exhibitions have expanded the predominantly Western European and North American field of contemporary art, primarily by introducing non-Western examples grouped by national identities.[12] Internationally traveling exhibitions including "China's New Art, Post-1989" (Hanart TZ Gallery, 1993), "Inside Out: New Chinese Art" (San Francisco MOMA, 1998), and "Art and China After 1989: Theater of the World" (Guggenheim, 2017) classify artworks based on artists' Chinese origins and the generally agreed-upon period of contemporary Chinese art: post-1989.[13] Paradoxically, numerous artists in these contemporary Chinese art exhibitions left mainland China after the 1989 Tiananmen Square events; some have returned to, and others have always lived in, Chinese cities that arguably share more with Tokyo, London, and New York than rural places in mainland China. A *New York Times* review of the most recent Guggenheim exhibition reported that many of the show's artists "reject the label 'Chinese' … [and] express mixed feelings about a nation-themed show. Most consider themselves international artists who have contributed mightily to the global avant-garde art movement."[14] "Global avant-garde art," while not explicitly defined, suggests the incorporation of certain artistic frameworks, such as conceptualism, and an ability to transcend national borders. Other recent group exhibitions have embraced even broader cultural categorizations (e.g., Asian, African, Islamic, Latin American) that, when unquestioned, become essentializing and as deceptively monolithic as the term *global* itself. For instance, curator Alexandra Munroe's exhibition "The Third Mind: American Artists Contemplate Asia, 1860–1989" (Guggenheim, 2009) problematically cast Asian cultures across time, nations, philosophical traditions, and religious affiliations as inherently mystical, populated by spiritual gurus of sage wisdom that would guide US artists dabbling in Zen Buddhism, ink abstraction, and other *Asian-y* motifs.

When faced with cultural essentialism, contemporary art historians and professionals must not abandon efforts to diversify the field but rather provide more nuanced ways of looking at non-canonical art. The current international political climate, wherein the United States and North Korea appear on the brink of war, offers a grave reminder of the need for deeper cross-cultural understanding. Some historians of art and architecture have begun tackling broad cultural categories, exposing their constructions and complexities. Michelle Antoinette and Caroline Turner's *Contemporary Asian Art and Exhibitions: Connectivities and World-making* discusses interconnected contemporaneities across late twentieth and early twenty-first-century art from diverse contexts such as those within the PRC, Japan, India, and the Philippines.[15] Antoinette and Turner bring together scholars including John Clark, Chaitanya Sambrani, Oscar Ho, and Marsha Meskimmon to effectively challenge Euro-American-dominated narratives of twentieth and twenty-first-century art while critiquing the supposed unity of Asian art. In *Hybrid Modernities: Architecture and Representation at the 1931 Colonial Exposition, Paris*, Patricia Morton probes the internal conflicts and porous boundaries between the supposedly distinct labels of *French, native, colonizer,* and *colonized*.[16] Morton's focus on Paris is especially instructive. Apparent in the current rise of sanctuary city movements, cities and networks between cities, as urban theorist Saskia Sassen observes, effectively challenge the power of nations.[17] World cities and, not coincidentally, financial centers, as art historian Julian Stallabrass argues, constitute the primary terrain for the circulation and consumption of contemporary art, while also functioning as critical sites of artistic contemplation, intervention, and resistance.[18]

Many artists today work transnationally and produce artworks most closely tied to the cities, rather than the nations, from which they spring. Consider Ai Weiwei, the best known contemporary Chinese artist outside of mainland China, and his city-specific artworks for Kassel (where he brought 1,001 Chinese tourists to "Documenta 12"), Chengdu (where he collected the names of local children killed by the collapse of shoddily constructed school buildings during the 2008 Sichuan earthquake), Beijing (where he created sculptures responding to his house arrest and imprisonment there), San Francisco (where he designed installations concerning political persecution around the world tailored to the site of Alcatraz Island), New York City (where he reflected on rising nationalism and border erections by installing fences and cage-like structures in public spaces), and Shanghai (where he orchestrated an impromptu river crab feast to protest the official demolition of his Shanghai studio).[19] Art historians in North American and Western European universities, following professionals working in museums, galleries, auction houses, and art media, have begun acknowledging China's vast field of contemporary art, canonizing contemporary Chinese artists, especially Ai Weiwei, and writing about recent Chinese artworks in relation to theories of Empire and the historic avant-garde. Ai Weiwei, whom Pamela Lee has deemed "a global artist par excellence," is the first Chinese artist to appear in Hal Foster et al.'s two-volume textbook *Art Since 1900: Modernism, Antimodernism, Postmodernism*, added with just a few others in the last entry of the second edition.[20] David Joselit writes in *After Art* that Ai Weiwei's arrest and subsequent release following international pressure suggests the political efficacy of twenty-first-century art "may lie in cultural diplomacy as opposed to the invention of avant-garde forms as new content."[21] What remains to be studied in more depth are the local urban contexts, visual cultural histories, and sociopolitical conditions that fuel and illuminate the stakes of contemporary Chinese art's international dissemination. There already exists a robust body of literature that addresses how urban landscapes shape artistic subjectivity in the modern and postmodern eras. But the geographical focus of the canonical texts—populated by Charles Baudelaire's Parisian *flâneur*, Michel de Certeau's New York pedestrian, and Fredric Jameson's dislocated wanderer in Los Angeles—underscores the need to contemplate visual culture in a non-Western European or North American city, especially in our current age, in which megacities of the so-called Global South foster immense flows of financial and cultural capital.[22]

Cultural capital

Shanghai—an international center of finance and culture and the PRC's largest city (with a current estimated population of twenty-four million)—constitutes a logical site through which to interrogate assumptions about global contemporary art and global China. The city's exponential growth at the turn of the twenty-first century resulted from the PRC's Open Door Policy and the economic reforms enacted under post-Mao-era leader Deng Xiaoping. In 1993, Shanghai annexed Pudong, a vast region comprised primarily of farmland east of the Huangpu River, as a New Development Zone open to overseas investment and less restricted trade.[23] Pudong's annexation expanded Shanghai's size by over seven times and effectively transformed Shanghai into the PRC's, and one of the world's, most powerful financial capitals.[24]

By the early 1990s, the PRC's economy, fueled by phenomenal growth in its eastern coastal cities, such as Shanghai and the first Special Economic Zone of Shenzhen, effectively competed with and soon overtook the economies of the so-called four Asian Tigers (Hong Kong, Singapore, South Korea, and Taiwan), which had achieved rapid industrialization and growth since the 1960s. The PRC claims sovereignty over two of the Asian Tigers—Hong Kong, which was officially returned from British colonial rule in 1997; and Taiwan, whose 1949 establishment as the Republic of China by the Nationalist Party remains unrecognized by the CCP. Singapore, Taiwan, and Hong Kong, while detached from mainland China as islands (with national autonomy in the cases of Singapore and Taiwan, albeit contested in the latter), share aspects of culture and language with the PRC and house millions of *overseas Chinese* (华侨/*huaqiao*).[25] The appellation *overseas Chinese* is commonly used to reference the enormous population of ethnically Han Chinese people residing in places outside of mainland China (as immigrants and/or by birth), such as Hong Kong, Taiwan, Singapore, Malaysia, Indonesia, the United States, and Canada. In the early 1990s, many overseas Chinese began coming to mainland China—for some returning home—to a landscape they would play a significant role in remodeling. Overseas Chinese entrepreneurs like Sir David Tang, the Hong Kong-born founder of fashion brand Shanghai Tang and an avid collector of contemporary art from mainland China, believed that once Shanghai broke free from decades of Maoist socialism, the city could return to and capitalize on the qualities and values of its former self. These values, presumably safeguarded in places like Hong Kong, as it developed as a consumer society under British colonialism, include an appreciation for Chinese craftsmanship and enthusiasm for more internationally minded economic innovations, such as globalized production. By the time Shanghai hosted the 2010 World Expo, an event that signaled the city's tremendous financial and cultural prowess, the PRC was considered the largest economy in Asia (ahead of Japan) and the second largest in the world, second only to the United States.[26]

Aside from achieving swift economic growth based on overseas investments and exports, Shanghai, unlike many of the world's major urban financial centers, operates not in tandem with a neoliberal democratic political system (self-governing or colonialist) but under the one-party rule of the CCP, which invests heavily not only in the expansion of Chinese cities but also in creative industries. Since the early 1990s, the CCP, with support from local municipal and district governments, has steadily sponsored numerous initiatives in Shanghai intended to flex China's soft power and the cultural capital of its largest metropolis. When I first moved to Shanghai in 2003, I knew of a few contemporary art galleries and underground art spaces, and there were two state-run modern art museums, Shanghai Fine Arts Museum in People's Square and the Duolun Museum of Modern Art, the latter of which opened during my stay.

By the time I returned five years later to begin fieldwork, Shanghai had dozens of museums, galleries, and art districts, both publicly and privately funded, all devoted to contemporary Chinese art, which was widely celebrated for its East-meets-West qualities linked to Shanghai's cosmopolitan legacy.

Spawned from the city's uneven semicolonialism of the Republican era, Shanghai's projected status as mainland China's most East-meets-West metropolis continues to resonate today. An old-fashioned relative of the global buzzword, the trope of East-meets-West abounds both in Shanghai's contemporary art scene and the wider burgeoning field of contemporary Chinese art. In the summer of 2008, amid the world financial crisis, Pace Gallery opened a branch in Beijing inaugurated by a display of Chinese paintings paired with Western counterparts, and the Shanghai Museum of Contemporary Art (MOCA) drew links between contemporary Chinese and Greek art. Shanghai's Zendai Museum of Modern Art (now Himalayas Museum) held a forum titled, "Los Angeles vs. Shanghai: Who is the Art Capital of the Pacific Rim?" demonstrating how the city's art is often placed in dialogue and even competition with Western foils, strategically utilized to promote Shanghai as an international cultural capital.[27] Meanwhile, countless media blurbs laud Chinese-born artists for combining traditional Chinese/Eastern motifs (e.g., dragons, calligraphy) with heretofore primarily Western frameworks of contemporary art (e.g., minimalism, land art).[28]

Take the Shanghai-born, contemporary international art star Gu Wenda, for whom I worked as a translator and project assistant. Gu Wenda is almost always labeled as a Chinese artist although he maintains studios in Shanghai, Beijing, and New York and lives, travels, and identifies himself as a "citizen of the world."[29] Today, Gu Wenda and the curators and critics promoting him will often speak of his unique ability to synthesize traditional Eastern elements, such as embroidery and ancient stone carving, with modern Western frameworks for art, usually referring to more conceptually inclined praxes.[30] These pairings—"traditional Eastern" and "modern Western"—fully loaded and constructed, as post-structuralist and postcolonial theories have helped elucidate, are nonetheless ubiquitously employed in the discourse surrounding modern and contemporary Chinese art, often as if they were entirely natural divisions.[31] In Chinese context, what makes oil painting modern and Western? Is it because the technique was imported from France? Did the Chinese artist, in turn, learn oil painting while studying abroad in France and if so, should she/he still be treated as a traditional Eastern artist? As art historian Michael Sullivan observed, Westernization figured more prominently for Shanghainese merchants in the early twentieth century in their embrace of imported foreign products, such as cars and radios—signs of technological progress and mass-produced status symbols of modernity—than in their support of fine art.[32] Such direct links between cultural hybridity and economic and trade ties should not be overlooked. In this vein, we might also ask, does the contemporary Chinese artist's use of traditional stone-carving techniques, even as he outsources the labor like so many heads of multinational corporations, really provide us with a glimpse of an Eastern essence? While the notion of East-meets-West continues to inform the discussions surrounding contemporary Chinese art, resonating doubly in Shanghai as mainland China's historic capital of East-meets-West encounters, the phrase is often employed as a mere marketing tool in the promotion of new objects or a convenient mode for producing fresh historical insight. What is really at stake, at least in the realm of contemporary art and perhaps in Republican Shanghai too, where artists had to negotiate between professional and literati camps, is the hybridizing of fine art and product design, seen in art's increasingly divided modes of production and promotion within an international market.

Past East and West

Today, Chinese tour books and civic promotional materials present Shanghai's glorious economic and cultural ascension as a reemergence linked to the city's illustrious international past.[33] But what is known of this past? Thrust open as a semicolonial treaty port following Britain's victory in the First Opium War (1839–42), Shanghai was subsequently forcefully occupied by British, US, French, and Japanese forces. These foreign powers carved the city into districts and concessions and imported their own governing bodies, policing systems, and economic, social, and cultural values until the communist establishment of the PRC in 1949. During China's Republican era, Shanghai sheltered numerous US and European émigrés, including White Russian and Jewish refugees, as well as Christian missionaries, entrepreneurs, and all types of expatriates. The city swiftly became known as the nation's most foreign-influenced and modern metropolis, with its modernity paradoxically connected to both the city's semicolonialism and position as progenitor of anti-colonialist communist revolution (the first meeting of Chinese communists was held in Shanghai in 1921).

In recent years, numerous scholars working in the fields of history, sociology, and Asian studies have considered how Shanghai's semicolonialism and the sociopolitical transformations of the twentieth century developed the city's distinct culture. Shu-mei Shih's *Shanghai: The Lure of the Modern*, Hanchao Lu's *Beyond the Neon Lights: Everyday Shanghai in the Early Twentieth Century*, Bryna Goodman's *Native Place, City, and Nation: Regional Networks and Identities in Shanghai, 1853–1937*, Jie Li's *Shanghai Homes: Palimpsests of Private Life*, and Yingjin Zhang's anthology *Cinema and Urban Culture in Shanghai, 1922–1943* utilize non-Western-centric approaches to provide penetrating analyses of Shanghai's modern literature, quotidian realities, vernacular architecture, and film.[34] I seek to extend these efforts as an intervention into contemporary art discourse by focusing on art and design created in Shanghai during the post-1989, so-called post-socialist, period.[35]

Shanghai-based art, absent from Western-dominated modern and contemporary art histories, also gets overshadowed within Chinese art histories by the country's more traditional cultural and political capitals like Beijing, Hangzhou, and Xi'an. Apart from important non-translated Chinese texts, such as writings by Shanghai-based scholars Gu Zheng and Zhu Dake, and English-language studies of modern art and visual culture in Shanghai, including Roberta Wue's *Art Worlds: Artists, Images and Audiences in Late Nineteenth-Century Shanghai* and Samuel Liang's *Mapping Modernity in Shanghai: Space, Gender, and Visual Culture in the Sojourners' City 1853–98*, the abundant artistic output of Shanghai, as mainland China's chief financial center, has been grossly neglected.[36] Yet it is precisely Shanghai's international economic might and the corresponding rise of its commercially driven creative industries (it was the capital of film production in the 1920s-30s and is currently pitched as the "Hollywood of China"[37]) that make a critical study of visual culture in this city so crucial today as art, now a multibillion-dollar industry, has become increasingly bound by late-capitalist modes of production and distribution.

Haipai/modern Shanghai style

In order to more fully understand Shanghai's contemporary art and design, we must probe the city's modern cultural histories, tied to its position as a semicolonial treaty port and the birthplace of China's internationally aspiring communist revolution. In *Shanghai Modern: The Flowering of a New Urban Culture, 1930–1945*, East Asian Studies scholar Leo Ou-fan Lee observes that it was in Shanghai where the English and French words *modern(e)* were first transliterated into the Chinese term 摩登/*modeng*, meaning novel and fashionable.[38] Indeed, Shanghai's modernity was intimately linked to the city's occupying forces and influences and to the foreign products that flooded the local market.

This modernity should also be understood as based on unequal power divisions. Against the rampant clichés of Shanghai as "the Paris of the East" or "the New York of the West,"[39] US-educated Chinese sociologist Fei Xiaotong wrote in 1948:

> Modern metropolises are the products of industrialization, [but] a country which has not been industrialized cannot have urban centers like New York or London. The treaty port brought about the invasion of an industrialized economy into an economically inferior area … creating a peculiar community which should not be classed with modern urban centers.[40]

The sociologist derisively characterizes Shanghai (and China's other foreign-controlled treaty ports) as economic "rat holes," where the import and consumption of foreign goods far exceeds Chinese exports, creating an imbalance based on unfair trade relations.[41] Despite these imbalances, Shanghai did have its own thriving industries; by the 1920s, a majority of the city's industrial enterprises were Chinese-owned. Nonetheless, as geographer and historian Rhoads Murphey observed, Shanghai became "the outstanding symbol of the economic exploitation of China by Western commercialism, and … the principle reminder of China's unequal-treaty status with the Western powers."[42]

Today, contemporary Shanghai-based artists and designers often claim inspiration from *old Shanghai* (老上海/*lao Shanghai*), referring specifically to the 1920s–30s, when the city bred a particular aesthetic and cultural sensibility referred to as *Shanghai style* (海派/*haipai*, literally *sea style*).[43] Differentiated from the capital of Beijing and its more traditional, dynastically rooted *Beijing style* (京派/*jingpai*, literally *capital style*), *haipai* described Shanghai's flourishing artworks and other cultural products, from opera to fashion, which combined Western European and Chinese influences and multiple forms of media (e.g., fine art, print, architecture, film). Also implicit in the *haipai* label was fine art's growing commercialism, supported by Shanghai's new private galleries and rising merchant-class collector base.

In 1934, the aforementioned revolutionary writer and cultural critic Lu Xun helped define and defend *haipai*, sketching out the major artistic and cultural differences between Shanghai and Beijing, rival cities that would continue to rise as China's largest and most powerful metropolises:

> Beijing was the imperial capital of the Ming and Qing Dynasties, Shanghai is where various foreign powers have concessions. The old capital swarms with officials, the concessions with businessmen. Thus the types in Beijing are akin to officials, those in Shanghai to merchants. Those akin to officials help officials win fame, those akin to merchants help merchants make money, filling their own bellies in the process. In a word, the sole difference between them is Beijing types are the protégés of officials, while Shanghai types are the protégés of businessmen.[44]

As described by Lu Xun, the emergence of "Shanghai types" and *haipai*, as opposed to "Beijing types" and *jingpai*, marked the monumental shift in the role of artists and intellectuals that accompanied China's 1911 transition from a dynasty to a republic. While Chinese artists were traditionally considered elite literati supported by dynastic courts, the emergence of Shanghai as a prominent cultural center at the turn of the twentieth century paved the way for a new type of artist, supported and influenced by the city's rising merchant class, foreign commodities and values, and Western European and US-imported capitalism. Traditionalists defended *jingpai* and discredited *haipai* as impure and crudely commercial. For revolutionary writers like Lu Xun, *haipai*, despite or actually because of its mercantile and outsider associations, had the potential to shape a more accessible and politically engaged art.

Scholar Chen Sihe has recently written of *haipai* as comprising two dimensions, referring, on the one hand, to Shanghai's bustling sensual life and, on the other, to the rise of Chinese working-class consciousness.[45] These distinct dimensions operate together within certain strands of *haipai* art, such as the proletarian woodcut movement spearheaded by Lu Xun. The movement aimed to raise awareness and empower denizens by promoting widely circulated prints in expressionistic and streamlined styles, as seen in Li Hua's iconic woodcut *Roar, China* (1931), depicting a man, blindfolded, bound, and struggling for a dagger, a symbol of the nation under colonialism; and Hu Yichuan's *To the Front!* which depicted an anti-imperialist uprising in the aftermath of the 1932 Japanese bombing of Shanghai's Zhabei District.[46] Unencumbered by China's deeply entrenched dynastic legacies and Confucian hierarchies, *haipai* art could more directly represent and sway the nascent Republic's pressing political concerns, including Japan's rising military aggression, civil unrest between the ruling Nationalist Party and underground communists, and economic inequalities and power imbalances between locals and European and US occupiers and their supporters. Even while engaging these national issues, *haipai*—defined in direct contrast to Beijing style and vis-à-vis Shanghai's mercantilism and Western influence—constituted a distinctly urban style that fashioned a cross-cultural model of modernity stretching beyond national categorizations long before the term *global* came into parlance.

Cross-cultural revolution

While conjured today as precursors to the city's cosmopolitan present, Shanghai's Republican-era history and *haipai* were rejected as imperialist and bourgeois by official cultural policies of the Mao era. Following the 1949 establishment of the PRC by Chairman Mao Zedong, Shanghai stood as a hotly contested landscape wherein nationalist and socialist goals collided with the city's colonial and capitalist past. In the aftermath of the Second Sino-Japanese War (1937–45), Chinese Civil War (1945–49), and over one hundred years of semicolonialism, still referred to today within mainland China as "the century of humiliation," the citizens of Shanghai—a city once carved up by foreign powers and made into the country's chief bastion of imported capitalism—felt acutely the reframing of the self-governing socialist nation. While experiments in foreign-influenced modernity abounded in Republican Shanghai, the quest to redefine China's nationhood and a unified, collective sense of the *new*—set against traditional Chinese and Western bourgeois values—dominated the city's artistic production during the Mao era.

The emphasis on establishing an entirely new culture reached its peak during the Great Proletarian Cultural Revolution (文化大革命/*Wenhua da geming*) (1966–76), a movement spearheaded by Chairman Mao, allies including his fourth and last wife Jiang Qing, and an army of Red Guards, comprised mostly of young radicalized students.[47] A 1966 issue of *Peking Review* described Shanghai's altered landscape during the Cultural Revolution:

> In this huge city which has the largest concentration of capitalists in the country and which, until the liberation, had long been under the rule of the imperialists and domestic reactionaries, the revolutionary students and the broad masses of workers and staff have taken up their iron brooms to sweep away all old habits and customs. The show windows of the Wing On Co., one of the biggest department stores in the city, are plastered with big-character posters put up by the Red Guards and workers and staff of the store, proposing that "Wing On" (Eternal Peace) should be changed into "Yong Hong" (Red For Ever) or "Young Dou" (Struggle For Ever).[48]

In February 1966, Jiang Qing held a nearly twenty-day long forum in Shanghai that established the chief principles of the Cultural Revolution's artistic policy, all of which echoed points made by Mao in his previous writings and speeches.[49] Jiang Qing advised her audience, which was comprised of People's Liberation Army soldiers, to immerse themselves fully in both politics and culture, and to rally against "black," or anti-socialist, counter-revolutionary influences, such as those, she argued, that had polluted Republican Shanghai.[50] Despite condemnations of past Shanghai-based art, Jiang Qing, reiterating a key point made by Mao, praised the literature of Lu Xun, calling him "the leader of the fighting, Left-Wing cultural movement," and advocating the writer's emphases on "truthful writing" and "the deepening of realism."[51] In contrast to this rhetoric, the ideals of the Cultural Revolution clearly broke with Lu Xun's models. In the context of the woodcut movement, Lu Xun advocated an antiheroic realism that rejected idealized figures and represented suffering individuals— "a different kind of people, not 'heroes' perhaps, but more approachable and more sympathetic."[52] Mao and Jiang Qing, however, insisted on heroic realism, proclaiming, "The basic task of socialist literature and art is to … create heroic models of workers, peasants and soldiers," and "Life as reflected in works of literature and art can and ought to be on a higher plane … nearer the ideal, and therefore more universal than actual everyday life."[53] While Lu Xun's work was relentlessly praised throughout the Cultural Revolution, many of the living artists who pioneered *haipai* were denounced and persecuted for creating bourgeois imperialist art.[54] *Haipai*'s initial artistic application and liberating promises of the 1920s–30s, the style's violent rejection during the Maoist years, and its reappearance in the 1990s–2000s hint at buried histories of imperialist inequalities and nationalist agendas, which, so long as they remain suppressed, threaten to recur—even, and perhaps especially, amid the enthusiastic embrace of global contemporary art in global China.

Cases and counter-tours

This book aims to challenge the cultural assumptions and overgeneralizations frequently made within global contemporary art histories and global China studies by focusing on art and design produced in and about Shanghai during the 1990s–2000s, the city's most intense period of post-socialist development. Rather than attempt to provide a comprehensive survey of Shanghai's contemporary visual culture, each chapter presents a set of case studies linked by particular glamorizing strategies and/or tactics of critical resistance: (1) pastiche and the idealization of *old Shanghai*; (2) hybridization and the rise of a contemporary Chinese art/fashion system; (3) biennialization-as-banalization and subversive artistic and curatorial practices; and (4) worlding and exposing the hidden tensions behind spectacular civic installations. Inspired by collage-like urban studies, such as Walter Benjamin's consideration of Parisian modernity in *The Arcades Project*, Michel Foucault's disciplinary critiques, and publications like *The Young Companion Pictorial* (良友/*Liangyou*), the most popular magazine of Republican Shanghai, my study spans art, urban culture, and sociopolitical analyses.[55] The first two chapters begin by discussing an urban design project and fashion brand, respectively, before exploring cultural histories from Shanghai's romanticized Republican-era past and the suppressed period of the Cultural Revolution. I subsequently examine related contemporary artworks and exhibitions, which serve as the primary focus of the book's latter half (though I interweave references to design, film, and Republican and Mao-era visual culture where relevant). This organization intentionally subverts conventional contemporary art histories, highlighting the importance of modern precedents and increasingly intimate relations between art, architecture, fashion, and urban design, so prevalent in Shanghai and other cities around the world.

Chapter 1 examines *pastiche* (recreating Shanghai's modernist past) in the urban development/architectural project *Xintiandi* (新天地, literally *New Heaven on Earth*) (built 1997–2002), before discussing the site's buried modern art histories marred by cross-cultural conflicts.[56] This popular outdoor shopping mall and cultural heritage complex physically surrounds China's first communist meeting site (1921), today memorialized as a museum. *Xintiandi* was designed with reference to the vernacular homes of its formerly foreign occupied French Concession setting, and it is officially celebrated for its "East-meets-West" and "Old-meets-New" architecture, even while the construction demolished most of the site's existing homes and dislocated thousands of working-class residents. I analyze how *Xintiandi*'s apparently benign East-meets-West facades mask collusions between the CCP's autocratic state power and capitalist development while romanticizing Shanghai's modern cosmopolitan legacy. I then analyze examples of *Xintiandi*'s repressed cultural histories, including leftist writings and art promoted by Lu Xun (who described Shanghai's colonial neighborhoods during the 1920s–30s, the period romanticized by *Xintiandi*'s marketers); the revolutionary art and design experiments of Pang Xunqin, founder of the 1930s avant-garde collective The Storm Society (决澜社/*Juelanshe*) (1931–35) (whose studio once neighbored present-day *Xintiandi*); and the major Cultural Revolution–era debate sparked by Michelangelo Antonioni's 1972 documentary *Chung Kuo* (中国/*Zhongguo*) *Cina* (*China*, first in Chinese and then in Italian), which features footage of the site of the first communist congress that *Xintiandi* now encompasses. I argue that the official admonishment of Shanghai-based cultural projects by Pang Xunqin and Michelangelo Antonioni speak to collisions between Shanghai's semicolonial past, Maoist socialism, and Cultural Revolution–era totalitarianism that, however repressed by *Xintiandi*, still resonate in Shanghai today.

In Chapter 2, I consider hybridization (combining traditional and modern influences, diverse media, and temporal registers) as embodied in Shanghai Tang (established 1994), a Hong Kong-founded fashion brand with a concept store in *Xintiandi*. I argue that, as in *Xintiandi*, Shanghai Tang uses pastiche and idealized references to *old Shanghai* to exploit the city's imagined cosmopolitan legacy toward the building of a multinational luxury brand. Here, I account for the rising political tensions between Hong Kong and Shanghai, as Hong Kong was handed over from British to mainland Chinese rule in 1997, and Shanghai threatened to usurp Hong Kong's position as the region's leading financial center. I analyze a 1997 Shanghai Tang advertisement featuring mainland Chinese actress Gong Li, addressing how the image signals the return of class-based society, while sanitizing the PRC's immediate socialist past. This chapter also examines the powerful influence of Shanghai Tang's founder, art collector David Tang, on the international dissemination of contemporary Chinese art, exploring key Shanghainese painters promoted by Tang, including Yu Youhan, Wang Ziwei and Ding Yi. Referencing these artists' connections to Shanghai Tang, and also the French fashion brand, Christian Dior (which held an art exhibition and launched an advertising campaign in Shanghai in 2010), I observe the rise of a contemporary Chinese art/fashion system. The final section of Chapter 2 focuses on Shanghai-based sculptor Liu Jianhua, who has been supported by both David Tang and Christian Dior, and his subversion of mainland China's presumed role as "the factory of the world" through his ceramic-based practice. I present a series of Liu Jianhua's artworks, including an assemblage of mass-produced commodities displayed at the 2006 Shanghai Biennial; sculptural installations utilizing artisanal labor in the country's historic porcelain capital and the artist's hometown of Jingdezhen; and *Export—Cargo Transit* (2007) exhibited at the Shanghai Gallery of Art, a project that comments on and harnesses the negative impacts of globalization by repackaging and exhibiting as art some of the millions of tons of trash that China imports annually from foreign nations like the United States and England. I argue that Liu Jianhua's Shanghai-based projects confront the globalization of art and the artist's own conflicted position within a transnational art world.

Chapter 3 investigates the turn of the twenty-first-century expansion of Shanghai's contemporary art vis-à-vis the first international iteration of the PRC's premier contemporary art event: the CCP-sponsored 2000 Shanghai Biennial. I begin by interrogating what I call *biennialization-as-banalization* in relation to contemporary exhibition practices and the curatorial promotion and marketing of global contemporary art, and especially contemporary Chinese art. I argue that the Shanghai Biennial's curators' hopes of harnessing the "spirit of Shanghai" were ultimately supplanted by a generic brand of art that neglected the city's unique historical features and current concerns. This chapter then examines critical responses to the 2000 Shanghai Biennial and critiques of the globalization of Shanghai's contemporary Chinese art as seen in Ai Weiwei, Feng Boyi and Hua Tianxue's counter-exhibition "Fuck Off" held in Shanghai's East Link Gallery in the Moganshan Arts District, and in two related works: Zhou Tiehai's video *Will* (1996) and Yang Fudong's multipart film *Seven Intellectuals in a Bamboo Forest* (2003–07).[57]

Chapter 4 considers *worlding*, or the city's positioning as a cosmopolitan center on an international stage, as a philosophical construct (theorized by Gayatri Spivak, Aihwa Ong, and Ananya Roy) and tangible phenomenon tied to the development and promotion of present-day Shanghai and contemporary Chinese art. I present three Shanghai-based installations: (1) Gu Wenda's *Heavenly Lantern* (2003–present), a proposal to cover Shanghai's iconic Jin Mao Tower in red Chinese lanterns as a celebration of the fusion of international architecture, modern progress, and national tradition; (2) Xu Bing's *Tobacco Project* (1999–present), a multipart exhibition commenting on Shanghai's past as mainland China's primary importer of foreign-brand cigarettes and its present as a capital of consumer luxury goods; and (3) Cai Guo-Qiang's *APEC Cityscape Fireworks* (2001), a state-sponsored fireworks spectacle honoring the Asia-Pacific Economic Cooperation (APEC) conference and heralding Shanghai as a global financial capital in the aftermath of 9/11. All three projects respond to and engage with globalization in the context of China, and specifically Shanghai, by utilizing cross-cultural content while navigating transnational networks. Disrupting the East-meets-West soundbites surrounding discussions of these works, I recognize the privileged subject positions of Gu Wenda, Xu Bing, and Cai Guo-Qiang as overseas

Chinese artists and argue that in some cases these artworks strategically function as branding campaigns that *world* Shanghai and China. The chapter also discusses the loaded cultural geographies of these installations' shared sites: the Bund, once the heart of Shanghai's British and US-controlled International Settlement; and the Pudong Skyline, considered the shining jewel of the PRC's post-socialist economic rise. I then look to a more recent project by Cai Guo-Qiang, his 2010 exhibition "Peasant Da Vincis," which acknowledges the PRC's post-socialist hidden peasant class and the migrant labor that fuels Shanghai's urbanization. "Peasant Da Vincis" critiques the concurrent 2010 Shanghai World Expo (上海世博会/*Shanghai shibohui*), which I, in turn, examine as an event underscoring the official promotion and international reception of contemporary Chinese art. The chapter finally considers the demolition of Ai Weiwei's Shanghai studio and his critical artistic response and reasserts the importance of studying twenty-first-century art in urban context.

I conclude by observing the continued proliferation of the staid East-meets-West trope within the aforementioned Metropolitan Museum of Art exhibition, "China: Through the Looking Glass" (2015). Co-organized by curators in the museum's Costume Institute and Department of Asian Art, the exhibition, which explored traditional Chinese influence on modern and contemporary Western European and North American fashion, exemplifies how claims of bridging cultures remain rooted in melding media and international business partnerships. Ruminating on the afterlives of East-meets-West exoticizations, this chapter synthesizes the preceding ones by examining the exhibition's loaded cross-cultural hybrids of art–fashion–celebrity culture and Chinese-US corporate sponsorship. I argue that "China: Through the Looking Glass" might have countered the critique that the exhibition did not adequately present contemporary Chinese culture by including some of the projects presented in previous chapters—projects that signal increasing intertwinements between art and design, including fashion; artisanal craftsmanship and mass-production; and governmental support and private commercial patronage.

Throughout this book, I investigate Shanghai's post-socialist visual culture as it represents, obscures, and fashions the global city. The ensuing case studies may initially appear to embody East-meets-West syntheses, but upon further inspection they actually illuminate frictions between local and overseas identities, uneasy relations between mainland China and purportedly more developed nations, and the stakes of contemporary Chinese art's international dissemination, challenging basic assumptions about East and West. What do Shanghai's seemingly global art and design projects promise, reveal, and disguise? To answer such questions hovering *above sea*, we must start by looking locally …

Notes

1 See Jean-Hubert Martin, *Magiciens de la Terre* [*Magicians of the Earth*] (Paris: Centre Pompidou, 1989). Huang Yongping emigrated from the PRC to France in 1989.

2 Terry Smith, "General Introduction: Contemporary Art in Transition: From Late Modern Art to Now," in *Contemporary Art: World Currents* (Upper Saddle River, New Jersey and Hong Kong: Prentice Hall, 2011), 8.

3 Wong Kar-wai in conversation with Andrew Bolton in *The First Monday in May*, directed by Andrew Rossi (New York: Relativity Studios, 2016), DVD.

4 David E. Pollard, *The True Story of Lu Xun* (Hong Kong: The Chinese University Press, 2002), 25. Lu Xun initially hoped to introduce Western medicine into China as a way to help modernize old-fashioned Chinese medical practices that he believed to be hindered by superstition.

5 Some of the Chinese artists discussed in this book were born in Shanghai (e.g., Ding Yi, Gu Wenda), but many come from different cities, such as Jingdezhen (e.g., Liu Jianhua), Beijing (e.g., Xu Bing), and Quanzhou (e.g., Cai Guo-Qiang). Most or all of them travel and/or exhibit extensively in cities around the world.

6 Édouard Glissant defines "Relation Identity" as "produced in the chaotic network of Relations and not in the hidden violence of filiation … not devising any legitimacy as its guarantee of entitlement, but circulating, newly extended … not thinking of a land as a territory from which to project toward other territories but as a place where one gives-on-and-with rather than grasps," while positing the necessity for Relation Identity in the face of urban experience: "In New York or Lagos" [and] "the shantytowns and ghettos of even the smallest cities the same gears engage: the violence of poverty and mud but also an unconscious and desperate rage at not 'grasping' the chaos of the world," Édouard Glissant, *Poetics of Relation*, trans. Betsy Wing (Ann Arbor: The University of Michigan Press, 2010), 144, 141.

7 Glissant writes further, "For though this experience made you, original victim floating toward the sea's abysses, an exception, it became something shared and made us, the descendants, one people among others. Peoples do not live on exception. Relation is not made up of things that are foreign but of shared knowledge. This experience of the abyss can now be said to be the best element of exchange. … Our boats are open, and we sail them for everyone," Glissant, *Poetics of Relation*, 6–9.

8 David Summers, Introduction to *Real Spaces: World Art History and the Rise of Western Modernism* (London: Phaidon, 2003), 43.

9 Ibid.

10 For a theorization of the Global South and the PRC's unique role within it, see Arif Dirlik, "Global South: Predicament and Promise," in *The Global South* 1, no. 1 (Winter 2007): 12–23.

11 Scholars have responded by questioning the very possibility of a global art history, but these responses are often entrenched in self-reference, as in James Elkins' multiauthored anthology, *Is Art History Global?* (New York and London: Routledge, 2006), which stems from Summers' *Real Spaces*. For fruitful

discussions of Chinese modernities and contemporaneities vis-à-vis global contemporary art discourse, see Jonathan Hay, "Double Modernity, Para-Modernity," Gao Minglu, "'Particular Time, Specific Space, My Truth': Total Modernity in Chinese Contemporary Art," and Wu Hung, "A Case of Being 'Contemporary': Conditions, Spheres, and Narratives of Contemporary Chinese Art," in *Antinomies of Art and Culture: Modernity, Postmodernity, Contemporaneity*, eds. Terry Smith, Okwui Enwezor, and Nancy Condee (Durham, NC: Duke University Press, 2008), 113–132; 133–164; 290–306.

12 For an alternative example of a contemporary art exhibition and catalogue focused on Asian cities, see Hou Hanru and Hans-Ulrich Obrist's pioneering *Cities on the Move: Urban Chaos and Global Change—East Asian Art, Architecture, and Film Now* (London: Hayward Gallery, 1999).

13 While 1945, the year of the end of the Second World War, or the 1960s usually designate the start of contemporary art in European and American contexts, 1989 generally stands as the beginning marker of contemporary Chinese art. In addition to the pivotal events in Tiananmen Square, which ended a relatively open interim reform era, the PRC continued rapid liberalization of its economy in 1989. For information on contemporary Chinese art in the 1980s and its relations to the PRC's pro-democracy movement, see, among others, Gao Minglu, *Total Modernity and the Avant-Garde in Twentieth Century Chinese Art* (Cambridge, MA: MIT Press, 2011).

14 Jane Perlez, "Where the Wild Things Are: China's Art Dreamers at the Guggenheim," *New York Times* (September 20, 2017), https://www.nytimes.com/2017/09/20/arts/design/guggenheim-art-and-china-after-1989.html?mcubz=0, accessed September 29, 2017.

15 See Michelle Antoinette and Caroline Turner, eds., *Contemporary Asian Art and Exhibitions: Connectivities and World Making* (Canberra: Australian National University Press, 2014), as well as Antoinette's *Reworlding Art History: Encounters with Contemporary Southeast Asian Art after 1990* (Amsterdam and New York: Brill Academic Publishers, 2015). For an excellent, nuanced study of modern and contemporary art in twentieth-century India, see Sonal Khullar, *Worldly Affiliations: Artistic Practice, National Identity, and Modernism in India, 1930–1990* (Oakland: University of California Press, 2015). See also Wang Hui, "Imagining Asia: A Genealogical Analysis" (2003) and David Clark, "Contemporary Asian Art and Its Western Reception" (2002), both reprinted in *Contemporary Art in Asia: A Critical Reader*, eds. Melissa Chiu and Benjamin Genocchio (Cambridge, MA and London: MIT Press, 2011), 87–106; 154–162.

16 See Patricia Morton, *Hybrid Modernities: Architecture and Representation at the 1931 Colonial Exposition, Paris* (Cambridge, MA: MIT Press, 2000).

17 For a groundbreaking discussion of powerful world cities and the networks between them, see Saskia Sassen, *The Global City: New York, London, Tokyo* (Princeton, NJ: Princeton University Press, 2001).

18 For penetrating analyses of the relations between global financial centers and contemporary art production and distribution, see Julian Stallabrass, *Art Incorporated: The Story of Contemporary Art* (Oxford: Oxford University Press, 2004).

19 For more information on Ai Weiwei's Shanghai river crab feast, see Chapter 4. Ai Weiwei's presence in the scope of research I have undertaken is nearly inescapable. Indeed, I include several of his projects in this book. However, Ai Weiwei's role here is mostly a supporting one, as I foreground less ubiquitous practitioners.

20 Pamela M. Lee, *Forgetting the Art World* (Cambridge, MA: MIT Press, 2012), 190. In addition to Ai Weiwei, *Art Since 1900* includes Zhang Huan and Wang Guangyi, all three under the heading "2010a: Chinese contemporary art," and Cao Fei under the heading, "2010b: The avatar as artistic strategy." See Hal Foster, Rosalind Krauss, Yves-Alain Bois, and Benjamin Buchloh, *Art Since 1900: Modernism, Antimodernism, Postmodernism, Volume 2: 1945–Present*, 2nd edition (New York: Thames and Hudson, 2011), 758–769.

21 David Joselit, *After Art* (Princeton, NJ: Princeton University Press, 2013), 6.

22 See Charles Baudelaire, "The Painter of Modern Life" (1863), in *The Painter of Modern Life and Other Essays*, trans. and ed. Jonathan Mayne (New York: Da Capo Press, 1986); Michel de Certeau, *The Practice of Everyday Life*, trans. Steven Rendall (Berkeley: University of California Press, 1984); Fredric Jameson, *Postmodernism, or, the Cultural Logic of Late Capitalism* (Durham, NC: Duke University Press, 1991); and other texts that read modern and contemporary art vis-à-vis particular cities, including Timothy J. Clark's study of modern art in Paris, *The Painting of Modern Life: Paris in the Art of Manet and his Followers* (Princeton, NJ: Princeton University Press, 1984); and the exhibition and catalogue on contemporary art in New York City, *Mixed Use Manhattan: Photography and Related Practices, 1970s–Present*, eds. Douglas Crimp, Lynne Cooke, and Kristin Poor (Cambridge, MA: MIT Press, 2010).

23 Hence the name *Pudong*; *Pu* refers to the Huangpu River and *dong* means east.

24 Robin Visser, *Cities Surround the Countryside: Urban Aesthetics in Postsocialist China* (Durham, NC: Duke University Press, 2010), 2.

25 Aihwa Ong has studied the importance of overseas Chinese investments, overseas/local relations, and the perceptions, within mainland China, of a cosmopolitan overseas culture, what is called *Blue Ocean culture (lanhai wenhua)*. See Aihwa Ong, *Flexible Citizenship: The Cultural Logics of Transnationality* (Durham, NC: Duke University Press, 1999).

26 For a discussion of China's economy in international context, see, among others, Charles Wolf, Brian G. Chow, Gregory S. Jones, and Scott Harold, *China's Expanding Role in Global Mergers and Acquisitions Markets* (Santa Monica, CA: RAND Corporation, 2011).

27 "Los Angeles vs. Shanghai: Who is the Art Capital of the Pacific Rim?" forum held as part of the Zócalo "Public Square" Lecture Series, Zendai Museum of Modern Art, Shanghai, 2008.

28 See, for instance, popular writing on internationally renowned Chinese-born artists Cai Guo-Qiang, Gu Wenda, Xu Bing, and Zhang Huan, who are discussed in Chapter 4 of this book.

29 Gu Wenda, interview by author, August 22, 2008, audio recording, Gu Wenda's studio, Shanghai, China.

30 Here I am thinking specifically of Gu Wenda's ongoing project *Forest of Stone Steles*, though similar artworks that utilize the stone-carving labor of expert Chinese

artisans have been produced by a number of contemporary artists, including Yang Fudong (discussed in Chapter 3) and Yutaka Sone. For a related analysis, see Chapter 2's discussion of Liu Jianhua's artworks produced in Jingdezhen, China's historic capital of porcelain production. For more general reflections on the relations between internationally recognized "non-Western" artists and their utilization of artisanal labor from "developing" nations, see Miwon Kwon, "Is it a Small World After All?" (unpublished conference paper), presented at the conference *Empire/Globe: Art in International Networks*, Yale University, Whitney Humanities Center, April 10, 2004.

31 For particularly fruitful discussions on postcolonialism and poststructuralism and their possible applications within fields of cultural studies and criticism, see Homi Bhabha, *The Location of Culture* (New York: Routledge, 1994) and Gayatri Chakravorty Spivak, "Can the Subaltern Speak?" in *Colonial Discourse and Postcolonial Theory*, eds. Patrick Williams and Laura Chrisman (New York: Columbia University Press, 1994), 66–112.

32 Michael Sullivan writes, "In China westernization was a slow and at first almost haphazard process, and until the Revolution of 1911, and the establishment of the Republic, it was scarcely reflected in art at all. Well into the twentieth century Western-style art was confined largely to the treaty ports, and above all to the French Concession in Shanghai. What went on in these enclaves was not thought of as having much to do with China, and high Chinese officials and others in positions of power ... tended to be conservative and anti-Western in cultural matters. Western railways and machine guns were one thing, Western painting—unless realistic and utilitarian—was quite another," Michael Sullivan, *The Meeting of Chinese Eastern and Western Art* (Berkeley: University of California Press, 1973), 172. See, also, the seminal survey-like exhibition catalogue, Wen C. Fong, *Between Two Cultures: Late-Nineteenth-and Twentieth-Century Chinese Paintings from the Robert H. Ellsworth Collection in The Metropolitan Museum of Art* (New York: Metropolitan Museum of Art, 2001).

33 See, for instance, Li Xin, ed., *Shanghai Glamour* (Shanghai: Shanghai People's Fine Art Publishing House, 2010).

34 See Shu-mei Shih, *The Lure of the Modern: Writing Modernism in Semicolonial China, 1917–1937* (Berkeley and Los Angeles: University of California Press, 2001); Hanchao Lu, *Beyond the Neon Lights: Everyday Shanghai in the Early Twentieth Century* (Berkeley and Los Angeles: University of California Press, 2004); Bryna Goodman, *Native Place, City, and Nation: Regional Networks and Identities in Shanghai, 1853–1937* (Berkeley, CA: University of California Press, 1995); Jie Li, *Shanghai Homes: Palimpsests of Private Life* (New York: Columbia University Press, 2015); and Yingjin Zhang, *Cinema and Urban Culture in Shanghai, 1922–1943* (Stanford, CA: Stanford University Press, 1999).

35 For theorizations of post-1989, post-socialist China, see Zhang Xudong, *Whither China? Intellectual Politics in Contemporary China* (Durham and London: Duke University Press, 2001); and Arif Dirlik and Xudong Zhang, *Postmodernism & China* (Durham and London: Duke University Press, 2000).

36 For Chinese language texts on art in Shanghai, see, among others, Gu Zheng, 城市表情/*Chengshi biaoqing/Expressions of the City* (Shenyang: Volumes

Publishing Company, 2009); and Shi Dawei's edited volume 上海中国画院/ *Shanghai Zhongguo huayuan/Shanghai Chinese Painting Academy: 1956–2004* (Shanghai: Shanghai Renmin Meishu Chuban Shi, 2005). In addition to Roberta Wue's *Art Worlds: Artists, Images and Audiences in Late Nineteenth-Century Shanghai* (Hong Kong: Hong Kong University Press, 2014) and Samuel Liang's *Mapping Modernity in Shanghai: Space, Gender, and Visual Culture in the Sojourners' City 1853–98* (New York: Routledge, 2012), see the rich anthology Jason Kuo, ed., *Visual Culture in Shanghai, 1850s–1930s* (Washington DC: New Academia Publishing, 2007); the journal article by Francesca Dal Lago, "Crossed Legs in 1930s Shanghai: How 'Modern' the Modern Woman?" *East Asian History* 19 (June 2000): 103–144; and valuable art exhibitions and (related) catalogues, including Jo-Anne Birnie Danzker, Ken Lum, and Zheng Shengtian, eds., *Shanghai Modern, 1919–1945* (Munich: Museum Villa Stuck and Hatje Cantz, 2005); Michael Knight and Dany Chan, eds., *Shanghai: Art of the City* (San Francisco: Asian Art Museum of San Francisco, 2010); and Biljana Ciric, *A History of Exhibitions: Shanghai 1979–2006* (Manchester: Centre for Contemporary Chinese Art, 2014).

37 For a recent study of Chinese-US film collaborations and related marketing campaigns, which acknowledges Shanghai's importance as a center of film production and branding, see Aynne Kokas, *Hollywood Made in China* (Berkeley and Los Angeles: University of California Press, 2017).

38 Leo Ou-fan Lee, *Shanghai Modern: The Flowering of a New Urban Culture in China: 1930–1945* (Cambridge and London: Harvard University Press, 1999), 5.

39 "Shanghai, sixth city of the World!/Shanghai, the Paris of the East!/Shanghai, the New York of the West!" So begins the frequently cited *All About Shanghai: A Standard Guidebook* (Hong Kong: Oxford University Press, 1935), an English tour book published in 1935. These catchy comparative labels epitomize the city's unique position as doubly (dis)located between "East and West." For a theorization of Shanghai's "doubly located" position, see Meng Yue's Introduction to *Shanghai and the Edges of Empire* (Minneapolis: University of Minnesota Press, 2006), which quotes the opening of *All About Shanghai*.

40 Fei Xiaotong, "Village, Town, and City," in *China's Gentry* (1948), ed. Margaret Park Redfield (Chicago and London: University of Chicago Press, 1953), 107.

41 Ibid., 105.

42 Rhoads Murphey, *Shanghai: Key to Modern China* (Cambridge, MA: Harvard University Press, 1953), 25.

43 For an insightful overview of "Haipai," see Lynn Pann, *Shanghai Style: Art and Design Between the Wars* (Hong Kong: Joint Publishing Co., 2008).

44 Lu Xun (under the pen name Luan Yanshi), "京派与海派"/"Jingpai yu Haipai" ["Beijing Style and Shanghai Style"], in 申报自由谈/*Shenbao ziyou tan* [*Shenbao Free Talks*, the Shenbao newspaper supplement] (January 17, 1934): 15. Translation is based on original text and modified from Lu Xun, "Shanghai Types and Peking Types," in *Selected Works of Lu Hsun*, vol. 4, trans. Yang Hsien-yi and Gladys Yang (Beijing: Foreign Language Press, 1959), 17–18.

45 Chen Sihe, "工人题材是海派文化的一个传统"/ "Gongren ticai shi haipai wenhua de yige chuantong" ["The Subject Matter of Workers is a Tradition of

Shanghai Style"], in 文匯报/*Wenhui bao* [*Wenhui Newspaper*] (February 25, 2013): 10.

46 In line with his beliefs, Lu Xun spearheaded the Shanghai-based revolutionary woodcut movement, aimed at fighting oppression in Republican China. For more information on the Shanghai-based woodcut movement, see Xiaobing Tang, *Origins of the Chinese Avant-Garde: The Modern Woodcut Movement* (Berkeley: University of California Press, 2007).

47 Aside from Mao Zedong, the primary group of political leaders responsible for the Cultural Revolution, disparagingly labeled as the "Gang of Four" after their denunciation and arrest in 1976, included Jiang Qing (born Li Shumeng, 1914–1991), Yao Wenyuan (1931–2005), Zhang Chunqiao (1917–2005), and Wang Hongwen (1935–92).

48 人民日报/*Renmin Ribao/People's Daily* editorial, "Guided by Mao Tse-tung's Thought: Red Guards Destroy the Old and Establish the New," *Peking Review* 9, no. 36 (September 2, 1966): 18. See also "上海天津掀起新的革命热"/"Shanghai, Tianjin xianxi xinde geming re" ["Shanghai and Tianjin Stir Up New Revolutionary Heat"], 博尔塔拉报/*Bo er ta la bao* [*Bortala newspaper*] (August 26, 1966): n.p.

49 See Jiang Qing, "Summary of the Forum on the Work in Literature and Art in the Armed Forces with Which Comrade Lin Piao Entrusted Comrade Chiang Ching," *Peking Review* 10, no. 23 (June 2, 1967): 10–16. Under Jiang Qing's art policy of the Cultural Revolution, based on Mao Zedong's watershed "Talks at the Yan'an Forum on Literature and Art" (May 1942), artists were required to align themselves with workers, peasants, and soldiers as per one of Chairman Mao's most frequently reproduced statements, "All our literature and art are for the masses of the people, and in the first place for the workers, peasants and soldiers; they are created for the workers, peasants and soldiers and are for their use," Mao Zedong, "Talks at the Yan'an Forum on Literature and Art" (May 1942), reprinted in *Quotations from Mao Tsetung* (Beijing: Foreign Language Press, 1972), 300.

50 During the "Shanghai Forum," Jiang Qing persistently repeated statements against the "black line" of art and literature: "In accordance with the instructions of the Central Committee of the Party, we must resolutely carry on a great socialist revolution on the cultural front and completely eliminate this black line. After we are rid of this black line, still others will appear and the struggle must go on. Therefore, this is an arduous, complex and long-term struggle which will take decades, or even centuries. It is a cardinal issue which has a vital bearing on the future of the Chinese revolution and the future of the world revolution," Jiang Qing, "Summary of the Forum," 11–12.

51 Ibid., 13.

52 Lu Xun, "Written in Deep Night: Introducing Käthe Kollwitz" (1936), in *Selected Works of Lu Hsun,* vol. 4, 255.

53 Mao Zedong quoted in Jiang Qing, "Summary of the Forum," 15–16.

54 For information on the denunciation and harsh treatment of artists during the Cultural Revolution, see, among others, Ellen Johnston Laing, *The Winking Owl: Art in the People's Republic of China* (Berkeley and Los Angeles: University of California Press, 1998); and Julia F. Andrews, *Painters and Politics in the People's*

Republic of China, 1949–1979 (Berkeley and Los Angeles: University of California Press, 1994).

55 For a series of fascinating reflections on *Liangyou*, see Paul Pickowicz, Kuiyi Shen, and Yingjin Zhang's *Liangyou, Kaleidoscopic Modernity and the Shanghai Global Metropolis, 1926–1945* (Leiden: Brill, 2014).

56 For a rich study of *Xintiandi*, which attends to the site's relationship to Shanghai's wider urban developments, see Samuel Liang, "Amnesiac Monument, Nostalgic Fashion: Shanghai's New Heaven and Earth," *Wasafiri* 23, no. 3 (September 2008): 47–55. See, also, Samuel Liang's "Where the Courtyard Meets the Street: Spatial Culture of the Li Neighborhoods, Shanghai, 1870–1900," in *Journal of the Society of Architectural Historians* 67, no. 4 (December 2008): 482–503, for an important foundational analysis of the architectural and urban developments within Shanghai's foreign settlements.

57 While the curators gave the exhibition its "Fuck Off" English title, the exhibition's Chinese title, 不合作方式/*Bu hezuo fangshi*, translates more closely in English to "Uncooperative Approach."

1   From the ruins of heaven on earth

New dreams for old Shanghai

In the early 1990s, Hong Kong-based development firm Shui On Land, one of the first overseas companies to enter mainland China, began devising a construction project that would radically transform a neighborhood in Shanghai's former French Concession into the city's leading commercial and residential zone. Today, the neighborhood houses *Xintiandi*, a shopping complex said to epitomize cosmopolitan Shanghai. Promising consumers a fuller life enriched by luxury goods, art, cultural heritage, international foods, and East-meets-West, Old-meets-New encounters, *Xintiandi* marks a pseudo-return to Shanghai's pre-socialist era, a time, its marketers tell us, that will inform the city's bright future. Within *Xintiandi*, there is no acknowledgment of the bloodshed leftist intellectuals endured in the 1920s–30s, though these stories are recounted with nationalist bombast in the adjacent museum honoring Chairman Mao and the first communist congress. Absent, too, are the manifold modern art histories of *Xintiandi*'s surrounding neighborhood, which in the early 1930s housed the studio of China's first self-proclaimed avant-garde art group, The Storm Society.[1] Claiming to integrate art, design, and everyday living, *Xintiandi* perversely plays out the avant-garde dreams of collectives like Shanghai's Storm Society and League of Left Wing Artists, yet the complex's convergence of art and life lacks these groups' socialist spirit, creating instead a system of total design that supports rampant privatization. In this chapter, I look beyond *Xintiandi*'s glamorizing surfaces, first to the socioeconomic conditions and political stakes surrounding the complex's construction in the 1990s–2000s, and then to examples of the site's untold cultural histories from two volatile periods that *Xintiandi* romanticizes and suppresses: the art, design, and ambivalent experiences of The Storm Society's founder, Pang Xunqin, in the 1930s, Shanghai's so-called "modernist heyday," plagued by civil war and the impending Second Sino-Japanese War; and the rise of socialist realism and ensuing debates surrounding Italian filmmaker Michelangelo Antonioni's documentary about China, made in 1972 amid Cold War tensions and the violent extremism of the Cultural Revolution. I reveal that *Xintiandi* does provide connections to *old Shanghai*, though less through the complex's recreated vernacular facades and more through the site's lingering cultural collisions and social contradictions.

Developed by Shui On and designed by US architectural firms Wood and Zapata; Skidmore, Owings, and Merrill; and the Singapore office of Japanese firm Nikken Sekkei International, *Xintiandi* comprises upscale boutiques, restaurants, hotels, and multinational chains housed in reconstructed *shikumen* (石库门) and *longtang* (弄堂)—the stone gate homes and alleyways commonly found in Shanghai's foreign districts beginning in the mid-nineteenth century (Plate 1).[2] This major urban development project included overhauling 30,000 square meters of residential land south of Huaihai Road, bounded by Taicang Road to the north, Xizhong Road to the south, Huangpi Road to the east, and Madang Road to the west. *Xintiandi* is the central node of a larger 520,000-square-meter area, Taipingqiao Zone, which includes luxury hotels and apartment towers, corporate offices, and additional retail outlets. Shui On's headquarters, housed in a steel and glass skyscraper, sits just south of Huaihai Road on Xing'an Road. Literally surrounding the historic site of China's first communist meeting of 1921, *Xintiandi* is widely celebrated as embodying Shanghai's East-meets-West and Old-meets-New character, even though the development, fueled by cutthroat capitalism, destroyed hundreds of original *shikumen* homes and displaced thousands of working-class residents. In both concept and design, *Xintiandi* exemplifies a pervasive tendency within contemporary Shanghai-based visual culture: the embrace of romantic visions of *old Shanghai*, meaning pre-socialist, Republican-era Shanghai, and the emulation of 1920s–30s *haipai* (*Shanghai style*) toward the projection of a cosmopolitan, global urban identity.

Urban development projects like *Xintiandi*, which stylistically reference certain, often mythologized facets of history toward the creation of spaces full of multinational chains promoting capitalist consumption, are pervasive in cities throughout the world. In the United States, we find romanticized references to industrial pasts and bohemian creative lifestyles deployed in the marketing of exclusive, uniformly designed apartments branded as New York "loft living,"[3] and signifiers of Mediterranean villas harkening back to the days of Spanish colonialism in outdoor Californian shopping malls/residential complexes such as the Americana at Brand in Glendale and Santana Row in San Jose. North of Shanghai in Beijing, the capital of the People's Republic of China (PRC), stands the now famous commercial hub 798 or Dashanzi Art District (大山子艺术区/*Dashanzi yishu qu*), once a sprawling Mao-era factory complex designed by East German architects and built with Soviet support.[4] In the mid-1990s, artists began converting factories at 798 into studios. These were soon followed by bookshops, cafés, and galleries, and then clothing stores and tourist stalls promoted by government officials, who evicted many artist tenants even while purporting to celebrate the site's artistic spirit and Bauhaus-inspired architecture. Like these counterparts, *Xintiandi*, with its return to *old Shanghai* style, operates as pastiche, following the cultural logic of postmodernism as detailed by theorists since the late 1980s. Marxist literary critic Fredric Jameson has notably analyzed pastiche, the imitation of preceding styles, as a primary mode of postmodernist art, literature, and design, which "expresses the inner truth of that newly emergent social order of late capitalism."[5] For Jameson, pastiche emerges from postmodernism's critique of authorship and originality—values prized under modernism. He writes, "In a world in which stylistic innovation is no longer possible, all that is left is to imitate dead styles, to speak through the masks and with the voices of the styles in the imaginary museum."[6] Jameson argues that pastiche stems either from the belief, rooted in a linear view of history, that in our current age of corporate capitalism, modernist bourgeois subjectivity no longer exists; or from the more radical, poststructuralist position that individual subjectivity never existed and was always a myth. Exemplifying historical pastiche, *Xintiandi* relies on nostalgia for Republican Shanghai toward the crafting of a popular space of consumption and the successful projection of a positive image of the city as a contemporary global capital and rightful heir to its long-standing cosmopolitan legacy.

In Shanghai's particular urban context, the embrace of *old Shanghai* also sheds light on mainland China's post-socialist (post-1989) economic system, a highly prevalent but still relatively understudied component of what we now call *late capitalism*. The entire *Xintiandi* project, as a pastiche of semicolonial and pre-socialist Shanghai, reveals how the Chinese Communist Party (CCP) no longer promotes national socialism but stands in support of a globally oriented capitalism, constituting a new and powerful union between an autocratic state and a free-market economy. *Xintiandi* is today widely celebrated for its East-meets-West and Old-meets-New architecture—hybrids that cloud the underlying conflicts between Shanghai's socialist past and a present defined by rampant consumerism. Testament to *Xintiandi*'s great popularity and financial success, since opening, the complex's chief designer, Benjamin Wood (previously of Wood and Zapata), has received invitations from municipalities throughout China to transform rundown city centers by "xintiandi-ing" (used as a verb) them.[7] Similar mixed-use complexes subsequently undertaken by Wood, such as Hangzhou's *Xihutiandi* (西湖天地, West Lake Heaven on Earth) and Chongqing's *Chongqing Tiandi* (重庆天地, Chongqing Heaven on Earth), all aim to meet the demands of a rapidly growing class of young and wealthy Chinese urbanites who, in numerous developers and investors' eyes, comprise the world's future. For Wood, *Xintiandi* signals "a very good name for China, for Chinese people; it literally means new sky or heaven and earth … but to them [the Chinese people] it means a new place, a new day."[8]

Ironically, *Xintiandi*, the construction of which destroyed hundreds of original *shikumen* homes and displaced over 8,000 working-class inhabitants, literally sprang from communist roots. The historic site of China's first communist congress of 1921 (Figure 1.1) sits sandwiched between *Xintiandi*'s "Tomorrow," its modern southern block designed by Nikken Sekkei, which is dominated by a glass-clad shopping mall, cinema, boutique hotel, and souvenir stalls; and its "Yesterday" northern block, designed by Wood and Zapata. *Xintiandi*'s "Yesterday" comprises the complex's signature terrain of partially preserved and reconstructed *shikumen* housing international shops, restaurants, and chains, such as Starbucks (Figure 1.2). To many outside observers, this arrangement marks a striking paradox: a memorial to the origins of

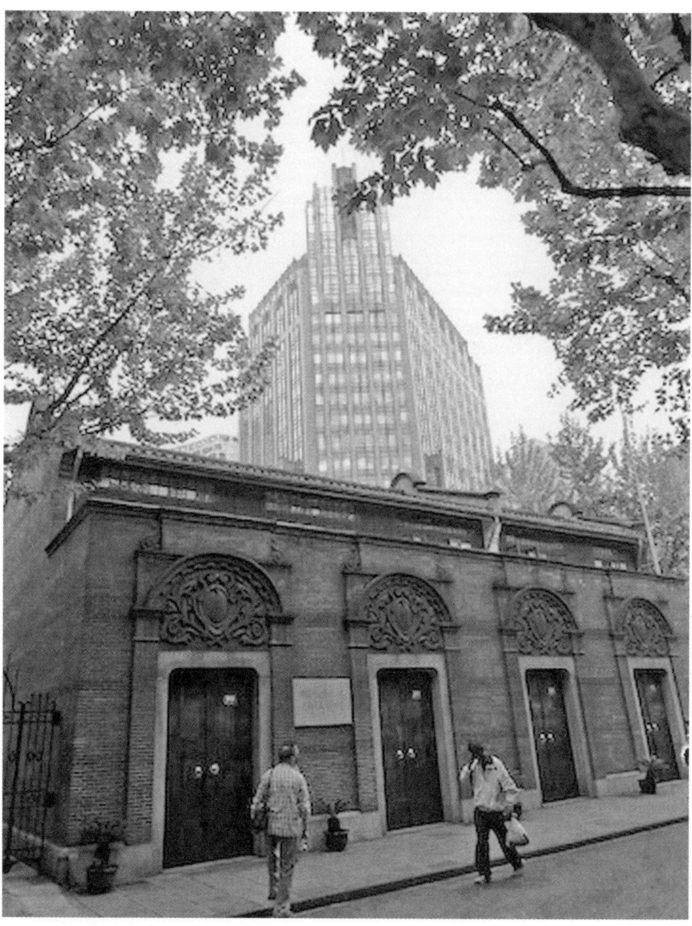

Site of China's First Communist Congress, held 1921.   **1.1**

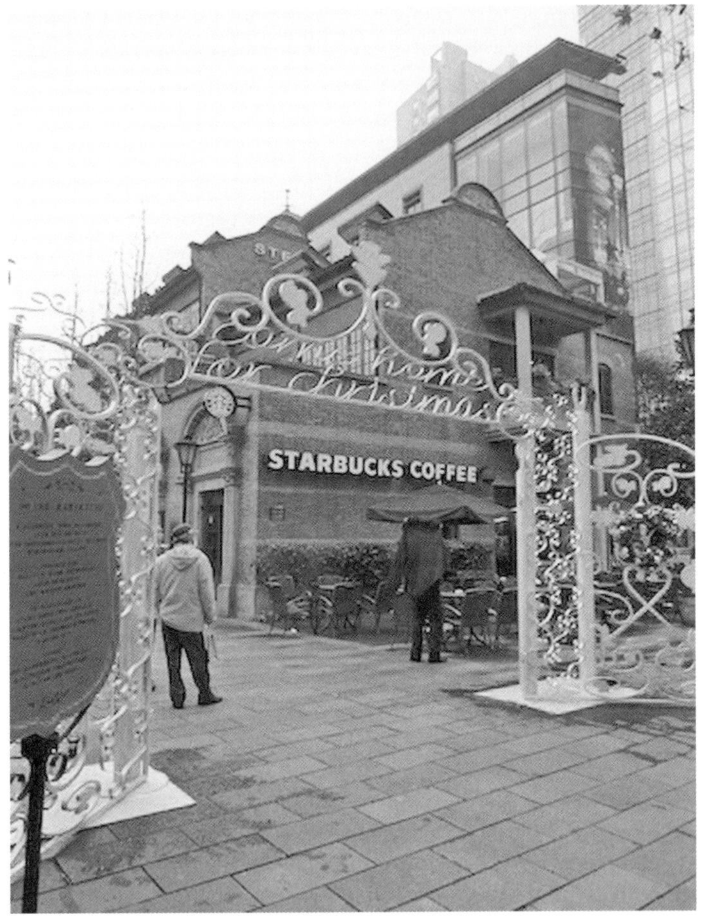

1.2   Starbucks at *Xintiandi*, developed by Shui On Land and designed by Wood and Zapata; Skidmore, Owings, and Merrill; and Nikken Sekkei International, built 1997–2002.

Chinese communism stands amid a consumerist mecca and center of unabashed global capitalism and ruthless development. For a growing number of Chinese studies scholars, however, the coexistence of free-market capitalism and China's Communist Party rule is not thought of as inherently paradoxical but as the reality of a new global order. Prominent Beijing-based scholar and cultural critic Wang Hui has described China's, and the world's, post-1989 situation in this way:

> Two worlds became one: a global-capitalist world. Although China's socialism did not collapse as did the Soviet Union's or Eastern Europe's, this was hardly a

barrier to China's economy from quickly joining the globalizing process in the arenas of production and trade. Indeed, the Chinese government's persevering support for socialism does not pose an obstacle to the following conclusion: in all of its behaviors, including economic, political, and cultural … China has completely conformed to the dictates of capital and the activities of the market.[9]

Xintiandi exemplifies this new order. While the CCP continues to pay lip service to China's socialist past, referring to its current economic system as "socialism with Chinese characteristics," it simultaneously promotes and participates in a capitalist economy and development projects, such as *Xintiandi*.

As Wood described to me in an interview, Shanghai's municipal and Lu Wan District governments, under Beijing's central state authority, granted Shui On the commission to develop *Xintiandi* on the stipulation that the developers improve the area surrounding the adjacent site of the first communist congress.[10] According to Wood, the real motivation behind this "act of social responsibility" (often obligatory for foreign companies working in China) arose from then Chinese president Jiang Zemin's planned visit to the historic site of the first communist congress, scheduled for October 1, 1999, to honor the fiftieth anniversary of the founding of the PRC.[11] In response, Shui On's plans included clearing out rundown buildings and poor tenants, landscaping a public park, and leaving intact the original site of China's first communist congress, which was revamped as a public museum, complete with wax figures of Mao and the meeting's other attendees. A didactic display inside the museum tells how the modest home served as the revolutionary breeding ground for the CCP, which would become an all-powerful governing entity over which Chairman Mao presided. As the now oft-recounted story goes, all of the meeting's attendees, who were reportedly caught and forced to continue their discussions on a boat, were eventually killed, save for Mao, who would rise to become the PRC's supreme leader. *Xintiandi's* mutually beneficial fusion of commercial development and governmental power, strengthened through historical memorialization and monumentalization, reveals that the complex's hybridity exists not simply in its East-meets-West or Old-meets-New aesthetics but also in its production of a space in which the CCP's hegemony blends together with localized gentrification and global capitalism. Posited as a beautification project that helped transmit a positive image of the site of the first communist congress and, by extension, a positive image of the CCP, *Xintiandi's* development eliminated all traces of China's failed socialist project, namely the overcrowding and squalid conditions of the neighborhood's preexisting communal-style housing.

A number of critics and scholars have recognized *Xintiandi's* promotion of a contrived hyper experience, lacking in authenticity and covering over

China's post-socialist politics of displacement. Historian of art and architecture Samuel Liang observes:

> It is not by chance that the themed shopping complex and the CCP memorial are combined perfectly at Xintiandi. Each advocates a falsified revolution: the former spatialises a playful consumer revolution, while the latter monumentalises the revolutionary history as a static ideological superstructure, contradictory to genuine revolution as a dynamic process from down below.[12]

Paul Goldberger, architectural critic for *The New Yorker*, characterizes *Xintiandi* as "a stage set of an idyllic past, created so that people in China can experience the same finely wrought balance of theme park and shopping mall that increasingly passes for upscale urban life in the United States."[13] In 2006, filmmaker Shu Haolun produced *Nostalgia*, a documentary detailing his grandmother's life in the Shanghai *shikumen* where he was raised, and which was soon to be demolished. Chinese studies scholar Robin Visser observes that *Nostalgia*'s director/narrator defends traditional Shanghai living, particularly in the face of pseudo-preservation projects like *Xintiandi*, citing Shu Haolun's lament, "If [this shikumen alley] has any chance of being 'preserved' it will only be as a Xintiandi-type yuppie place."[14] *Nostalgia* crafts a longing farewell to a fondly remembered spatial arrangement and the sense of community it bred.

It should also be noted that while many Shanghai residents carry nostalgic feelings about *shikumen* living, its communal nature and slower pace of life, others I spoke with complained of the deteriorating shared bathrooms and kitchens and cramped living quarters, preferring their lives in the city's ubiquitous modern high-rises and private flats, now housing the majority of Shanghai's denizens. Those select people who gained rapid and immense financial success since leader Deng Xiaoping's economic reforms might enjoy living in Shanghai's luxury apartment towers, like *Xintiandi*'s "Rich Gate," which represents Shanghai's most expensive real estate.[15] Wood, who was living in a penthouse apartment in "Rich Gate" when I met with him, defends his architectural design by emphasizing *Xintiandi*'s use of local materials (efforts were made to use original bricks, tiles, and timber salvaged from the demolition site) and the historical specificity of the site's architectural referents.[16] The architect recalled his appeal to Shui On's chairman, Vincent Lo, who, before selecting Wood and Zapata's reconstructed *shikumen* design, considered a proposal by Skidmore, Owings, and Merrill that would demolish every trace of all of the buildings on site and construct *Xintiandi* as a series of glass, steel, and concrete high-rises. Wood pleaded:

> Look past the obvious, the dirt, the decay, the crowded, unsanitary conditions and see [this neighborhood] as what it is, a cultural artifact that could for generations come to symbolize the meeting of East and West. ... *Xintiandi*

> is a turning point because a building type [*shikumen*] that's quintessentially
> Shanghainese took on emotional importance. *Xintiandi* made Shanghai realize
> that the greatest commodity Shanghai has is itself.[17]

Instead of reproducing the international architectural vocabulary of generic towers (which dot Shui On's greater Taipingqiao Zone) or constructing a postmodern patchwork of transhistorical and trans-geographical signs, false signifiers without referents for philosophers like Jean Baudrillard, *Xintiandi* conjures a localized history particular to Shanghai. As such, the complex embodies the cooptation of the activist tagline "Think Global, Act Local," operating on a more sophisticated level than many global chains, such as McDonald's, which originally opened at *Xintiandi* but was rumored to have been kicked out for not fitting the complex's elite identity. It is true that anything resembling a preservationist strategy was an anomaly in the overheated atmosphere of urbanization that engulfed many major Chinese cities in the 1990s–2000s. In Shanghai, it was extremely common to hear stories of entire neighborhoods being leveled, seemingly overnight, to make way for high-rises built up almost as fast as the old homes were destroyed. While some of Shanghai's most upscale hotels or financial towers incorporate postmodern flourishes that broadly reference Chinese aesthetics, such as pagoda-like crowns, the majority of high-rises in Shanghai match their low-cost, standardized concrete counterparts in cities across the globe. Furthermore, *Xintiandi*'s presence did help spur an architectural preservation movement where none had existed; the area around *Xintiandi* is now among the best preserved in Shanghai. The crux of the issue is not that *Xintiandi* neglects to account for Shanghai's urban specificity or unique past, but rather that the exclusive complex reconstructs an idealized and aestheticized past that tempers the conflicts and tensions of Shanghai's Republican era, Maoist years, and evolving CCP-controlled capitalist present.

In 2005, marketers at Shui On launched a concept-driven branding campaign aimed at promoting *Xintiandi* by connecting the complex to the "spirit of Shanghai," defined as a cosmopolitan urban identity. As one of the campaign's chief marketers earnestly told me, echoing the primary goal of historic avant-garde groups, "At Xintiandi we aim to unite art and life."[18] Supporting this campaign, Shui On began publishing *Zing* (新/*Xin*, literally *new*), a bilingual Chinese/English lifestyle magazine featuring international art, architecture, and fashion.[19] In an issue devoted entirely to *longtang* alley living, an essayist writes:

> In the old days, flirting between servants happened in the back lanes. Men
> came to reunite with wives who worked as nannies here, lingering in the back
> lane waiting, one cigarette after another. For those wandering in the city to collect second-hand copper kettles and candleholders, the back lane was the ideal
> business setting. Time has not weakened the strategic importance of the back

lane: strange faces will immediately stir up notice; sweet lovers kiss goodbye here at night; young nannies from the same hometown share family letters and photos here. Today's back lane is like a lonely island in an ocean of modern buildings, yet its strong Shanghai flavor still shapes the soul of the city.[20]

This romantic portrayal of the old French Concession's back lanes links Shanghai's pre-socialist past (signaled by the presence of servants and small businesses) to its post-socialist present. We are told that today "nannies from the same hometown" find personal connections at *Xintiandi*, forging moments of intimacy in an otherwise isolating modern city. Never mind that Shanghai's nonlocal nannies—members of mainland China's vast "floating population" of migrant urban workers who fuel post-Mao economic development—rarely frequent *Xintiandi*, the establishments of which are among the most expensive in the city.

Also related to *Xintiandi*'s branding campaign, Shui On, in consultation with architectural historians from Shanghai's prestigious Tongji University, established the Shikumen Open House Museum on the site's premises. Located in a reconstructed *shikumen*, the museum is designed to look like the private home of a bourgeois family living in Shanghai's elite French Concession during the Republican era. At the museum's entrance, wall plaques detail how dilapidated the *shikumen* homes had been before *Xintiandi*'s construction began, praising the development project for restoring the neighborhood to its *old Shanghai* glory:

> Built in the 1920s and 30s, most of the shikumen houses in Xintiandi were in a deplorable state of decay. … In these crowded and dilapidated houses lived about 2,800 families and more than 8,000 people. To salvage the city's remaining heritage houses from bulldozers, the developers, mainly the Shui On Group from Hong Kong, decided to keep the old houses as the theme of the Xintiandi Project. It made painstaking efforts to maintain the original looks of the exteriors while boldly remodeling the interiors. The result is a beautiful fusion of the old and new, appealing to people of various tastes and backgrounds. Xintiandi stands as a good example of the balance between historical protection and urban development.[21]

Predictably, the plaques do not explain that the construction project destroyed a great deal of the site's preexisting *shikumen*, while also displacing thousands of residents.

The museum's interior is staged with photographs, furniture, and daily household items, many of which are originals from the 1920s–30s (Figure 1.3). One room is modeled to look as if it had belonged to a young woman. On her vanity sit makeup containers and jewelry boxes, photographs of smiling young girls, a lamp, and an oil painting of birds. A magazine featuring a Chinese

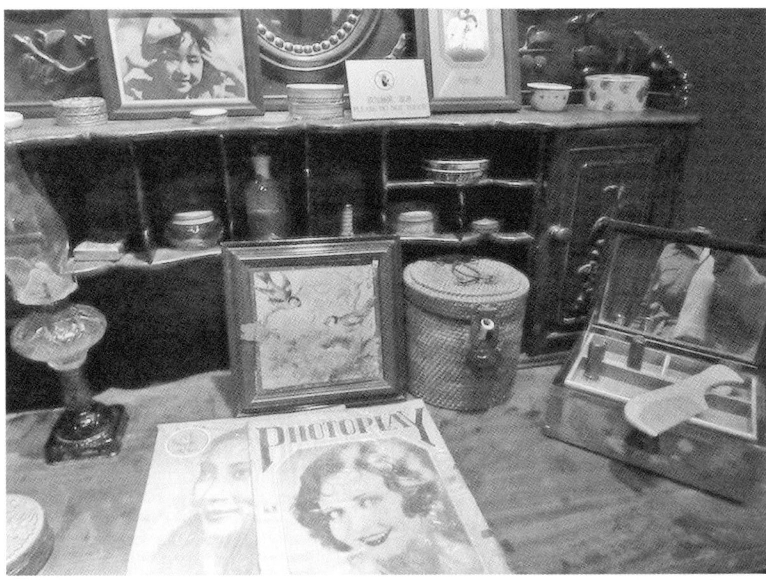

Shikumen Open House Museum at *Xintiandi*, developed by Shui On Land and designed by Wood and Zapata; Skidmore, Owings, and Merrill; and Nikken Sekkei International, built 1997–2002.   **1.3**

cover star is laid out just beneath an issue of *Photoplay*, a US film magazine featuring a Hollywood starlet. This display conjures the cosmopolitan modernity of Republican Shanghai as it was defined through the figure of the young modern woman and fashions that fused Chinese tradition and foreign influence. In contrast to the museum's lavishly decorated rooms, there is one small chamber set at the staircase's bend that contains nothing more than a modest bed, chair, and wooden desk with all the necessary tools for writing: brush, ink, and paper. A plaque tells visitors that, beginning in the early 1920s, many of the writers associated with the New Culture Movement (新文化运动/*Xin wenhua yundong*) rented out and worked in these small rooms.[22] The room is presented as the perfect private space for unencumbered creative freedom, nowhere referencing the bloody persecutions these revolutionary writers endured.

Modernist writer and art critic Lu Xun, a leader of the New Culture Movement who lived in Shanghai in the 1920s–30s, reminds us that violence and torture existed as dangerously invisible undersides of Shanghai's modernity during the period recreated by the Shikumen Open House Museum. Lu Xun wrote from Shanghai in the aftermath of the White Terror campaign of 1931–1934, when Nationalist Party forces, aided by the foreign districts' police officers, severely crippled the communists' Shanghai base by conducting over 100,000 arrests and numerous executions of those accused of leftist agitation.

He compared Shanghai's realities to Dante's *Inferno*: "I was amazed by the tortures [Dante] had conceived. But now with more experience I understand that he was kind; he never conceived of a hell so cruel that nobody can see it, which is so common today."[23] For Lu Xun, one of the most alarming parts of Shanghai's fractured social structure in the 1930s was how easily the city's poverty and violence could be hidden from view.

In 1937, Lu Xun's contemporary, League of Left Wing Artist Group member Cai Ruohong, depicted Avenue Joffre (present-day Huaihai Road—the main commercial road just north of *Xintiandi*) as a site of extreme disparity where overfed foreigners shop for imported fashions while Chinese children, reduced to the status of dogs, subsist in rags, women work as hardened prostitutes and begging mothers, and young men are violently hauled off by the French-run police force. Cai Ruohong's cartoon *Avenue Joffre* (Figure 1.4) was published in the Shanghai-based journal 天下/*Ti'en Hsia Monthly*, and it was accompanied by an article on young Shanghai-based artists whose "keen social outlook was most strongly affected by the brutalities of the Shanghai jungle."[24] The cartoon appears heavily influenced by German artist George Grosz, whose satirical sketches criticizing bourgeois Weimar culture were advocated by Lu Xun, reproduced, and circulated widely in Shanghai's journals. *Avenue Joffre* depicts a busy urban scene, showing a twisted tree recalling the imported London plane trees lining the avenues of Shanghai's French Concession, and in the foreground a woman wearing a traditional Chinese dress (*qipao*/旗袍), with a hardened stare. A foreign policeman aggressively throws someone into a truck, while a portly man carrying a parcel stands idly in the background, a destitute mother and child behind him. A scrawny boy with torn clothing and two ragtag dogs are juxtaposed against the foreigner and a store sign advertising a "SALE" in English. The Chinese boy is more closely aligned in scale to the dogs near his side than the foreigners free to play and consume in the uneven city. It is a scene recalling the oft-cited racist exclusion of Chinese people from Shanghai's foreign-run parks, seen in an early placard placed outside the British and US–run International Settlement's Bund Park, stating both "No Chinese (excluding Chinese servants of foreigners)" and "No dogs."[25] The cacophonous sketch reveals the injustices lurking below Avenue Joffre's material allures, echoing Lu Xun's descriptions of the dichotomies between Shanghai's main commercial roads and side streets:

> Walk into any lane in the residential district, and you will see buckets of nightsoil … flies swarming in all directions and children milling around, some engaged in active devilry—a microcosm of utter chaos. On the main roads, however, your eyes are caught by the splendid, lively foreign children playing—you see scarcely any Chinese children at all. Not that there are none, but with their tattered clothes and lackluster expression they pale into insignificance.[26]

Through the creation of idealized scenes, *Xintiandi* obfuscates the inequalities of Republican-era Shanghai while glossing over the economic disparities that continue to characterize post-socialist China. *Xintiandi* strategically fashions a pastiche of pre-Mao-era Shanghai that buries the site's violent struggles and problematic cross-cultural histories, while aligning the city's contemporary identity with a romanticized version of its semicolonial and capitalist past. In the following two sections, I examine case studies from *Xintiandi*'s underlooked cultural histories: (1) the work and experiences of Pang Xunqin, a Chinese artist living in Shanghai in the 1930s, the period celebrated by *Xintiandi* marketers as the city's golden age, and (2) a contentious debate

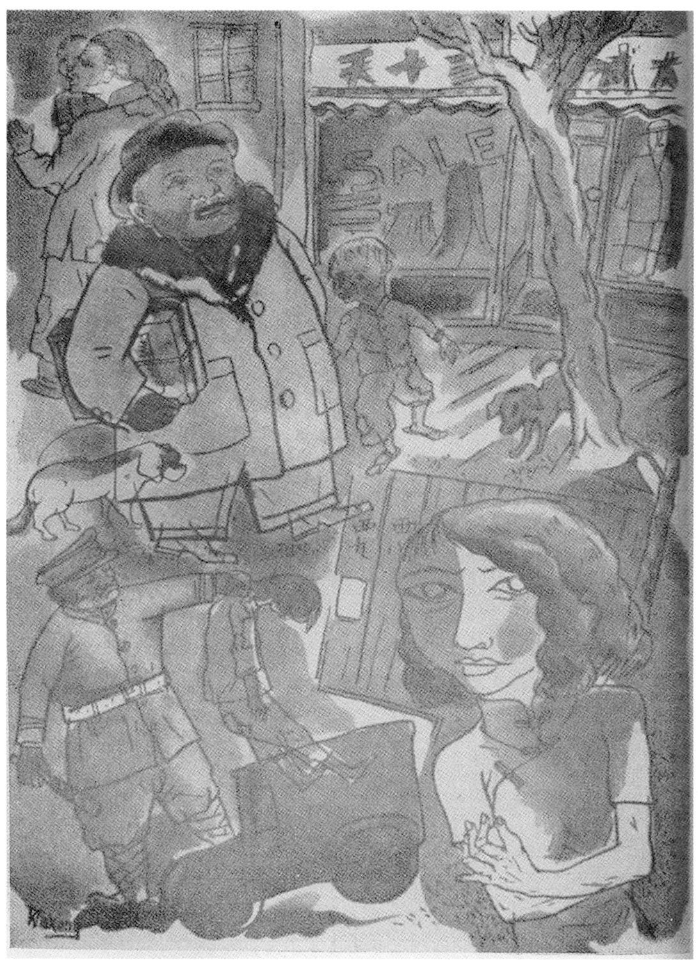

Cai Ruohong, *Avenue Joffre*, 1937. In *T'ien Hsia Monthly* 5, no. 2 (September 1937).   **1.4**

surrounding documentary footage of the first communist congress site shot by Italian director Michelangelo Antonioni in 1972 during the turmoil of the Cultural Revolution.

Buried modern art histories

In 1931, the artist Pang Xunqin had just returned to China after studying painting in Paris for five years. That year he set up the studio of China's first self-proclaimed avant-garde art and design collective, The Storm Society, at 90 Rue Marcel Tillot (present-day Xing'an Road of *Xintiandi*) in what was then Shanghai's French Concession.[27] The neighborhood comprised the vernacular architecture celebrated by *Xintiandi*—row after row of *shikumen* homes arranged in *longtang*, residential alleyways closed to street traffic. The *shikumen* homes' solid stone facades, decorated with floral bas-reliefs in classical Western European styles, opened onto central communal courtyards in keeping with both traditional Chinese residential arrangements and Western row-house layouts. Inside, the *shikumen* utilized Chinese timber roof construction, an engineering system that employed interlocking wooden beams as structural supports without the need for adjoining fixtures. While the design of the *shikumen* and *longtang* radiated a harmonious balance between Chinese and Western aesthetic motifs, the neighborhood was, in reality, an incendiary hotbed of anti-colonialist, revolutionary political activity.

The local French-run police force, aligned with the Nationalist Party, monitored The Storm Society's studio while keeping a massive file on Pang Xunqin. They had already arrested the artist once for his activities with the Société des Deux Mondes/Two Worlds Society (苔蒙画会/*Taimeng huahui*), a painting society that forged ties between the Parisian and Shanghainese art scenes, which the police suspected of leftist leanings.[28] That unobtrusive building on Rue Marcel Tillot, which has since become entirely forgotten, stood as one of Republican Shanghai's most experimental artistic centers and intensely policed sites. As described by Pang in his memoirs, The Storm Society's building was shared by a first-floor bookstore frequented by young communists questioning the role that art should play in their underground revolution. The third floor served as a rehearsal space for some of Shanghai's best-known left-wing actors and filmmakers, including director Yuan Muzhi,[29] whose 1937 film *Street Angel* narrates the plights of working-class denizens and reveals dire contrasts between Shanghai's glamorizing signs of cosmopolitan modernity and destitute slum-level realities.

Street Angel's opening credits run over urban scenes flashing in rapid succession: neon signs in English and Chinese, birds flying over the city, people strolling in a park, moviegoers, a band on parade, churches' pointy spires, fireworks, dancehalls, crowded trams, bright street lamps, the neoclassical Customs House, and the chief symbol of Shanghai's imported capitalism—a pair of bronze lions flanking the Hong Kong and Shanghai Banking Corporation on Shanghai's Bund, the city's colonial waterfront and the heart of the International Settlement.[30] Following this montage, viewers face a gleaming white Art Deco skyscraper, most likely a model of the Hamilton House or Metropole Hotel in the International Settlement.[31] The camera films the model skyscraper from top to bottom, before plunging underground; the subtitles, "The Slums of Shanghai," appear.[32] Based loosely on the 1928 Hollywood film of the same title by US director Frank Borzage, *Street Angel* portrays a young working-class woman trying to make her way in the vice-ridden city. The young woman, Xiao Hong, nearly falls victim to Shanghai's seedy underworld when her greedy adoptive parents scheme to sell her to a wealthy gangster. Xiao Hong's boyfriend and his buddies finally save her, but her older sister, who had already been forced into prostitution, ends up stabbed, freed from judgment only as a martyr. At the film's conclusion, Xiao Hong and her friends huddle around the dying sister—exemplar of the moral that one's socially imposed role does not necessarily reflect personal character. They are shown through the shabby windows of their squalid tenement before the screen fades to darkness. Viewers are transported back underground, where the narrative began, and finally return to the Art Deco skyscraper. Representing the city's modern cosmopolitan architecture as rooted in destitute poverty, *Street Angel* sharply departs from the popular modern myths of Shanghai (perpetuated by sites like *Xintiandi*) as site of harmonious East-meets-West encounters.

In line with *Street Angel's* representations, the living conditions surrounding The Storm Society's studio highlighted the city's many inequalities. While a number of foreign expatriates (businessmen and their wives, missionaries, diplomats and the like) and also wealthy Chinese compradors occupied the apartment hotels and mansions of the main boulevards of Shanghai's French Concession, the *shikumen*, densely packed down side streets, housed the far more substantial population of lower-middle and working-class Chinese families who would often share a single home with other families.[33] In addition to secret communist meetings and avant-garde art experiments, these crowded dwellings housed droves of Shanghai's Chinese citizens fleeing civil unrest and increasing incursions by Japan's military forces. As such, the *shikumen* existed in the shadows of what English author James Graham Ballard, who was raised in Republican Shanghai, described as "French built Provençal villas and Art Deco mansions," "German Bauhaus white boxes" and "English … half-timbered fantasies of golf-club elegance," together comprising a "bright but bloody kaleidoscope" where

> unlimited venture capitalism rode in gaudy style down streets lined with beggars showing off their sores and wounds … fierce street battles … between

the Communists and Chiang Kai-shek's Kuomintang forces (were) followed by frequent terrorist bombings, barely audible … against the background music of endless night clubbing, daredevil air shows and ruthless money-making.[34]

Within this volatile urban milieu, The Storm Society—co-founded by Pang Xunqin and Tokyo-educated painter and writer Ni Yide, an avid translator and promoter of French Surrealist texts—was conceived of as a radical art group devoted to "hitting the rotten art of contemporary China with a powerful wave."[35] The group maintained its headquarters at Pang Xunqin's French Concession studio, where they also tried, but failed, to establish an experimental art academy. The academy was to be styled after the Parisian academies and salons that Pang Xunqin had attended, the Académie Julien and especially the large public studio La Grande-Chaumière, where he ended up after leaving Julien over his dissatisfaction with its conservative academic training. The Storm Society's manifesto broadcasts the group's rebellious spirit, their disgust with the current state of Chinese art, and their embrace of European avant-garde predecessors, such as the Futurists, Dadaists, and Surrealists, toward their goal of creating a transgressive new Chinese art and a bold new world:

> The air around us is too still, as mediocrity and vulgarity continue to envelop us. Countless morons are writhing around and countless shallow minds are crying out. Where are the creative talents of the past? Where are the glories of our history? Impotence and sickness are what prevail throughout the entire artistic community today. No longer can we remain content in such a compromised environment. No longer can we allow it to breathe feebly until it dies. Let us rise up! With our raging passion and iron intellect, we will create a world interwoven with color, line and form!
>
> We acknowledge that painting is by no means an imitation of nature, nor a rigid replication of the human body. With our entire being, we will represent, unconcealed, our bold and daring spirit. We believe that painting is by no means the slave of religion, nor a mere illustration of literature. We will freely, and cohesively, construct a world of pure shapes. We detest all the old forms and colors, as well as all mediocre and rudimentary techniques. We will represent the spirit of a new era with new techniques. Since the beginning of the 20th century, a new atmosphere has emerged in the European artistic community, comprised of the outcries of the Fauvists, the twists of the Cubists, the vehemence of the Dadaists and the cravings of the Surrealists. … It is time for a new atmosphere to emerge throughout the 20th-century artistic community of China. Let us rise up! With our raging passion and iron intellect, we will create a world interwoven with colour, line and form![36]

The manifesto reacts to what The Storm Society members saw as stagnation in the prominent Chinese art practices of the day. While ancient masters, such as

China's most famed fourth-century calligrapher, Wang Xizhi, were celebrated for their spontaneous freehand calligraphy, most Chinese art academies by the early twentieth century required art students to copy these masters for years, often leading to, as the manifesto diagnosed, "mediocrity" and "shallow minds." The manifesto also articulates a disapproval of the importation of classical Western European notions of art as defined by mimesis and art made in the service of religion. Aligning their socially oriented goals with those of the European avant-garde groups the manifesto references, The Storm Society makes a passionate cry to inject art into life and life into art. In fact, Ni Yide and Pang Xunqin go even further than many of their Western counterparts by calling not only for the blurring of art and life but also for the making of a new world, and in particular a new nation, through their art.

Describing his philosophy of art and life in relation to Lu Xun's revolutionary art criticism and within the context of a war-ravaged China, Pang Xunqin writes:

> In front of us,
> There are still unlimited ditches as roadblocks
> They prevent us from moving forward
> In this time of necessity, I can use my own body
> To pave the ditches
> Let the future generation step on our bodies
> And quickly move forward.[37]

Pang Xunqin and The Storm Society sounded the call of an art revolution in between and in direct relation to China's twentieth-century social and political revolutions: the 1911 overthrow of the Qing Dynasty and the establishment of the Republic of China, the ensuing New Culture Movement that originated in 1919, and the 1949 Communist victory and establishment of the PRC. In 1946, amid a devastating climate wrought by China's civil war and in the aftermath of the Second Sino-Japanese War (1937–45), Pang Xunqin ruminated on the differences between Chinese and Western European art. In a letter to his friend Michael Sullivan, a pioneering British art historian of Chinese art, Pang Xunqin wrote: "I want to draw for the heavily burdened Chinese. That's why Chinese modern art will never be on the same path as French or British art."[38] In Pang Xunqin's work, it is not only the integration of Chinese and foreign aesthetics that matter, but the new hybrid art/life forms developed and revolutionary paths forged, especially as the artist critically inhabited and represented Shanghai, while developing an avant-garde strand of *haipai*.[39]

In 1931, the same year as the founding of The Storm Society and the establishment of its studio at 90 Rue Marcel Tillot, Pang Xunqin created a watercolor bearing two titles, *Such is Shanghai* and *The Riddle of Life* (Plate 2). The watercolor integrates the lessons Pang Xunqin gleaned while living in Paris, including his translation abilities. As recounted to me by his daughter, the artist Pang Tao, Pang Xunqin was fluent in French, more so than most of his Chinese artist peers.[40] His familiarity with Latin-based languages and Western customs shows in the signature "Xunqin Pang," a Romanized transliteration that reverses the standard Chinese ordering of placing one's surname before one's given name. The watercolor also integrates artistic tactics aligned with the French Surrealist artworks and writings Pang Xunqin had studied, such as the transformation of everyday objects into occult symbols, the creation of a diaphanous oneiric tableau, and the picturing of chances lost in the modern city through the figure of the enigmatic woman. Despite these nods to the current French culture, in which the young artist had just been immersed, the watercolor fashions a multivalent landscape particular to Shanghai by layering imagery associated with the city's reputation as China's most international, cosmopolitan, sexually open, and vice-ridden metropolis. Of the young women pictured in *Such is Shanghai*, two have Han Chinese features. The other, blonde and blue-eyed, has a floral crown-like detail above her head that makes her resemble a queen of hearts. Superimposition crafted through skilled watercolor technique makes the women's faces appear and dissolve all at once. They might be dancing girls (common subject matter in Pang Xunqin's oeuvre), movie starlets (like the famous Ruan Lingyu), or prostitutes (nothing shocking in a city in which one in 130 people worked in prostitution).[41] Here, we find a clue in the flower tucked behind the most prominent face in the foreground and by the petals clenched in the candle-lit fist in the painting's bottom left corner; flowers in Chinese visual culture and literature often suggested sexual availability by punning on the term *flower girl* (花娘/*huaniang*)—a Chinese euphemism for prostitute.[42] While resisting singular classifications, the women in *Such is Shanghai* all share up-to-date hairdos and cosmetics. Between these women's seductive faces emerges another of an opera performer in full stage makeup. So-called *painted faces* (花脸/*hualian*) such as these were traditionally associated with Beijing Opera, popular in Republican Shanghai, and may also have appeared in the city's own brand of opera, 沪剧/*huju*; these two theatrical forms played a key role in constructing the city's cosmopolitan culture. The watercolor's partially disguised faces—made-up women and a painted-face opera performer—alternate between disguising and being disguised by the blemishes of the city's underside. *Such is Shanghai* conjures the city's infamous underground gangster-operated mahjong parlors and casinos with a coin, a target, and Western-style playing cards that sink lightly, just like the women's faces, into the watery recesses of the paper. The entire watercolor appears as if structured around a playing card's axis, with parallel symbols occupying its opposing corners: a hand grasping a deathly dagger at the top, and a hand clutching a candle at the bottom. Along with brothels and opium dens, game rooms, by the early 1930s, housed one of Shanghai's most characteristic and ubiquitous vices. The city's commercial gambling was said to be more rampant than in any other urban center in the world.[43] Existing between fantastical and nightmarish dreamscapes, the latter made manifest in a chain of bondage bordering the woman in the bottom right and the dagger seeming to plunge into a dismembered body form, Pang Xunqin's watercolor characterizes Shanghai's new, foreign-influenced culture as glamorous and enticing on one side and menacingly sinister on the other; glimmers of quick financial gains and fleeting beauty bleed into traces of violence, drugs, unfulfilled lust, and money lost.

Such is Shanghai was exhibited in Pang Xunqin's 1932 solo exhibition at the Chinese Art Students Society on Aimay Yuxian Road.[44] On the occasion of the exhibition's opening, art and literary critic Fu Lei (1908–66) published an article entitled "Xunqin's Dream." The article postulates that artists like Pang Xunqin hold the unique ability to conjure deeply meaningful dreams, which exist outside of the "false dreams" of consumer society and help shape an improved world:

> The dreams of artists shape the environment, whereas the dreams of non-artists are false fantasies, shaped by our environment and beholden to everyday demands and distractions. We believe we are clearheaded and aware, but in reality we are seduced by today's current situation, blinded by materialism. Only artists who are outside this contemporary dream fueled by materialism, can truly know reality.[45]

For Fu Lei, Pang Xunqin's artworks create new realities, reshaping the world into a creatively charged utopia (极乐世界/*jile shijie*).[46] This utopia is not entirely imaginary; rather, it is built from the tangible urban experiences offered by the city of Shanghai.[47] By Fu Lei's estimation, Pang Xunqin, stimulated by enveloping urban enticements and repulsions, embraces all of his environment's subjects toward the crafting of dreamlike cityscapes. But what kind of dream confronts us? Fu Lei cites, among Pang Xunqin's many sources of inspiration, 妖艳的魔女/*yaoyan de monü*. This term, best translated as *bewitching seductress*, carries the connotations of a beautiful woman who is fraudulent and deceptive. More than metaphor, this figure, which takes center stage in *Such is Shanghai*, defines the artist's view of Shanghai as full of alluring but ultimately specious facades.

Pang Xunqin's relationship with Shanghai was deeply ambivalent. In his memoirs, the artist expresses his disdain for Shanghai's rampant materialism, his disappointment over the city's lack of a bohemian culture like that in Paris, and his frustration over the dearth of a sustainable interest in modern Western art. He recounts how when he first moved to Shanghai from Paris, he wore Western-style suits and hats. After realizing that in Shanghai the appetite for Western fashions and commodities far overshadowed any interest in Western art, Pang Xunqin quietly protested by swapping his Parisian-inspired fashions for simple Chinese robes, only to find himself scorned.[48] He recalls a party held in his honor and hosted by a wealthy US art collector, in which everyone, especially the Chinese servants and guests, shot him disdainful glances. The artist laments:

> Shanghai! Shanghai! For many years in France I had also worn lousy things, but never had people looked down on me as they did in Shanghai. If you go to the movie theater in Shanghai and you can't speak English, they will refuse to sell you tickets, exclaiming, "You can't understand foreign films!"[49]

For Pang Xunqin, Shanghai was consumed by shallow snobbery and status symbols like expensive clothing, modern Western clothing, and colloquial English. In defiance of the city's East-meets-West veneers and emphases on appearances, *Such is Shanghai*'s deep layers expose the threats lurking beyond Shanghai's dazzling faces.

Such is Shanghai, like so many of the artworks created in Shanghai in the first half of the twentieth century, was destroyed during the Second Sino-Japanese War, which ravaged the city.[50] The tragic loss does little to negate the revolutionary promises of *haipai* as figured by Pang Xunqin in this watercolor and others. In addition to the multilayered cosmopolitan content of *Such is Shanghai*, the work's reproduction and transnational circulation in Shanghai-based magazines such as *The Young Companion*, the city's most popular lifestyle pictorial, began to share, on a scale at once urban and international, a more complicated picture of Shanghai. Pang Xunqin's interest in design and embrace of both cultural and media hybridity supported The Storm Society's broader goal of uniting art and life. Pang Xunqin championed the European Decorative Arts and German Bauhaus movements, which he studied firsthand in Europe. He described his enchantment by the 1925 International Exposition of Modern Industrial and Decorative Arts in Paris, writing animatedly of the "beauty of the furniture, carpets, drapes and the industrial design halls. … It was then I realized, art is not only painting, everything in life needs beauty."[51] A dazzling scene of colorful electric lights reflected in the Exposition's fountain especially struck Pang Xunqin because of the lights' stark contrast to the kerosene lamps of local, poor-quality oil (and later only slightly better imported oil) that he remembered using as a boy.[52] He would come to champion the unification of art and industry, arguing that design must play a prominent role in modernizing the newly formed Republic of China. As the artist's son, Pang Jun, later wrote, "Pang Xunqin … not only brought … his artistic practice and aesthetic thinking in line with … Western modernism and the movements of Art Nouveau and Art Deco, but also recognized that 'an industrial country requires modern design.'"[53]

In 1939, living in Kunming after escaping war-torn Shanghai, Pang Xunqin embarked on an ambitious art/design project entitled *Chinese Traditional Patterns* (Figure 1.5).[54] The project came to comprise dozens of loose-leaf painted designs, which combine ancient Chinese decorative motifs with the aesthetics of Art Deco that had so struck the artist in Paris and Shanghai. The designs of *Chinese Traditional Patterns* incorporate colorful streamlined geometries and patterns culled from Chinese bronze wares of the 商代/Shang Dynasty (1700–1027 BCE) and 周代/Zhou Dynasty (1027–221 BCE), lacquers of the 春秋/Spring and Autumn Period (770–467 BCE), and stone reliefs of the 汉代/Han Dynasty (202 BCE–220 CE). The designs stand as a culmination of Pang Xunqin's intensive studies of ancient Chinese motifs, such as mythical and real animals, weapons, and masks, matched with his passion for the promises of the 1925 Paris Exposition and the Bauhaus School that he wished to emulate. Intended for application to a variety of everyday items, including lacquer trays, carpets, umbrellas, and decorative boxes, these designs were left unrealized amid war and tempestuous political turmoil. While this project has been mostly overlooked, the designs stand out as some of the most daring cross-cultural experiments of early twentieth-century China. Rather than

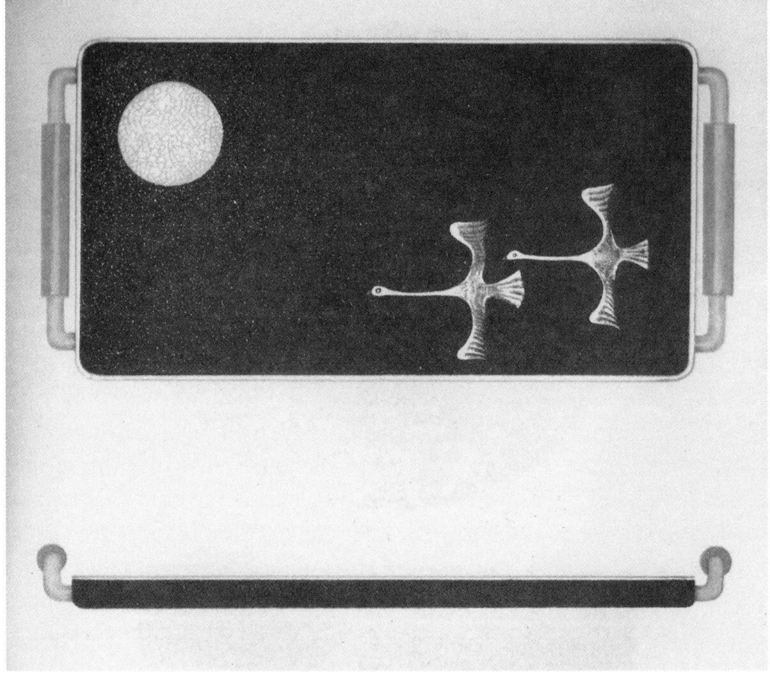

1.5

Pang Xunqin, *Long Tea Tray*, design from *Arts and Crafts Collection*, 1941. Ink on paper. 38 × 29.2 cm.

simply applying Western European art styles to the depiction of Chinese content, Pang Xunqin's designs fluidly integrate well-researched ancient Chinese motifs with international styles, such as Art Nouveau and Art Deco, which had already appeared and distinctly developed in Shanghai. As dedicated attempts at bridging art and life, Pang Xunqin's art/design hybrids should be understood as a radicalization of *haipai* aesthetics and as an extension of his work in establishing China's first avant-garde movement.

In 1956, Pang Xunqin began to realize his life's dream of the creation of an industrial arts movement in China when he helped establish the China Industrial Art Institute (中央工艺美术学院/*Zhongyang gongyi meishu xueyuan*) in the suburbs of Beijing. During the Cultural Revolution, he fell victim to an administrative struggle for power over the academy, was dismissed from his position, and was "condemned as the most 'radically anti-party rightwinger' in the Chinese art world."[55] He was not fully reinstated as a professor at the academy until 1979. Designing *Xintiandi* as a picturesque after-image of *old Shanghai* erases the stories of artists like Pang Xunqin, who once haunted the streets on which the complex now sits. *Xintiandi* further obscures the volatile climate of China's and Shanghai's more immediate socialist past, especially the decade of the Cultural Revolution (1966–76), when many artists were labeled as bourgeois rightists, exiled, publicly ridiculed, beaten, and forced to destroy their works by their own hands.

Realities of cultural collision

In the mid-1960s, students began seizing control of established art academies, while young Red Guard artists, with the support of officials, established new art schools throughout the PRC. In 1966, a Catholic cathedral not far from China's first communist meeting site and the bygone Storm Society studio was converted into the campus of the Shanghai Oil Painting and Sculpture Workshop, the city's most active art institution during the 1960s–70s.[56] The Workshop produced art in the officially mandated style of the Cultural Revolution—heroic socialist realism based on the Soviet Union's Stalinist model—which exalted the primary subjects of Mao and peasants, workers, and soldiers through grand stature, idealized musculature, rosy cheeks, and bold postures usually set amid bright color palettes and in monumentally scaled compositions.[57] In 1968, Workshop artists erected the public mural *Portrait of Chairman Mao throughout the Ages* (毛主席各个时期的肖像/*Mao zhuxi gege shiqi de xiaoxiang*) at Huaihai Road. The multipanel mural heroically depicted Mao in eight key moments of his life, including his leadership during the Long March—a 1934 military retreat in which the CCP's Red Army successfully escaped an attack from Nationalist Party forces—and his 1949 speech at the PRC's founding ceremony in Beijing. All the portraits were adapted from pre-existing photographs and/or paintings. Under each portrait appeared a quote culled from Mao's philosophical writings and poems, reproduced in the leader's ubiquitously published calligraphy. A handwritten slogan at the top of the mural read: "To be sure, a complete collapse of colonialism, imperialism, and all systems of exploitation, the complete rising up of the world's oppressed people, and the complete emancipation of all oppressed nations, is not far off."[58] In using extant materials to collaboratively produce the explicitly political public mural, Workshop artists followed Mao's cultural directive, rejecting "art for art's sake."[59] The mural on Huaihai Road offered just one glimpse of the city's pervasive surface-level transformations.

In line with the values of the Cultural Revolution, including the purported aim of eliminating China's *four olds* (四旧/*si jiu*) (old ideas, old customs, old habits, and old culture), Shanghai became a target of attack. Even while celebrating the city's legacy as the origin site of Chinese communism and a hotbed of left-wing literature and art in the 1920s–30s, CCP officials and Red Guards decried Shanghai's historic position as primary seat of semicolonial occupation and imperialist corruption. By 1966, the condemnation of Shanghai's decadent past had reached a powerful crescendo, and the city was aggressively, visibly transformed. Protestors plastered over foreign street signs, centers of material consumption, colonial-style architecture, and any facade that served as a reminder of Shanghai's imperialist, bourgeois past. Statements about Chinese communism, which had in the first half of the twentieth century existed only as hushed murmurs and idealistic dreams, became codified into slogans, such as *Long Live Chairman Mao* (毛主席万岁/*Mao zhuxi wansui*). A number of Shanghai's most iconic buildings of the formerly British and US–run International Settlement were covered in large red flags and banners celebrating Mao, the CCP, and the Cultural Revolution, and decrying imperialism, especially Japanese and US military aggression. Large-scale public murals like *Portrait of Chairman Mao throughout the Ages* and others portraying heroic revolutionaries saturated the landscape, as did *big character posters* (大字报/*dazibao*)—bold posters handwritten in easily legible characters, which denounced feudalist and colonialist culture and criticized individuals suspected of counter-revolutionary activities.[60] As local documentary photographer and historian Er Dongqiang recalled from his childhood spent in Shanghai during the Cultural Revolution, "The city could be characterized by a literal veiling over of its internationalist past."[61]

Amid the nationalist extremism of the Cultural Revolution, Chinese premier Zhou Enlai (a more moderate politician than Mao) offered Italian filmmaker Michelangelo Antonioni the rare opportunity to make a documentary in and about the PRC. The resultant film, *Chung Kuo Cina* (hereafter *Chung Kuo*), comprises 220 minutes of footage divided geographically into five locations where the director and his crew were brought over the course of five weeks: Beijing, Linxian County in Hunan Province, Suzhou, Nanjing, and Shanghai, where Antonioni visited the site of the first communist congress beside present-day *Xintiandi*.[62] According to cultural critic Umberto Eco, the documentary's airing on Italian television in 1973 "manifested … an act of justice on TV's part which revealed to millions of viewers a true China, human and peaceful outside of the western propagandistic schema."[63] Eco reasoned that *Chung Kuo* provided a humane portrait of China during a time when Cold War tensions were high and anti-Chinese news stories were prevalent in Western Europe and North America. In China, however, Mao, Jiang Qing, and their allies who led the Cultural Revolution denounced *Chung Kuo* as anti-socialist slander and banned its release. In 1977, *Chung Kuo* instigated another diplomatic debacle when a number of CCP officials, supported by some local Italian bureaucrats, almost succeeded in halting the film's planned screening at the Venice Biennial.[64] The Chinese government had tightly controlled Antonioni's access to locations and activities for shooting. Schoolchildren singing, historical monuments, state-of-the-art factories, and engineering feats mark some of the state's preferred *mise-en-scènes*.[65] Nonetheless, the director, through his focus on mundane moments, intimate gestures, and the particularities of personal presence, unwittingly acted against governmental wishes.[66] Unlike in the official heroic socialist-realist art of the Cultural Revolution, marked by idealized industrial land-scapes and aggrandized peasants, workers, and soldiers, *Chung Kuo* focuses instead on everyday details: ordinary individuals, empty rooms, mud-brick homes.[67] The realism with which Antonioni hoped to show Chinese social-ism was condemned as undercutting socialist progress, and the documentary was censured as a bombastic attack on the country and its people. In reflect-ing on the documentary project, Zhu Qiansheng, one of Antonioni's guides in Shanghai, reported the following: "It struck me that he was filming a lot of bad things. Things that reflected our backwardness. … [Antonioni] said, 'Everything I've seen is very good! What do you think is not good?' … Our standards were so different."[68] In filming those "bad things" that were officially excluded from the frames of China's Cultural Revolution–era documentaries, films, and artworks, Antonioni created a rare visual archive of everyday life under Maoist communism in 1972. The controversy surrounding *Chung Kuo*, and especially its Shanghai footage and that of the first communist congress site, reveals the tense cross-cultural circumstances of the Cold War, a period when Chinese communism and socialism violently collided with Western European individualism and capitalism.

Chung Kuo's Shanghai segment begins at the Bund—the city's Huangpu Riverfront and the former heart of the British and US-run International Settlement. Featured in *Street Angel*'s opening montage sequence, described in the previous section, the Bund is lined with monumental colonial-style build-ings, such as the old Hong Kong and Shanghai Banking Corporation (1923) and Customs House (1927) designed by British firm Palmer and Turner.

Chung Kuo's narrator, Italian news journalist Andrea Barbato, delivers this introduction:

> Ten million inhabitants, the second city of the world. The name of Shanghai evokes crime, drugs, corruption. But if Peking [Beijing] is the capital of pure revolution, Shanghai is the city of struggle and of the most evident transformation. In the space of only one generation, Shanghai changed with a profound turn around. The houses of the Western economic empires, which had their own concessions and general neighborhoods, are now public offices. The ex-slaves became an immense class of workers, who were the protagonists in the Chinese revolution in this half a century.[69]

Antonioni presents Shanghai, because of its semicolonial past, as the Chinese city that has undergone the most tremendous change since the communist takeover, and, in contrast with Beijing, a site of conflicted struggle as opposed to one of "pure revolution." In line with the Cultural Revolution's ideological position, Antonioni identifies Chinese workers under feudalism and colonialism as "slaves" and identifies socialist workers as revolutionary protagonists. However, unlike in the model heroic socialist-realist works of the Cultural Revolution, *Chung Kuo*'s commentary is narrated as anthropological-like observation. Filmed entirely on location, *Chung Kuo*'s accompanying imagery presents Chinese people as everyday individuals working and moving naturally through their environs.

The opening Shanghai sequence focuses on a number of small rickety fishing boats. When the director does show a larger ship, he zooms in to reveal workers on unsteady equipment, painting its rusty exterior (Figure 1.6). Shifting from the river to Shanghai's busy adjacent streets, the camera pans over details of the Bund's Western European neoclassical buildings and a facade covered by a propaganda poster depicting idealized portraits of revolutionary workers rising up against imperialist oppression (Figure 1.7). These images of the Bund's colonial architecture and propaganda art are then strikingly juxtaposed with an extended sequence focusing on throngs of people as they walk down the street. With the camera set in a fixed spot, Antonioni films Shanghai's crowd at great length, allowing dozens of individuals to filter in and out of the frame. In filming these pedestrians as they walk, without any staging, costumes, direction, or constructed sets, Antonioni reveals Shanghai's denizens as single individuals rather than part of a unified collective. Their eyes dart in different directions; some of them look directly into the camera inquisitively, others look away, and still others look forward or to the side, their sightlines unknown. These particularized bodies provide a human scale that contrasts with both the Bund's architectural grandeur and the heroic monumentality of the propaganda poster's figures. Similarly, at Shanghai's famous Yu Garden, window reflections of passersby appear immediately following a

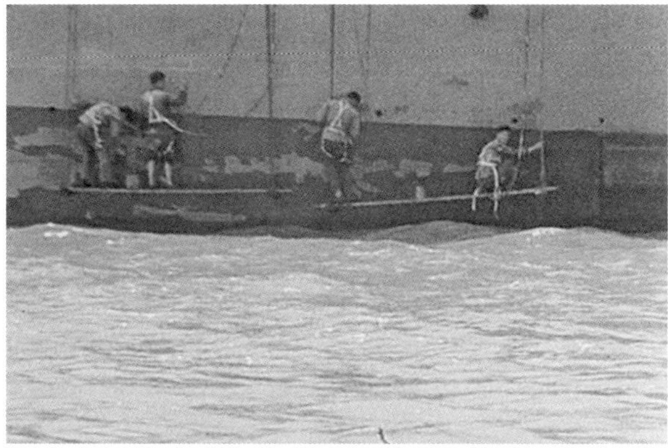

1.6   Michelangelo Antonioni, *Chung Kuo Cina*, 1972. 16 mm color film.

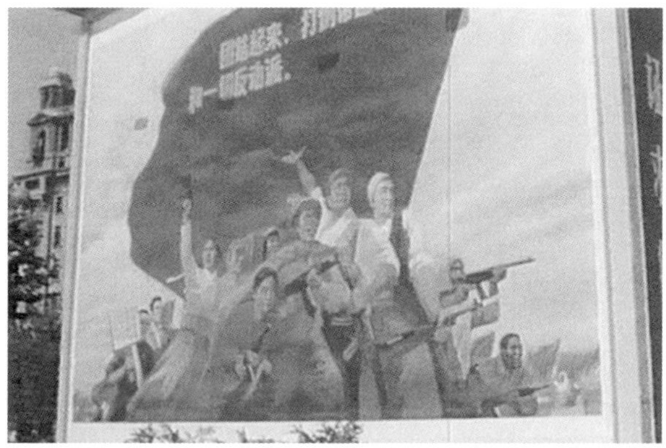

1.7   Michelangelo Antonioni, *Chung Kuo Cina*, 1972. 16 mm color film.

shot of a miniature replica of *Rent Collection Courtyard*, an officially approved socialist-realist artwork of the Cultural Revolution that comprised dozens of sculptures of life-like peasants forced to grovel at the feet of their corrupt landlord (the original work was installed in the courtyard of the landlord's seized property in Sichuan Province).[70] Soon after, a close-up shot of a public sculpture comprised of People's Liberation Army soldiers raising guns high in the air flashes to a rainy street scene in which pedestrians huddle under shared umbrellas. This is followed by a shot of children, clad in scraps and wearing straw hats, hauling wagons of hay through the street (Figure 1.8). For Antonioni, such scenes position non-idealized Chinese people as victors in the socialist dream of overcoming exploitation, while privileging personal experience over totalizing political messages and spectacular sights.[71]

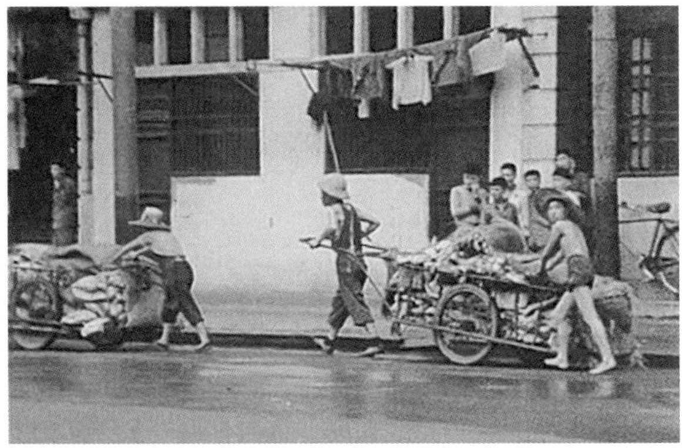

Michelangelo Antonioni, *Chung Kuo Cina*, 1972. 16 mm color film.   **1.8**

In an article written after the filming of *Chung Kuo* entitled "China and the Chinese," Antonioni explains:

> In reality I did not make a film about China, but about the Chinese. I remember having asked, on the first day of our discussions, what, according to them, mostly clearly symbolized the change which happened in the country after liberation. "Man," they had replied. Therefore, at least in this, our interests coincided. And I tried to look at man more than at his accomplishments or at the landscape.[72]

The director concluded that the foregrounding of China's people was the most honest way of representing the post-1949 nation and its socioeconomic structures.

Later in *Chung Kuo*'s Shanghai segment, viewers are brought to the site of China's first communist meeting (the semicolonial-era home that today sits amid *Xintiandi*). Here, Antonioni ruminates on Maoist socialism as an alternative to his own Western European capitalism, recounting the origin story of the CCP with a tone of longing. The camera moves into the site's courtyard and enters the meeting room. As the narrator describes the events of the secret meeting, an invisible hand opens the door so that viewers are made to feel as if they are walking in. The space appears haunted by the ghosts of Shanghai's underground revolutionary past. "Everything remains as it was (*Tutto è rimasto come era*)," the narrator says, referring to the teacups on the table where the young revolutionaries first met. Added, however, is a painted portrait of a young Mao, who had, in 1921, not yet come to power as the primary leader of China's then primitive communist network. The vacant space illustrates the narrator's tale of that first ill-fated meeting:

> At this house of brick at number 108 Wang Tze Road, the story of communist China began. The first of July of 1921, a spy, possibly sent by the French police,

entered in this second entranceway, across this hallway, and through this dark corridor. Then he entered into a room, blank and at that point empty. The men who had met there had just escaped. Those men were twelve, and that day they had held, in that room, the first congress of the Chinese Communist Party. Of the twelve men, only Mao resisted the storm of history, the others were all killed or remembered as traitors.[73]

The absence of any figures in this footage is a somber reminder of the assassinations of the meeting's attendees. Following this scene, the camera meanders into a poor neighborhood nearby, described as a reminder of the horrors of the city's semicolonial past. The camera fixates on old mud homes, while the narrator utters, "During the war with Japan, the people drank rain water that collected in holes dug out by bombs."[74] These traces of past tragedy and poverty become Antonioni's tools for thinking through China's socialist achievements.

Antonioni also took this approach when filming a factory on the outskirts of Shanghai. Here, the camera homes in on various pieces of equipment and on individuals laboring. The refinery appears shabby as the camera zooms in on rundown machines and a site shrouded in exhaust. The accompanying narration reads:

> The immense industrial periphery of Shanghai was not born today. In a certain sense, the city was industrialized over many decades. Shanghai's products go all over China, but the industries are often little more than large warehouses, built in a hurry. Even this refinery, the most major of the city, is a poor factory, made of materials that were almost discarded.[75]

For Antonioni, such depictions were not intended to be critical, but rather honest and even admiring. Calling the refinery a "poor factory" might be understood as a sort of misguided compliment, as Antonioni considered, "China's contemporary sociopolitical structure as a model … worthy of the most attentive study."[76] In Western Europe, such scenes and commentary were read as well-meaning reflections by those, like Antonioni, who looked to Maoist China as a promising alterative to consumerism, individualism, and capitalism and who considered the Chinese people to be resourceful and respectfully humble. However, for Chinese officials like Mao and Jiang Qing, who enforced the art of heroic socialist realism, these scenes and commentaries derided socialist achievement. *Chung Kuo*'s attention to squalid environments, even when described as signifiers of past colonial oppression, was read as a sign of Antonioni's inescapable rootedness in imperialist, capitalist conditions. Official criticism of *Chung Kuo* decried Antonioni's depiction of Shanghai not as an idealized industrial city but as a poor and destitute one:

> Antonioni presents Shanghai as "an industrialized city," only to sling mud at China's socialist industry. Shutting his eyes to the large numbers of big modern

enterprises there, the director concentrated on assembling unconnected scenes of poorly equipped hand-operated enterprises. There are, in fact, shipyards that build 10,000-ton vessels by the [Huangpu] River, and Chinese-made ocean-going ships that berth in Shanghai. However, under Antonioni's camera, all the freighters on the river are from abroad and China has only small junks. Taking an outright imperialist stand, the director asserts that Shanghai's industry "was not born today" and "as a city, Shanghai was literally built by foreign capital in the last century." … His vicious implication is that if Shanghai, China's major industrial city, is like this, imagine other areas![77]

Western European critics often interpreted these Chinese criticisms as examples of cross-cultural misunderstandings. As Eco observed in 1977:

> The *Cina* question reminds us that when political debate and artistic representation involve different cultures on a worldwide scale, art and politics are also mediated by anthropology and thus by semiology. … We see how the by now famous criticism in *Renmin Ribao* could consider the shot of the Nanking bridge as an attempt to make it appear distorted and unstable, because a culture which prizes frontal representation and symmetrical distance shots cannot accept the language of western cinema which, to suggest impressiveness, foreshortens and frames from below, prizing dissymmetry and tension over balance.[78]

Eco was right to acknowledge the undeniable semiotic problems of cross-cultural translation, but his argument also resorts to reductive cultural categorizations. For example, Eco's comment that "the Chinese culture is one which prizes frontal representation and symmetrical distance shots," while adequately characterizing the aesthetic policy of the Cultural Revolution, denied an entire tradition of Chinese painting and calligraphy based on asymmetrical relations between positive and negative space, as well as modernist embraces of collage and asymmetry. While correctly locating the CCP's criticism, Eco wrongly assumed that the critiques sprung from *Chung Kuo*'s failure to align with China's culturally bound system of signification, neglecting to account for the state power that artificially constructed that signification system in the first place.

Susan Sontag, who discussed *Chung Kuo* in her book *On Photography* (1977), also identified opposing representational systems as underlying the film's denunciation. Contemplating how photographic images operate within distinct cultures—*ours* (Western European and North American) and *theirs* (Chinese)—Sontag wrote,

> The Chinese circumscribe the uses of photography so that there are no layers or strata of images, and all images reinforce and reiterate each other. We make of photography a means by which, precisely, anything can be said, any purpose served. … To us, the difference between the photographer as an individual eye and the photographer as an objective recorder seems fundamental, the difference often regarded, mistakenly, as separating photography as art from

photography as document. But both are logical extensions of what photography means: note-taking on, potentially, everything in the world, from every possible angle.[79]

Sontag's discussion accurately identifies the locus of *Chung Kuo*'s denunciation. The film's images, shot from a variety of perspectives, do not present people, landscapes, or China as unified wholes but convey an overwhelming sense of the world as full of endless directions, permutations, and possibilities. This defied the CCP's insistence on a singular, idealized mode of realism to represent and promote Maoist doctrine. Sontag's writing on *Chung Kuo* escaped Eco's cultural reductivism by acknowledging that China's signification system was dictated by its authoritarian regime: "China offers the model of one kind of dictatorship, whose master idea is 'the good,' in which the most unsparing limits are placed on all forms of expression, including images."[80] Indeed, the *Chung Kuo* question was steeped less in vying Chinese and Western semiotic systems and more in divisions arising from two very different, particular notions of realism: the heroic socialist realism promoted by the leaders of the Cultural Revolution and *Chung Kuo*'s direct-cinema realism steeped in visual reality. The political-aesthetic obstacles of reconciling these two forms of realism resulted in the film's castigation in China and Antonioni's deep personal disappointment.

The attacks made against *Chung Kuo* and Antonioni were not only reflective of a disapproval of the film's non-idealized realism but also intimately linked to a concurrent struggle for power over China's cultural apparatus. By the early 1970s, the exuberance, wild abandon, and violence of the early years of the Cultural Revolution had begun to subside. It was suspected that even Mao, whose health began seriously waning in 1971, wished to temper the Cultural Revolution's radicality. Premier Zhou Enlai, the chief figure responsible for *Chung Kuo*'s commission, was growing concerned with China's reputation abroad and began promoting less overtly political art.[81] In 1973, Jiang Qing, sensing an usurpation of her absolute power over China's cultural sphere, launched a campaign against Zhou Enlai.[82] *Chung Kuo* was caught in the middle of this political struggle; as a target of attack, it revealed the hidden agendas underlying the Cultural Revolution's official art and the CCP's insistence on a singular model of realism. However unintentionally, *Chung Kuo*'s emphasis on individuals and quotidian details and capturing of what Antonioni defined as "visual reality" functioned in direct opposition to the Cultural Revolution's officially approved aesthetics.[83]

That which still haunts

Chung Kuo's final scene, shot in Shanghai, concludes,

> China opened its doors to us, but it remains, nevertheless, a remote world, for the most part unknown. We were not able to do much more than glance at it.

There is an ancient Chinese saying which goes, "You can draw the coat of a tiger, but not his bones. You can draw the face of a man, but not his heart."[84]

In filming China, and especially Shanghai, Antonioni had hoped to show the bones and the heart of socialism—China's communist roots and disparate realities. While filming at the site of the first communist congress, Antonioni was also unknowingly retracing the steps of artists like Pang Xunqin and filmmakers like Yuan Muzhi, who had occupied the French Concession neighborhood decades earlier, until their steps were silenced by war and the official mandates of the Cultural Revolution.

The Storm Society's model of *haipai*, characterized by cross-cultural art/design hybridity aimed at equitable social improvement, remained violently repressed throughout the Cultural Revolution. It would not be until after the market reforms of the late 1970s, which would eventually catapult Shanghai as the PRC's, and one of the world's, most powerful economic centers, that artists and designers would begin to deliberately conjure the modernist styles of Republican-era Shanghai, now affectionately called *old Shanghai*. Amid the development of CCP-sponsored capitalism, nostalgia for Shanghai's so-called modernist heyday of the 1920s–30s came to characterize the marketing of the city and its booming consumer culture, but with little attention paid to the actual art that was being produced in and about the city by artists like Pang Xunqin. At the turn of the twenty-first century, the modernity of pre-Mao Shanghai reemerged as a nondescript specter, now haunting the ruins of the old French Concession, wherein lies *Xintiandi*.

Notes

1 In the neighborhood surrounding *Xintiandi*, there is a small plaque honoring the home of the modernist painter and founder of Shanghai's first private art school, Liu Haisu (1896–1994). The plaque, however, does not reveal that this residence served as a hideout when Liu Haisu was persecuted for modernist tendencies in the 1920s; and a prison during the Cultural Revolution, when he, like so many other artists, was attacked and forced into house arrest.

2 As described in a Shanghai tour book, "The Shikumen (stone-framed gate) is a unique architectural style of Shanghai. The Shikumen houses appeared in the 1860s, when the local realty developers built townhouse-style residences for the sudden influx of population pouring into Shanghai to escape the Taiping Rebellion. By the 1920s, Shikumen accounted for three fourths of all Shanghai's houses. The most important feature of the Shikumen is the gate. While framed with stone slabs like the name suggests, the gate is usually topped with a triangular or semicircular pediment decorated with floral patterns. The Shikumen is praised for its perfect combination of the Western architecture with traditional Chinese elements," Li Xin, *Shanghai Glamour*, 89. As described by East Asian Studies scholar Jie Li in her compelling microhistory and memoir of life down Shanghai's lanes, most of the city's "alleyway homes were named after a

decorative motif called shikumen, or 'stone portal gate,' marking the front entrance of each alleyway and the front door of each house within the alleyway," Jie Li, Introduction to *Shanghai Homes: Palimpsests of Private Life*, 7. For further accounts of everyday life in Shanghai's characteristic *longtang*, see Zhang Zhen, "Worldly Shanghai, Metropolitan Spectators," in *An Amorous History of the Silver Screen: Shanghai Cinema, 1896–1937* (Chicago and London: University of Chicago Press, 2005), 42–88.

3 See Sharon Zukin, *Loft Living: Culture and Capital in Urban Change* (Baltimore: Johns Hopkins University Press, 1982).

4 See Wu Hung and Huang Rui, eds., *Beijing 798: Reflections on Art, Architecture and Society in China* (Beijing: Timezone 8, 2008).

5 Fredric Jameson, "Postmodernism and Consumer Society," in *The Cultural Turn: Selected Writings on the Postmodern, 1983–1998* (London: Verso, 1998), 194.

6 Ibid., 196.

7 Benjamin Wood, interview by author, April 1, 2010, audio recording, Benjamin Wood Studio, Shanghai, China.

8 Ibid.

9 Wang Hui, *China's New Order: Society, Politics, and Economy in Transition*, trans. Theodore Huters and Rebecca Karl (Cambridge, MA: Harvard University Press, 2003), 141.

10 Wood, interview by author.

11 Ibid.

12 Samuel Liang, "Amnesiac Monument, Nostalgic Fashion: Shanghai's New Heaven and Earth," 53.

13 Paul Goldberger, "Shanghai Surprise: The Radical Quaintness of the Xintiandi District," in *The New Yorker* (December 26, 2005), https://www.newyorker.com/magazine/2005/12/26/shanghai-surprise, accessed May 18, 2018.

14 Shu Haolun discussing his documentary 乡愁/*Xiangchou*/*Nostalgia*, cited in Robin Visser, *Cities Surround the Countryside: Urban Aesthetics in Postsocialist China* (Durham, NC: Duke University Press, 2010), 38.

15 While in 2010 the majority of those occupying flats in "Rich Gate" were foreigners, the demographics have steadily shifted as a number of mainland Chinese people are enjoying increasing levels of wealth, despite, or even because of, the alarmingly high rates of economic disparity and the fact that workers are still paid nominally.

16 To critics who label *Xintiandi* as theme park architecture, Wood counters, "[Not] if you take the traditional materials and you use them and you drop about half the decorative details, just use the materials, not the details. … Is a roof overhang that shelters an outdoor balcony a decorative detail? No, it's about function, and about providing shade and also providing a sense of shelter, making people comfortable. You can also up-light the roof at night and if it's a local wood, it warms up the place. So I don't consider that a theme park. A theme park is when you purposely copy buildings for the visual effect, which is not quite what I had in mind," Wood, interview by author.

17 Benjamin Wood cited in "Xintiandi in Shanghai," *Zing* (April 2006), 20.

18 Annie Ye, interview by author, March 1, 2010, Shui On Headquarters, Shanghai, China. In line with the values of this campaign, *Xintiandi*'s private clubhouse, *One Xintiandi*, hosted rotating exhibitions and cultural events for visiting VIPs,

while the complex's grounds featured public art, such as decorative fountains and temporary sculptures, and served as a venue for marketer-organized art exhibitions, such as "Be Inspired—Shanghai Xintiandi Art Fest" (2007).

19 Marketers transformed *Xintiandi's* standard promotional brochure into 新 (*Xin/New*), *Zing* in English, a registered lifestyle, arts, and culture magazine that included stories on and interviews with international artists, filmmakers, and designers as well as advertisements featuring the complex's retailers.

20 Cheng Naishan, "Life in the Slow Lane," *Zing* (April 2008): 13.

21 Introductory wall plaque, Shikumen Museum, *Xintiandi*, Shanghai, China, visited November 2010.

22 Wall plaque, Shikumen Museum. The New Culture Movement was an anti-imperialist, anti-feudalist movement led by intellectuals demanding the development of modern science, democracy, and culture in the recently established Republic of China. The movement came to a head with wide-scale public protests in Beijing's Tiananmen Square on May 4, 1919, and as such it is also referred to as the *May Fourth Movement*. Participants were protesting decisions made at the post-First World War Paris Peace Conference and especially the Versailles Treaty, which handed German rights to China's Shandong Province over to Japan. In addition to demanding a stronger domestic government that would stand up to foreign powers, the New Culture Movement called for the transformation of classical Chinese into more legible vernacular Chinese, women's liberation, anti-feudalism, the re-examination of Confucian texts using modern critical methods, modern science, and democratic values.

23 Lu Xun, "Written in Deep Night: On Dying in Secret" (1936), in *Selected Works of Lu Hsun*, vol. 4 (Beijing: Foreign Languages Press, 1960), 257. In 1931, Lu Xun introduced the Chinese public to Käthe Kollwitz's art by featuring her print *Sacrifice* from the series *War* (1922) on the cover of the inaugural issue of leftist journal *Beidou* (*Big Dipper*). The cover stood as a disguised homage to Lu Xun's former student and close collaborator and friend, Rou Shi (1901–1931), another ardent promoter of woodcuts who, along with 22 other left-wing intellectuals, had been secretly arrested and executed by the Chinese Nationalist Party earlier that year. For more information on The White Terror Campaign of 1931–1934, see Patricia Stranahan, *Underground: The Shanghai Communist Party and the Politics of Survival, 1927–1937* (Lanham, MD: Rowman & Littlefield Publishers, 1998).

24 Chen I-wan, "The Younger Group of Shanghai Artists," *T'ien Hsia Monthly* 5, no. 2 (September 1937): 148.

25 Frederic Wakeman Jr. and Wen-hsin Yeh, eds., *Shanghai Soujourners* (Berkeley: Institute of East Studies, University of California at Berkeley, 1992), 47. By the 1920s, these laws had changed.

26 Lu Xun, "Shanghai Children" (1933), in *Selected Works of Lu Hsun*, vol. 3, trans. Yang Hsien-yi and Gladys Yang (Beijing: Foreign Languages Press, 1959), 299.

27 Pang Xunqin, 就是这样走过来的/*Jiushi zheyang zou guolai de* [*This is the way it happened/This is the path I traveled down*] (Beijing: Shenghua, douxin, xin he sanlian shudian, 2005), 130.

28 Ibid., 122–123.

29 Ibid., 135–136.

30 See 马路天使/*Malu Tianshi*/*Street Angel*, directed by Yuan Muzhi (1937; Shanghai, China: Mingxing Film Company/Cinema Epoch, 2007), DVD. This opening montage credit sequence also appears in Yuan Muzhi's earlier film 都市风光/*Dushi fengguang*/*Cityscape* (1935).

31 The Hamilton House and its neighbor, the Metropole Hotel, are two iconic Art Deco buildings, both built in 1934, which were commissioned by Shanghai's wealthiest foreign industrialist, Sir Victor Sassoon, and designed by British architectural firm, Palmer and Turner. See Chapter 2's mention of the Metropole Hotel, which appears in David Lynch's short film for Christian Dior, *Lady Blue Shanghai*.

32 The full subtitles read, 一九三五年/秋/上海地下层/*Yi jiu san wu nian*/*qiu*/*Shanghai dixia ceng* [1935/autumn/ the slums of Shanghai]. 上海地下层 literally translates into *basement of Shanghai*.

33 According to historian Marie-Claire Bergère, by 1914, the last year in which the French Concession was allowed to expand its borders, the concessions housed 640,000 people, 98 percent of whom were Chinese. See Marie-Claire Bergère, "The Concession as a Model," in *Shanghai: China's Gateway to Modernity*, trans. Janet Lloyd (Stanford, CA: Stanford University Press, 2009), 111.

34 James Graham Ballard, *Miracles of Life: Shanghai to Shepperton, An Autobiography* (London: Fourth Estate, 2008), 5, 11.

35 Wang Jiyuan quoted in Zhu Boxiong and Chen Ruilin, eds., 中国西画五十年/*Zhongguo xihua wushi nian, 1898–1949* [*Fifty Years of Western Painting in China*] (Beijing: People's Art Publishing House, 1989), 302. Original members of The Storm Society included its founders, Ni Yide and Pang Xunqin, and Li Baoquan, Wang Jiyuan, Zhou Duo, Duan Pingyou, Zeng Zhiliang, Yang Qiuren, and Yang Taiyang. Later, Zhang Xian and female artist Qiu Ti, who would marry Pang Xunqin, joined the group. For an art-historical account of The Storm Society, see Ralph Croizier, "Post-Impressionists in Pre-War Shanghai: The Juelanshe (Storm Society) and the Fate of Modernism in Republican China," in *Modernity in Asian Art*, ed. John Clark (Sydney, Australia: Wild Peony, 1993), 135–154.

36 Ni Yide, "决澜社宣言"/"Juelanshe xuanyan" ["Storm Society Manifesto"], 艺术旬刊/*Yishu xunkan*/*L'Art* 1, no. 5 (October 11, 1932): 8. *L'Art* was a short-lived art journal (1932–1933) founded by Ni Yide and sponsored by Moshe/Muse Society. Using equally revolutionary and even more militaristic language, art theorist and Storm Society collaborator Li Baoquan wrote of the group: "They unite together … use their combined strength to forge ahead. Their goal is to create a *Xintiandi* [*New Heaven on Earth*] … under the flag of a new, modern 20th-century Chinese art. … They are not only a tide or a wave. They are a flood! … Of all the warriors of The Storm Society, some are veteran teachers, some just came back from France or Japan, some are just planning to go overseas for many years, after which they will return to marry their lovers. … They want to rage past the dead environment. They use their passion in this depressing world, becoming its illuminating beacon. In the darkness, they bend their backs. Their faces flush and grow sweaty. Their eyes grow bloodshot. They look down on everything in the past. They are only thinking about the great mission

they have amidst this darkness. … The creation of twentieth-century Chinese art," Li Baoquan, "洪水翻了"/"Hongshui fan le" ["A Great Flood Rises"], in 艺术旬刊/*Yishu xunkan/L'Art* 1, no. 5 (October 11, 1932): 9.

37 Pang Xunqin, *Jiushi zheyang*, 140.

38 Pang Xunqin, 庞薰琹文选：论艺术设计美育/*Pang Xunqin wenxuan: lun yishu sheji meiyu* [Pang Xunqin's *essays: on art, design, fine arts education*] (Jiangsu: Jiangsu Jiaoyu Chu Ban Shi/Jiangsu Education Publishing House, 2007), 108.

39 See Introduction for an overview of *haipai*.

40 In reflecting on her father's art practice, Pang Xunqin's daughter, Pang Tao, commented that Pang Xunqin's fluency in French set him apart from most of his peers, even those who had studied in France. Pang Tao, interview by author, September 6, 2011, audio recording, private residence and studio of Pang Tao, Beijing, China.

41 "In 1934, a local Chinese newspaper estimated that Shanghai led the world's cities in prostitution as a specialty: in London, one person in 960 was a prostitute, in Berlin one in 580, in Paris one in 481, in Chicago one in 430, in Tokyo one in 250, and in Shanghai, one in 130," Rhoads Murphey referencing the newspaper, *Shun Pao* (December 3, 1934), in *Shanghai: Key to Modern China*, 7.

42 Women pictured with flowers insinuating sexual availability had long been a popular motif in the history of Chinese art, as seen, most closely to Pang Xunqin's time, in turn-of-the-twentieth-century courtesan portraits, which were ubiquitous in Shanghai beginning in the late 1800s. For an important examination of the role the courtesan played in shaping Shanghai's visual culture and urban identity, see Catherine Yeh, *Shanghai Love: Courtesans, Intellectuals, and Entertainment Culture, 1850–1911* (Seattle: University of Washington Press, 2006).

43 Murphey, *Shanghai: Key to Modern China*, 8.

44 The exhibition displayed a wide variety of Pang Xunqin's works. As both a solo artist's show and one with artworks for sale, this exhibition marked two kinds of art practices seldom before seen in China.

45 Fu Lei, 薰琹的梦/"Xunqin de Meng" ["Xunqin's Dream"], 艺术旬刊/*Yishu xunkan/L'Art* 1, no. 3 (September 1932): 12–13, reprinted in Pang Xunqin, *Wenxuan lun yishu sheji meiyu*, 31. Fu Lei's article references a myriad of artists, musicians, and philosophers, comparing their unique ability to dream in an unencumbered way with Pang Xunqin's mental and material exercises. The vast range of figures Fu Lei mentions—from Greek philosophers to Michelangelo to Beethoven to Debussy to Picasso—is reflective of the artistic landscape of 1920s–30s Shanghai, in which a torrent of art, music, and related writings from Western Europe were introduced all at once.

46 In a poetic essay entitled "艺术家的春梦"/"Yishujia de chunmeng" ["Artist's Spring Dream"], Storm Society co-founder Ni Yide also writes of an artist's dream and of a world filled with art and poetry, what he too describes as a utopia. The word Ni Yide uses for *utopia*, however, is 乌托邦/*wutuobang*, a transliteration from the Greek-rooted word Thomas More chose for the title of his sixteenth-century novel *Utopia*. See Ni Yide, "Yishujia de chunmeng" ["Artist's Spring Dream"], in 艺术随笔/*Yishu suibi* [*Art Essay*] (Shanghai: Wenyi Chufangshi, 1999), 21–23.

47 Material drawn from Pang Xunqin's everyday urban surrounds shows up not only in *Such is Shanghai* but also in the watercolor's Parisian counterpart, 如此巴黎/*Ruci Bali* (*Such is Paris*) (1931), created that same year. These two works share a great deal of imagery, such as decorative harlequin patterning, playing cards, and close-up faces representing various urban types. *Such is Paris* also features an upside-down urinal, a tribute to Marcel Duchamp's pivotal artwork *Fountain* (1917), and fragments of language, *HOT, CAF, BAL, NCING*, reminiscent of Picasso and Braque's cubist collage. It is revealing that Pang Xunqin included bits of language in *Such is Paris* but not in *Such is Shanghai*. Not only is the Chinese language pictorially based and thus inherently linked to visual culture, but Chinese painting is also closely related to calligraphy, traditionally considered the most elevated of all art forms. Chinese ink paintings usually included language in the form of poetry and/or imperial inscriptions and patrons' seal stamps. While the inclusion of language in painting broke the rules in Paris, its exclusion in Shanghai did the same.

48 Pang Xunqin, *Jiushi zheyang*, 118.

49 Ibid., 126. Similarly, Lu Xun, warned, "If you live in Shanghai, it pays better to be smart than dowdy. If your clothes are old, bus-conductors may not stop when you ask them, park attendants may inspect your tickets with special care, and the gate-keepers of big houses or hotels may not admit you by the main door. That is why some men do not mind living in poky lodgings infested by bedbugs, but insist on pressing their trousers under the pillow each night so that the creases are sharp the next day," Lu Xun, "Shanghai Girls" (1933), in *Selected Works of Lu Hsun*, vol. 3 (Beijing: Foreign Languages Press, 1959), 297.

50 Sadly, many of Pang Xunqin's artworks have been lost, either during the Second Sino-Japanese War or later during the Cultural Revolution.

51 Pang Xunqin, *Jiushi zheyang*, 43.

52 Within China, it was not until Pang Xunqin arrived in Shanghai that he first saw streets illuminated by gas lamps, which would soon be replaced by electric lights. Ibid., 42–43.

53 Pang Jun, "Illuminator of Modern Chinese Design: Pang Xunqin," in Wu Wenxiong, ed., 庞薰琹中国传统图案/*Pang Xunqin: Zhongguo chuangtong tuan* (*China Decoration Figure Pang Xunqin*) (Shanghai: Renmin Meishu Chubanshi and Changshu Fine Art Museum, 2009), 57.

54 See Pang Xunqin, 工艺美术设计/*Gongyi meishu sheji* [*Industrial and Fine Art Design*] (1940) (Beijing: People's Fine Arts Publishing Company, 1981), which published a limited number of the designs.

55 Pang Jun, "Illuminator of Modern Chinese Design: Pang Xunqin," 57.

56 The Shanghai Oil Painting and Sculpture Workshop was officially formed in 1965, on the eve of the Cultural Revolution, through a merging of the Chinese Sculpture Institute, founded by the minister of culture in 1957, and the Shanghai Art Design Company/Sculpture Division. In 1966, the Workshop moved its location from West Jianguo Road near Huaihai Road (formerly Avenue Joffre) to an old Catholic church at the corner of Changle Road and Ruijin Road, both sites set in the heart of the old French Concession. For a timeline of events surrounding the establishment of the Shanghai Oil Painting and Sculpture Workshop

(later called Institute), see Qiu Ruimin, ed., 上海油画雕塑院/*Shanghai Youhua Diaosu Yuan/Shanghai Oil Painting and Sculpture Institute: 1964–2005* (Shanghai: Shanghai Jiaoyu Chubanshe, 2005).

57 For information on artistic representations and visual culture during the Cultural Revolution, see, among others, Zheng Shengtian and Melissa Chiu, eds., *Art and China's Revolution* (New York and New Haven: Asia Society in association with Yale University Press, 2008); and Laikwan Pang, *The Art of Cloning: Creative Production during China's Cultural Revolution* (New York: Verso, 2017).

58 The phrase is written in Chinese characters: 可以肯定，殖民主义，帝国主义和一切剥削制度的彻底崩溃，世界上一切被压迫人民，被压迫民族的彻底翻身，已经为期不远了 (*Keyi kending, zhimin zhuyi, diguo zhuyi he yiqie boxue zhidu de chedi bengkui, shijie shang yiqie bei yapo renmin, bei yapo minzu de chedi fanshen, yijing weiqi bu yuanle*).

59 See Mao's popular quote, cited in Chapter 2: "In the world today all culture, all literature and art belong to definite political lines. There is in fact no such thing as art for art's sake, art that stands above classes, art that is detached from or independent of politics," Mao Zedong, "Talks at the Yan'an Forum on Literature and Art" (May 1942), reprinted in *Quotations from Mao Tsetung* and in *Mao Zedong's Talks at the Yan'an Conference on Literature and Art: A Translation of the 1943 Text with Commentary*, trans. and ed. Bonnie S. McDougall (Ann Arbor: Center for Chinese Studies, University of Michigan, 1980), 299.

60 Art historian Julia F. Andrews writes, "The most frequently seen, yet transitory, art form of the period may have the big-character posters (*dazibao*). … On June 1, [1966] Mao approved broadcast of the text of a big-character poster that denounced the president of Beijing University. In the view of the Red Guards, he personally launched the Cultural Revolution by this act," Andrews, "The Art of the Cultural Revolution," in *Art in Turmoil: The Chinese Cultural Revolution, 1966–76*, ed. Richard King (Vancouver and Toronto: University of British Columbia Press, 2010), 33. Mao, however, did not entirely condone *dazibao* as art, writing, "Works of art which lack artistic quality have no force, however progressive they are politically. Therefore, we oppose both works of art with a wrong political viewpoint and the tendency towards the 'poster and slogan style' which is correct in political viewpoint but lacking in artistic power," Mao Zedong, "Yan'an Forum," in *Quotations from Mao Tsetung*, 302.

61 Er Dongqiang, interview by author, 27 January 2009, audio recording, Deke Erh Centre, Shanghai, China.

62 *Chung Kuo Cina*, directed by Michelangelo Antonioni (1972; Milan, Italy: RAI Radiotelevisione Italiana, 2007), DVD. Over the years, *Chung Kuo* has been largely forgotten or mistakenly dismissed as a benign travel documentary. Recent exceptions include insightful discussions of *Chung Kuo* in Homay King, *Lost in Translation: Orientalism, Cinema, and the Enigmatic Signifier* (Durham, NC: Duke University Press, 2010); Jerome Silbergeld, "Photography Goes to the Movies: On the Boundaries of Cinematography, Photography, and Videography in China," in *Bridges to Heaven: Essays on East Asian Art in Honor of Professor Wen C. Fong*, eds. Jerome Silbergeld, Dora C. Y. Ching, Judith G. Smith, and Alfreda

Murck (Princeton, NJ: P.Y. and Kinmay W. Tang Center for East Asian Art and Department of Art and Archaeology, Princeton University, 2011), 875–906; Jiwei Xiao, "A Traveller's Glance: Antonioni in China," *New Left Review* 79 (January–February 2013): 103–20; and Rey Chow, "China as Documentary: Some Basic Questions (inspired by Michelangelo Antonioni and Jia Zhangke)," *European Journal of Cultural Studies* (February 2014): 16–30.

63 Umberto Eco, "De Interpretatione, Or the Difficulty of Being Marco Polo (On the occasion of Antonioni's "China" film)," *Film Quarterly* 30, no. 4 (Summer 1977): 9.

64 Ibid.

65 Antonioni did manage once to convince his escorts to let him break from the official schedule so as to film a roadside black market; such markets were technically illegal but widely overlooked. All the other scenes, however, were pre-established and officially approved.

66 The general criticism of *Chung Kuo* was published as follows: "The film 'China' by the Italian director Michelangelo Antonioni is an out-and-out anti-China film. Its appearance is a serious anti-China event and a wild provocation against the Chinese people. All Chinese who have national pride are greatly infuriated to see that this anti-China film attacks Chinese leaders, smears socialist New China, slanders China's Great Proletarian Cultural Revolution and insults the Chinese people," "Repudiating Antonioni's Anti-China Film," *Peking Review* 17, no. 8 (February 22, 1974): 13.

67 This is not surprising, as Antonioni's films had long been characterized not by their *distaste of* but their *ambivalence toward* contemporary Italian society. His well-known feature films, such as *L'Avventura* (*The Adventure*) (1960), *La Notte* (1961), and *L'Eclisse* (*Eclipse*) (1962), critiqued bourgeois subjectivity while positioning it as a seductive puzzle. In *Il Deserto Rosso* (*The Red Desert*) (1964), for instance, Antonioni anxiously focused on Italy's industrial urban outskirts, but his focus was always tender, homing in on details like the primary colors of a construction site, composed, framed and sometimes painted to look like dazzling abstract paintings. Antonioni approached China with this same ambivalent perspective, warning against blind faith in Maoist doctrine and trying as hard as possible to shoot something that simply captured his act of looking.

68 Zhu Qiansheng, interviewed in the documentary 海上传奇/ *Haishang chuanqi/ I Wish I Knew*, directed by Jia Zhangke (Shanghai: Shanghai Film Group Corporation, 2010), DVD. The literal English translation of the Chinese title is *Sea Legend*.

69 Michelangelo Antonioni, *Chung Kuo. Cina*, ed. Lorenzo Cuccu (Turin: Einaudi, 1974), 64. Andrea Barbato would have initially been accepted by the CCP, as he was known as a left-wing writer with experience in Asia as a foreign correspondent.

70 *Rent Collection Courtyard* was upheld for promoting the primary values of the art of the Cultural Revolution: collective production, life-like realism, and the articulation of an anti-feudalist, pro-socialist message. See *Rent Collection Courtyard: Sculptures of Oppression and Revolt* (Beijing: Foreign Language Press, 1968).

71 In another example from *Chung Kuo*'s Beijing segment, a close-up shot of a young woman on the Great Wall is accompanied by the following words: "Who built

Thebes of the seven gates? In the books you will find the name of kings. Did the kings haul up the lumps of rock?" Bertolt Brecht quoted in Antonioni, *Chung Kuo*, 17. These questions highlighting the implications of the Great Wall as the world's grandest marker of military prowess, border defense, and the harnessing of slavery to produce massive works were borrowed from Bertolt Brecht's "Questions from a Worker Who Reads" (1935), a poem that later asks, "Where, the evening that the Great Wall of China was finished, did the masons go?" Bertolt Brecht, "Fragen eines lesenden Arbeiters" ["Questions from a Worker Who Reads"], in *Bertolt Brecht, Poetry and Prose*, ed. Reinhold Grimm, trans. Michael Hamburger (New York: Continuum, 2003), 63. Antonioni's focus on a single face reduces the Great Wall to a nondescript stone background, supporting Brecht's suggestion that people are the greatest assets in revolutionary realism. Brecht wrote, "There is only one ally against growing barbarism—the people, who suffer so greatly from it. … Therefore it is obvious that one must turn to the people, and now more necessary than ever speak their language. Thus the terms *popular art* and *realism* become natural allies," Brecht, "Against Georg Lukács," in *Aesthetics and Politics*, trans. Stuart Hood (London: Verso, 1980), 80. First published in *Schriften zur Literatur und Kunst*, ed. Werner Hecht (Frankfurt: Suhrkamp, 1967).

72 Michelangelo Antonioni, "China and the Chinese," in *Michelangelo Antonioni: The Architecture of Vision: Writings and Interviews on Cinema*, trans. Allison Cooper, ed. Marga Cottino-Jones (Chicago: University of Chicago Press, 1991), 116. [Originally published as "La Cina e I cinesi," *Il Giornio* 22, no. 25 (26 July 1972)].

73 Antonioni, *Chung Kuo*, 65–66. Note that the date of July 1 that Antonioni gives is inaccurate. While the group had planned to meet in early July, they didn't end up meeting until the end of the month. Furthermore, they were run out of their first meeting place, a nearby girls' school on Rue Bourgeat.

74 Ibid., 66.

75 Ibid., 68.

76 Antonioni, "China and the Chinese," 116. Eco offered this interpretation, "[Antonioni was] not so much interested in seeing those cases where the Chinese were able to construct industries like western ones; we know that they even have the atomic bomb: but it seems to me more interesting to show you how they were able to construct a factory, or hospital, or child-care center from a few scraps, in working conditions based on reciprocal trust. … Where the film means 'simplicity' for 'poverty,' the Chinese viewer reads 'miseria' and 'failure,'" Umberto Eco, "De Interpretatione," 10. *Chung Kuo* produced multiple moments in which Chinese poverty was looked upon with admiration, as in the stated narration of the film's opening scenes: "The residents of Beijing seem poor, but not miserable, without luxury and without hunger. What is so striking is their quality of life, which is so far from ours," Antonioni, *Chung Kuo*, 7. Such commentary, coupled with footage of crowds riding old bicycles, rundown factory sites, and drably dressed individuals, received drastically diverging receptions within and outside China.

77 "A Vicious Motive, Despicable Tricks—A criticism of M. Antonioni's anti-China film 'China,'" *Peking Review* 17, no. 5 (February 1, 1974): 8.

78   Umberto Eco, "De Interpretatione," 9, 11. One of the most frequently cited criticisms referred to *Chung Kuo*'s footage of the Yangtze River Bridge set in Nanjing. The scene begins with an establishing shot that scans the bridge in its entirety. The camera zooms in on the middle of the bridge, revealing two bold red Chinese characters, 万岁/*wansui* (*long live*, part of a longer political slogan), before zooming in further on barely visible pedestrians walking across the bridge. Antonioni's camera then travels under the bridge before jump-cutting to the other side and shooting a close-up of a man on a boat hanging laundry to dry. This scene prompted the following criticism published in *Peking Review,* "In photographing the Yangtze River Bridge at Nanking, the camera was intentionally turned on this magnificent modern bridge from very bad angles in order to make it appear crooked and tottering," "A Vicious Motive, Despicable Tricks," 9.

79   Susan Sontag, "The Image-World," in *On Photography* (New York: Farrar, Straus and Giroux, 1977), 177.

80   Ibid., 178.

81   Zhou Enlai aimed to resuscitate traditional Chinese art and some modernist art that had been banned during the early years of the Cultural Revolution. In the early 1970s, Zhou supported older artists, who had been exiled or arrested, in the creation of what would come to be called *Hotel Art*, paintings intended for display in hotels where visiting foreign dignitaries would stay. For a discussion of Zhou's promotion of Hotel Art and its denunciation by Jiang Qing and her allies, see Art Research Center of the Literary and Arts Research Institute, "批黑画是假，篡党切过是真"/"Pi heihua shi jia, cuan dang qieguo shi zhen" ["Criticizing Black Painting Was False, Overthrowing the Party and Nation Was the True Intention"], 美术/*Meishu* [*Fine Arts*] no. 2 (1977): 7. In 1972, the year Antonioni filmed *Chung Kuo*, US president Richard M. Nixon visited China, where he and Zhou Enlai signed the "Shanghai Communiqué," now widely considered to have signaled the beginning of restored US-China relations after decades of tense divisions.

82   For information on Jiang Qing's "Criticize Lin Biao, Criticize Confucius" campaign, which took Zhou Enlai as a main target, see, among others, Wu Qington, 周恩来在文化大革命中:回忆周恩来同林彪江青两个反革命集团的斗争/ *Zhou Enali zai wenhua dageming zhong: huiyi Zhou Enlai tong Lin Biao Jiang Qing liang ge fangeming jituan de douzheng* [*Zhou Enlai in the "Cultural Revolution": Recalling Zhou's Struggle against Jiang Qing and Lin Biao, Two Counter-revolutionary Figures*] (Beijing: Chinese Communist Party History Publishing House, 2002).

83   Antonioni theorized the concept of visual reality through an experience he had while filming *Chung Kuo*. In Suzhou, a city south of Shanghai, the director decided that he wanted to film a wedding scene. His interpreter reported that none of the locals were planning to marry soon. Antonioni suggested that a boy and a girl could fake a wedding, to which the interpreter responded that it was not right that two people pretend to get married. Antonioni concluded, "maybe the interpreter was simply naïve, but I wanted to remember this small incident because it seems typical of the importance that one can give to the image and how it can be captured. The Chinese have a very earthly, concrete, *visible*

idea of reality." Michelangelo Antonioni, "*Chung Kuo. Cina*: Is It Still Possible to Film a Documentary?" in *Michelangelo Antonioni: The Architecture of Vision*, 114. [Originally published as "È ancora possibile girare un documentario?" in Antonioni, *Chung Kuo.*] Antonioni recounted this anecdote in response to an Italian review of *Chung Kuo* that claimed, "Socialism is not something one sees." Antonioni disagreed; he believed *Chung Kuo could* show socialism, so long as the film presented images that were concrete and readily visible, as opposed to those that were staged, feigned, or idealized, "Is It Still Possible," 114. This definition of visual reality reveals Antonioni's own naiveté, pronounced by his role as an admiring outside observer, all too eager to trust what he saw. In enthusiastically concluding that all Chinese people share a "*visible* idea of reality," Antonioni neglected to recognize the Cultural Revolution's artistic policy, which suppressed everyday images through the construction of idealized figures, universal symbols, and heroic narratives.

84 Antonioni, *Chung Kuo*, 71.

2 Shanghai's art in fashion

The contemporary Chinese art/fashion system

Since opening, the shopping mall and cultural complex *Xintiandi* has hosted a number of retailers claiming connections to *old Shanghai* or even more specific ties to the city's cultural heritage.[1] The complex has housed international hair salon Vidal Sassoon, owned by a descendant of Sir Victor Sassoon, a wealthy Sephardic merchant who played a seminal role in building Republican Shanghai's International Settlement; and Layefe, a designer housewares store and fashion label founded by Chen Yifei, a prominent Shanghai-based painter active during the Cultural Revolution and the first Chinese artist to gain international fame in the post-Mao era.[2] Yet the business most emblematic of *Xintiandi*'s self-proclaimed East-meets-West and Old-meets-New spirit is the fashion house and retailer Shanghai Tang (Figure 2.1), founded in 1994 by Sir David Tang, a Hong Kong–born, British-educated entrepreneur, author, and prominent collector of contemporary Chinese art. Claiming to be a "global ambassador of contemporary Chinese Chic" and "the only Chinese 'Haute Couture' house with a unique fusion of east meets west," Shanghai Tang combines details of traditional Chinese clothing with "imperial tailoring skills," *old Shanghai* style, and contemporary cosmopolitan fashions.[3] In Shanghai Tang, like at *Xintiandi*, pastiche tends to cover over present-day socioeconomic tensions, such as those arising from the reestablishment of class divisions, vying conceptions of local and global identities, and anxieties about Shanghai overtaking Hong Kong as the region's primary economic powerhouse. This chapter analyzes Shanghai Tang's hybrid imagery as an obfuscation of Shanghai's socialist past and a seductive promotion of its late-capitalist present. In the chapter's latter half, I examine the international promotion of contemporary Chinese, and especially Shanghai-based, art by Shanghai Tang's founder. I consider David Tang's art patronage as fueling what I call the contemporary Chinese art/fashion system, in which multinational fashion corporations sponsor contemporary Chinese artworks, often as glorified advertisements.[4]

The fashion industry, with its emphases on speedy turnover and maximum profits, has become infamous as one of the world's biggest polluters and exploiters of labor in developing countries.[5] In response, marketers devise

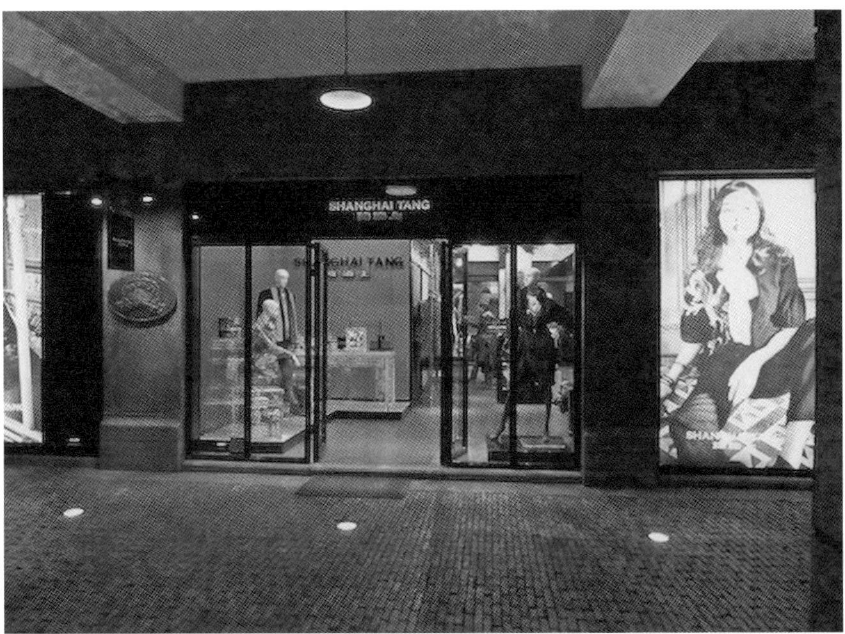

Shanghai Tang at *Xintiandi*, developed by Shui On Land and designed by Wood and
Zapata; Skidmore, Owings, and Merrill; and Nikken Sekkei International, built 1997–2002.   **2.1**

campaigns to promote fashion's softer side and cultural benefits, including
the corporate sponsorship of contemporary Chinese art. Since the late 1990s,
numerous Chinese artists have collaborated with overseas fashion designers:
Cai Guo-Qiang contributed to Japanese designer Issey Miyake's fall 1999 collection; Yang Fudong directed *First Spring*, a short film for Italian company
Miuccia Prada's 2010 menswear line; and Shanghai's Rockbund Art Museum,
in cooperation with German fashion house Hugo Boss, launched an award for
contemporary Asian artists.[6] It is important to recognize issues of cooptation
in relation to these collaborations, especially as fashion corporations tend to
exploit art trends and exoticize non-Western cultures.[7] Indeed, this chapter
discusses how Shanghai Tang and French fashion brand Christian Dior have
capitalized on Shanghai's modernist past, quelling the revolutionary strands of
1920s–30s *haipai* (*Shanghai style*) toward the propagation of consumer desire.
However, I also consider instances in which artists struggle to revive the *haipai*
belief that art and design hold the potential for social critique and transformation, even, or perhaps especially, while operating within a transnational
art/fashion system. I present a series of projects by Shanghai-based artist Liu
Jianhua, who has been supported by both David Tang and Christian Dior.
Resisting the fashionable aestheticization and depoliticization of the loaded
East-meets-West trope, Liu Jianhua's works critically confront globalization in

a Chinese context and the globalization of art in Shanghai. While embedded in contemporary art/fashion nexuses, Liu Jianhua's art nevertheless foregrounds disillusionment with altered cityscapes and environmental destruction, and in some cases subverts the norms of globalized manufacturing by reviving artisanal sectors left out of the twenty-first-century rise of the People's Republic of China (PRC) as the world's primary exporter of mass-produced goods.

Cultural hybridity and overseas exchange

As evidenced by Shanghai Tang and *Xintiandi*, numerous Hong Kong–based and other overseas Chinese investors and entrepreneurs have, since the early 1990s, been successfully claiming stakes in Shanghai's inevitable emergence as a competitive financial capital. In discussing the historical and current relations between Hong Kong and Shanghai, anthropologist Helen Siu singles out Shanghai Tang:

> In the late 1930s and early 1940s … Hong Kong and Shanghai, competitors and partners linked by historically global networks, shone behind the grim shadows of war and political terror with charged commercial energies. Taken for granted were the circulation of cosmopolitan populations and their brashly luxurious cultural styles—film, opera, fashion, cuisine, markets, and the underworld of crime and political intrigue. Such mutual modeling has continued in the non-fictional commercial world today. Shanghai Tang, a Hong Kong–based fashion chain founded by Cambridge-educated Sir David Tang, stands out in the global consumer market. It specializes in re-orientalizing Shanghai chic at the high end, with a colonial touch and a postmodern twist.[8]

This "re-orientalizing of Shanghai chic" depends upon Shanghai Tang's ability to embody multiple modes of hybridity—cultural, temporal, and sociopolitical. These modes of hybridity, formed within a retail enterprise, continuously capitulate to the fashion industry's demands of generating fresh products, consumer desire, and economic profit. In 2006, David Tang sold Shanghai Tang to Richemont, a Swiss luxury-goods company that owns numerous internationally sold high-end brands, including Cartier, Chloé, Dunhill, and Montblanc. As such, Shanghai Tang's brand of hybridity should be considered not only across cultures and times but also in terms of the transnational movement of capital. How does Shanghai Tang's hybrid style reflect mainland China's post-1989 economic shifts?

The fashion label operates a number of "Art Deco concept stores" in Shanghai, Hong Kong, New York, Paris, London, and Madrid, some of which include a Shanghai Tang Café. These concept stores stylistically align themselves with *old Shanghai* through the use of Art Deco interior design and architectural details prevalent in Shanghai's foreign concessions of the semicolonial era, as seen in the *Xintiandi* location. In describing the opening of Shanghai Tang Café at *Xintiandi*, a columnist for *Zing* magazine writes:

> Shanghai Tang presents something beyond fashion and food—an experience and a culture. It's saying that luxury is within reach and everywhere in details. … A subtle scent of ginger flowers … floats and mingles with the fragrance and the old Shanghai music, which builds a sensational connection and continuously lulls you back … The decorations are all about Chinese elements. … Chinese handicrafts like silk, embroidery uncovers and brings out the unique witty humor and richness of Shanghai culture to the fullest. Tradition and elegance combine, different yet harmonious … the perfect match with Shanghai Tang's concept of combining tradition with modern fashion.[9]

In addition to experiencing the combination of tradition and modernity in Shanghai Tang's luxurious multisensory stores, a shopper can order a tailor-made *qipao* (traditional Chinese dress commonly worn in Republican-era Shanghai), which will be updated through its form-fitting qualities (shorter and tighter than its historic counterparts), contemporary colors (e.g., bright fuchsia, orange, teal), and stylish additions, such as a waist-cinching belt. The company's tailors are described as multigenerational artisans employing "ancient techniques," and their fathers are identified as *old Shanghai* master tailors who successfully fled to Hong Kong during mainland China's volatile Maoist years. A company-issued statement reads, "Much of the Shanghainese tailoring skills and fashions were lost during the Cultural Revolution with now only a fragment of houses employing the ancient techniques, Shanghai Tang being one of the last bastions."[10] Shanghai Tang thus connects its brand both to traditional China and *old Shanghai*, while distancing itself from the PRC's socialist past and especially the Cultural Revolution. However, while rejecting the social and economic tenets of the Cultural Revolution, there are instances in which Shanghai Tang's designs and marketing campaigns stylistically reference Mao era fashions. These references transform the Maoist ideologies of the Cultural Revolution into commercialized aesthetics, while presenting a palpable veneer of stylistic and temporal hybridity that contributes to the reestablishment of Shanghai's cosmopolitan status.

In 1997, Shanghai Tang released an advertisement on the back cover of a special souvenir issue of *TIME Asia* (a subsidiary of *TIME* magazine), published just prior to the July 1 Hong Kong handover from British colonial rule to PRC sovereignty (Figure 2.2). As uncertainties about Hong Kong's post-handover identity mounted, Shanghai was emerging as an increasingly powerful financial capital. A number of overseas Chinese investors relocated from Hong Kong to Shanghai and/or increased travel between the two cities. In the early to mid-1990s, the relationship between Shanghai and Hong Kong hovered tenuously between one of threatening competition and mutual support.

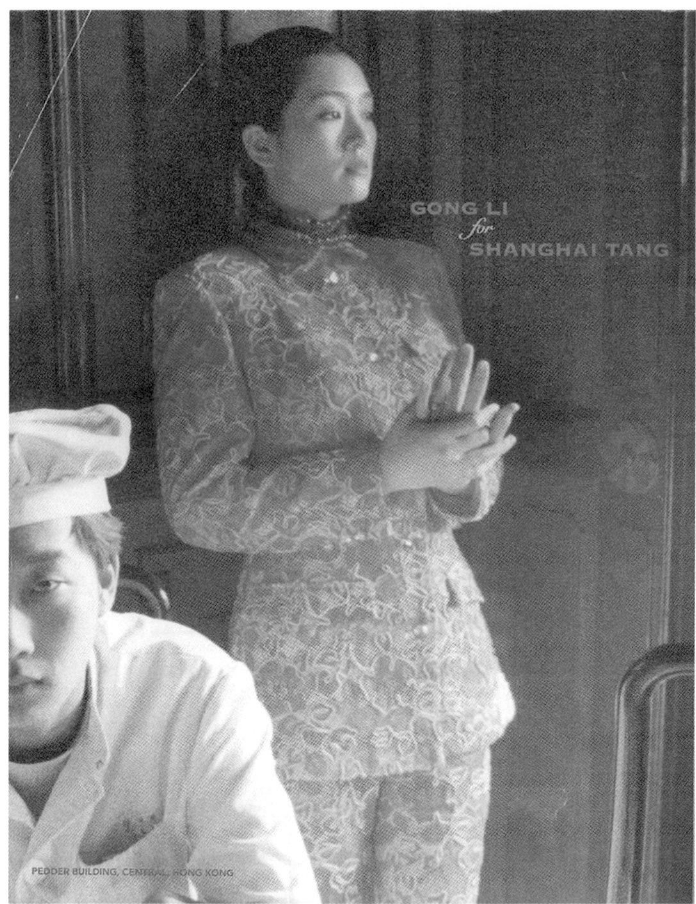

2.2   Advertisement for Shanghai Tang featuring actress Gong Li. On back cover of *TIME Asia* (Special Souvenir Issue: "Hong Kong 1997").

The *TIME Asia* issue focused on the anxieties and speculations surrounding the impending transfer of power. Major themes covered included the implications of the "One Country, Two Systems" policy that the PRC's central government promised would define relations between Hong Kong and mainland China for the next fifty years, Hong Kong's sustainable future as a leading international financial center, and the fears and biases of Hong Kong residents. The issue reported the results of a poll, which suggested that "at least one-third of Hong Kong's 6.4 million residents are prepared to leave if things go wrong," and "more than half the [Hong Kong] population believes mainland immigrants are rude, ignorant, unclean and unable to adapt to Hong Kong's culture. For their part, new arrivals [from mainland China] tell pollsters that their hosts are materialistic, selfish and uncaring."[11] Such comments betray prejudices informed by categories of class and cosmopolitan status, which had, during the PRC's socialist era, divided people from Hong Kong and mainland China, even while many of those living in Hong Kong would identify themselves as overseas Chinese.

The Shanghai Tang advertisement features the actress Gong Li—the first mainland Chinese actress to gain international renown in the post-Mao era.[12] Standing in the corner of a wood-paneled interior, the actress wears one of Shanghai Tang's characteristic hybrid fashions. Her outfit synthesizes a *power suit*, a tailored jacket and matching pants typically worn by professional women in the United States, and a *Mao suit* (中山装/*Zhongshan zhuang*), the obligatory uniform of the Cultural Revolution, as referenced in the jacket's centered line of buttons, high neckline, short turndown collar, and decorative details suggestive of flap pockets.[13] The Shanghai Tang suit, however, overturns the ideological underpinnings of the Mao suit, which embodied mass-produced uniformity, proletarian functionality, gender neutrality, and adherence to Maoist doctrine. While the Shanghai Tang suit is relatively modest (only the flesh of the actress's hands and face are exposed), it is, unlike intentionally loose-fitting Mao suits that aimed to shape a gender-neutral body, individually tailored to accentuate Gong Li's famed curves. Bright orange and dazzling gold replace the Mao suit's hues of workers' and soldiers' uniforms: grey, blue, and khaki. The Shanghai Tang suit appears made of embroidered silk or lace, and the jacket's buttons resemble opulent pearls. Gong Li's necklace, comprised of multiple strands of crystal balls worn tight like a choker, recalls Buddhist prayer beads. As opposed to the Mao badges ubiquitously worn during the Cultural Revolution to express loyalty to the nation's supreme leader, Gong Li wears a thick gold ring on her left ring finger, suggestive of wealth, and, following Western conventions, devotion to her husband.

Her styling recalls that of the jeweled movie starlets featured in Shanghai's Republican-era calendar posters and magazines, as exemplified by the January 1929 cover of *The Young Companion*, on which US-born Chinese actress Anna May Wong appears with a flapper bob, silk shawl over *qipao*, manicured nails, golden and pearlescent rings, and shiny gold bracelets (Figure 2.3).[14] Evoking Shanghai's extravagant 1920s–30s style, Gong Li, even while in a pseudo-Mao suit, stands in stark contrast to the values of mainland China's socialist period, especially defying the adamant rejection of luxury items as capitalist excess during the Cultural Revolution. In an oft-recounted anecdote, Wang Guangmei, the wife of leader Liu Shaoqi, was admonished for wearing pearls during her 1963 trip through Southeast Asia. When Liu fell out of favor during the Cultural Revolution, Red Guards publicly shamed Wang by dressing her like a prostitute and forcing her to wear clownish pearls made of

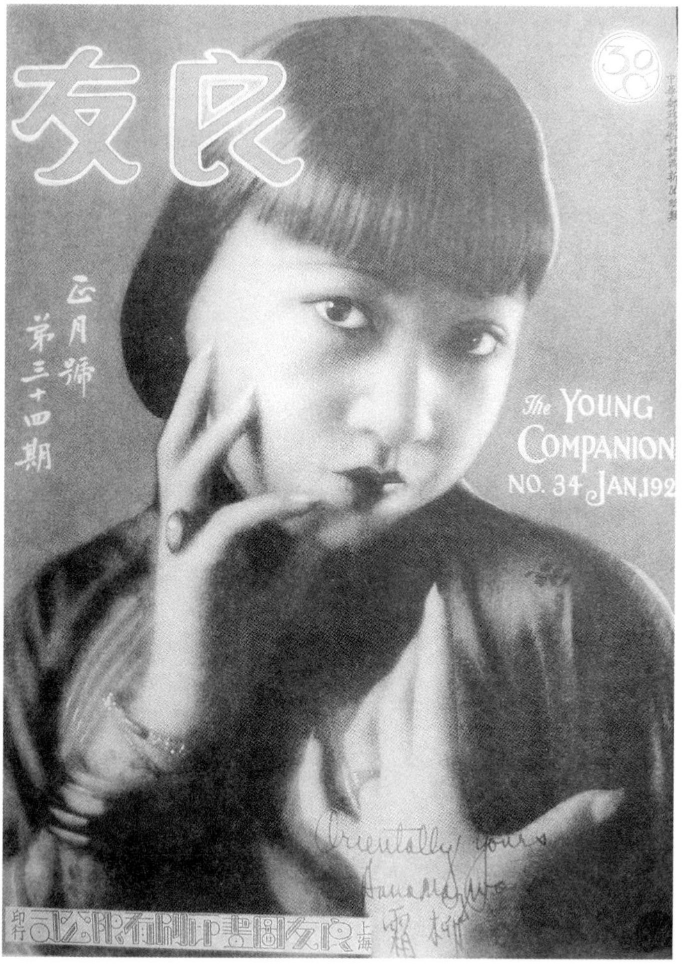

2.3 Cover featuring Anna May Wong. On *Liang You/Young Companion*, no. 34 (January 1929).

Ping-Pong balls. A 1966 *Peking Review* article described the mandates placed on individual style in Shanghai:

> The revolutionary workers and staff of Shanghai barber shops have adopted revolutionary measures in response to the proposals of the Red Guards: they no longer cut and set hair in the grotesque fashions indulged in by a small minority of people; they cut out those services specially worked out for the bourgeoisie such as manicuring, beauty treatments and so on. In those shops which sold only goods catering to the needs of a small minority of people, workers and staff have taken the revolutionary decision to start supplying the people at large with good popular commodities at low prices.[15]

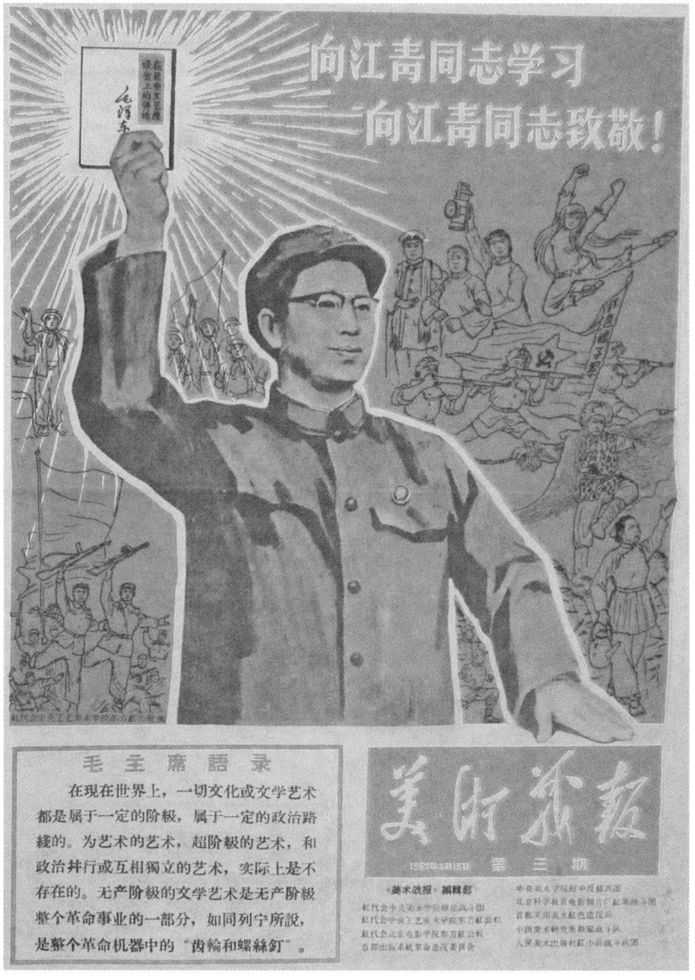

Cover featuring Jiang Qing, *Fine Arts War News*, no. 3 (May 1967). Chinese Cultural   **2.4**
Revolution collection, Box 6, Hoover Institution Archives.

A 1967 cover of the mainland Chinese bulletin, *Fine Arts War News* (美术战报/*Meishu zhanbao*), features Mao's wife and Cultural Revolution leader Jiang Qing. Clad in a unisex Mao suit, Mao badge, and communist cap, Jiang Qing visually embodies the model Maoist woman (Figure 2.4).[16] She appears in a black and white photographic cutout over a red background, on which are drawn characters and episodes from the Eight Model Plays (八个样板戏/*Ba ge yangban xi*)—a series of officially approved plays performed in the 1960s–70s that incorporated traditional Beijing opera and European-style ballet to tell stories of anti-feudalist and anti-imperialist uprisings. Her right hand clutches a radiating book, Mao's watershed 1942 "Talks at the Yan'an Forum on Literature and Art," and the cover quotes this popular excerpt:

> In the world today all culture, all literature and art belong to definite political lines. There is in fact no such thing as art for art's sake, art that stands above classes, art that is detached from or independent of politics. Proletarian literature and art are part of the whole proletarian revolutionary cause; they are, as Lenin said, cogs and wheels in the whole revolutionary machine.[17]

Comparing these images of Jiang Qing and Gong Li reveals how ideological battles have been fought by objectifying women's bodies both during the PRC's Maoist era, when the government mandated gender neutrality as a marker of socialist equality, and during the post-socialist period, when private companies re-sexualized women to propel capitalist consumption. In the Shanghai Tang advertisement, Gong Li stands tall and poised with clasped hands, a position that alludes to one of Mao's standard poses. Despite this and references to the Mao suit, the Shanghai Tang advertisement, like the brand, reveals the capitalist, individualist, and transnational values that reemerged forcefully within mainland China throughout the 1990s–2000s, and which came into collision with the preceding Mao era's socialism, communism, and nationalism. Gong Li's pensive gaze is directed off into the distance, suggesting a worldly outlook and contemplations of the future. In the foreground sits the movie star's foil—a young man in a cook's uniform. The picture is cropped so that only half of the cook's face, which gazes directly at the viewer, can be seen. Gong Li's wealth and high social standing, signaled by her international celebrity status, high-quality accessories, and upscale attire, stand in stark contrast to the cook's lowly position. Seated in front of the actress, who pays him no notice, the cook wears a white hat and slightly stained uniform. The juxtaposition between these two figures visually embodies the return of a class-based society and resulting economic inequalities of China's post-socialist years. By the mid-1990s, a strong domestic service economy had developed in mainland China, especially in cities like Shanghai, and those people of means hired servants, including nannies, cooks, and drivers, of which there was a labor surplus. By including the figure of a cook in the advertisement's frame, Shanghai Tang's purported stylistic references to *old Shanghai* become overshadowed by the economic similarities of China's pre-socialist semicolonial capitalism and turn-of-the-twenty-first-century Chinese Communist Party (CCP)-sponsored capitalism. While acknowledging the return of class hierarchies, the Shanghai Tang advertisement, through its seemingly harmonious blend of stylistic and temporal references, ultimately obfuscates the class-based and local/foreign tensions that defined Republican Shanghai and that reappeared in the city in the 1990s–2000s.

China's new art

As an avid art collector, David Tang, founder of Shanghai Tang, became one of the most influential figures in defining the field of contemporary Chinese art within an international context. Tang recalls that when he first began collecting contemporary oil paintings from mainland China, he stood alone amid a sea of "traditional snobbish collectors [who] maintained their aloofness with the classical ink scrolls. … Happily for me," he continues, "these snobs have all been proved wrong. … Chinese modern and contemporary art has risen like a meteorite. … Of course there is a difference between art and the market. But having a good market at least suggests good art." [18] For Tang, the sudden growth and market success of contemporary Chinese art, which peaked in the early 2000s, resulted in large part from a newfound sense of hope amid mainland China's economic boom. He writes:

> The nation of China, with its economic overdrive, has in the last 10–20 years become a nation of hope—hope amongst each and every individual—hope none dared to dream of, say, in the times of Mao. All this release of optimism has given artists across the country an opportunity to release their own imagination and expression. No wonder in recent years, that Chinese art has become unmistakably more imaginative and expressive.[19]

Chinese hope, as Tang describes it, is intimately linked with the post-socialist promise of financial success. Tang effectively notes a general shift among Chinese artists, who, after 1989, tended to abandon thinking of art as a political tool, unified through collective styles, in favor of conceiving of art as individualistic expression, and, as many Shanghai-based artists have reminded me, as a financially profitable enterprise.[20] In line with these new artistic and commercial values, Tang widely exhibits his private collection of contemporary Chinese artworks in exclusive commercial spaces. For instance, numerous pieces are displayed in Tang's illustrious China Club—an elite private dining club in Hong Kong's Old China Bank building, decorated in Shanghai Tang's signature *old Shanghai* style (Figure 2.5).[21]

In 1993, many of the artists represented in David Tang's collection were included in the watershed exhibition "China's New Art, Post-1989," the first major instance in which "non-official" Chinese art traveled outside of mainland China. The exhibition was initially held at Hong Kong's Hanart TZ Gallery, named after the gallery's owner and exhibition curator Johnson Chang Tsong-Zung, and later traveled to sites throughout the United States, Canada, and Australia.[22] Co-curated by Chang and Beijing-based curator Li Xianting and assembling works by fifty-three Chinese artists, the exhibition highlighted thematic categories, such as "Political Pop" and "Cynical Realism," that largely defined the canon of contemporary Chinese art as it is

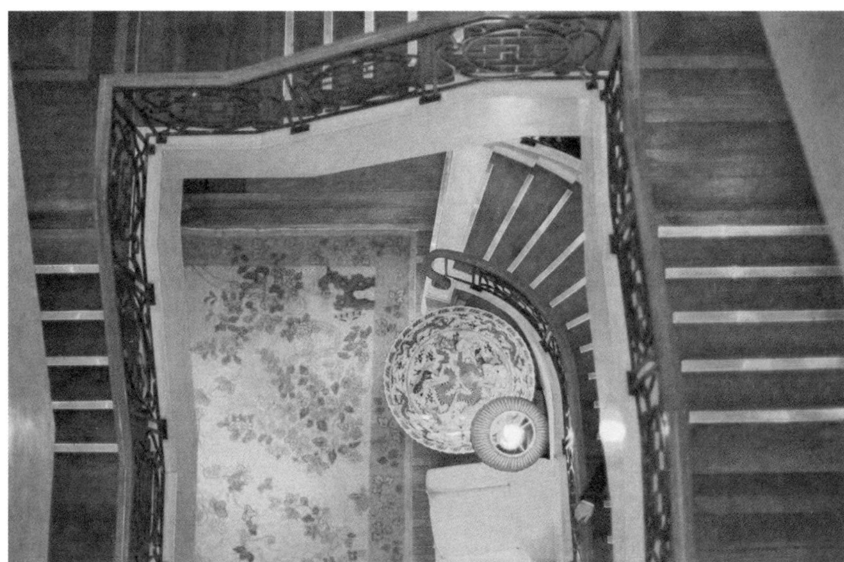

2.5 David Tang's China Club in Hong Kong displaying a sculpture from Liu Jianhua's series *Merriment*, 1999–2000.

now generally understood by foreign curators, collectors, gallerists, and other art professionals.

"China's New Art, Post-1989" supports a contemporary Chinese art/fashion system, in which fashion and garment-industry leaders such as David Tang, who received special thanks in the exhibition catalogue, play important roles. Many of the artworks included in the exhibition followed the hybrid logic of fashion brands like Shanghai Tang, integrating stylized references to China's socialist past. Featured in "China's New Art, Post-1989," Shanghai-based painter Yu Youhan and his student, Wang Ziwei, produce large-scale oil and acrylic paintings of Chairman Mao. Cast by the curators of "China's New Art, Post-1989" as among the most influential works in the late 1980s–90s "Political Pop" movement, paintings such as Yu Youhan's *Waving to the World* (1992) (Figure 2.6) combine iconic images of Mao, culled from the heroic socialist-realist portraits of the 1950s–70s, with flattened painted surfaces and decorative details, such as bright color planes, repetitive patterns, and floral motifs. In addition to referencing the popular imagery of the Cultural Revolution, namely the ubiquitous images of Mao, both series appropriate modernist and postmodernist aesthetic elements, including the expressionistic color palette of French artist Henri Matisse and US pop artist Andy Warhol's flattened surfaces. Warhol, who many contemporary Chinese painters tout as a model, culled materials from mass media and advertising and produced large

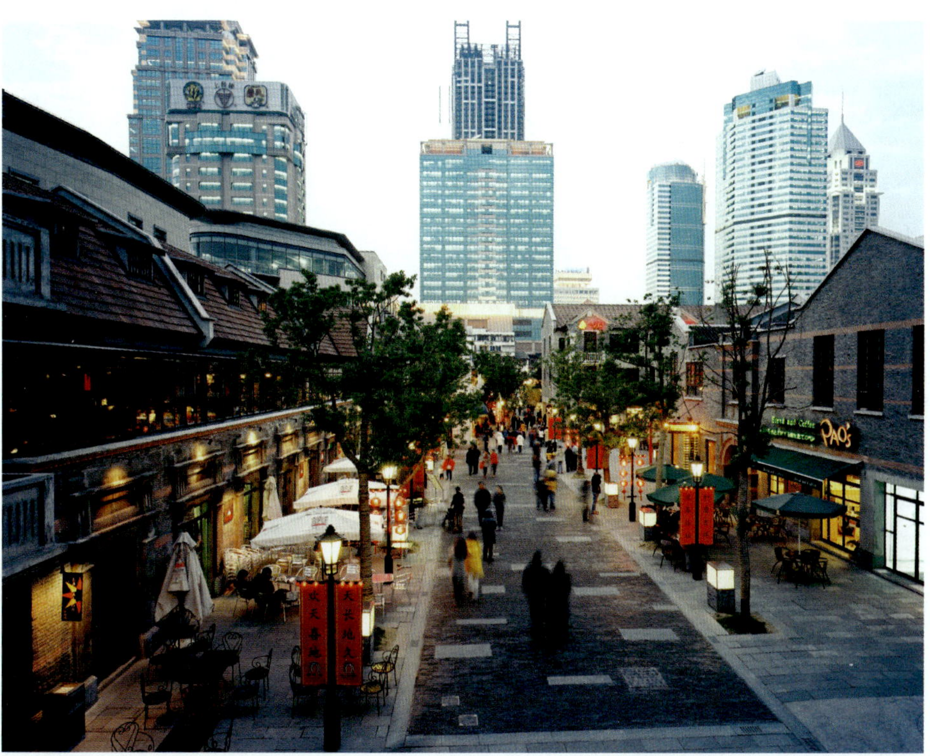

Plate 1 *Xintiandi,* developed by Shui On Land and designed by Wood and Zapata; Skidmore, Owings, and Merrill; and Nikken Sekkei International, built 1997–2002. Image courtesy of Benjamin Wood Studio.

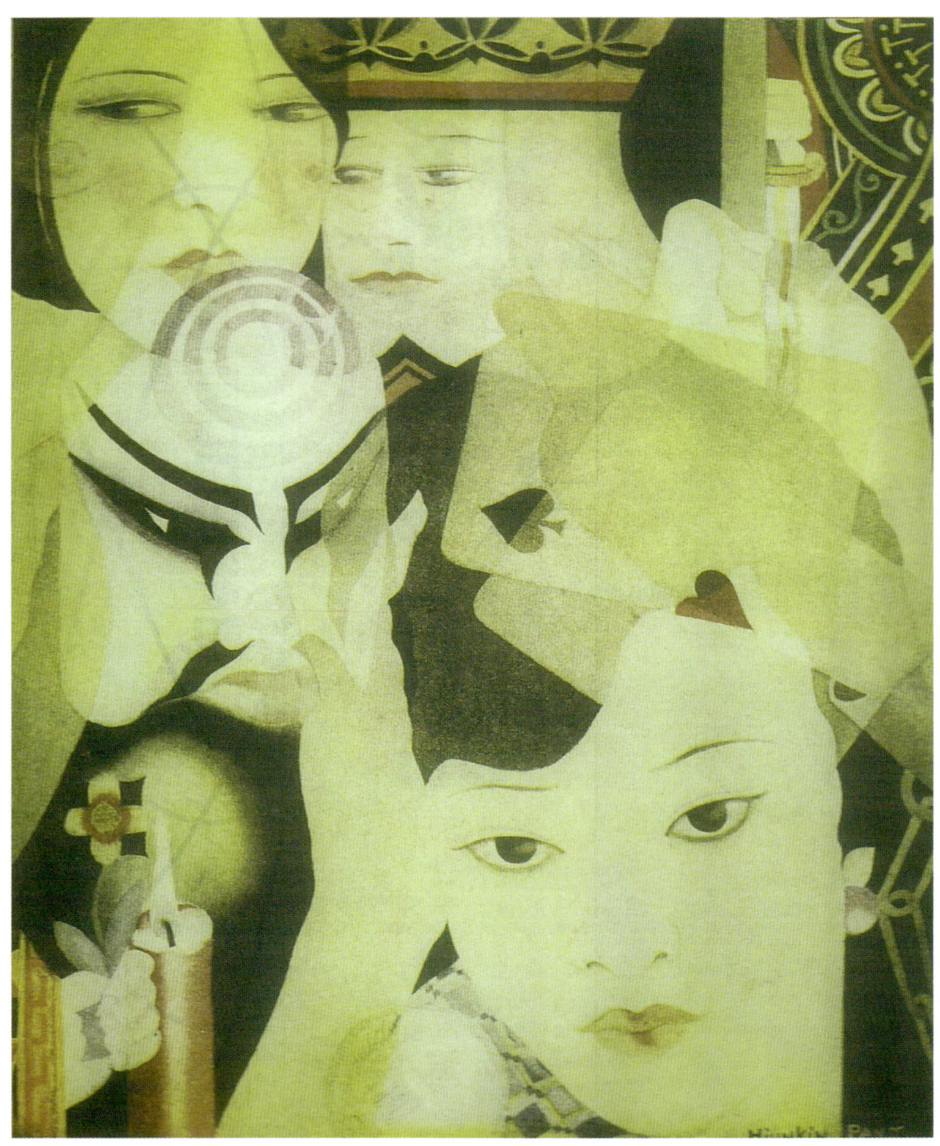

Plate 2 Pang Xunqin, *Such is Shanghai*, or *The Riddle of Life*, 1931. Watercolor on paper. Destroyed. Image courtesy of Changshu Art Museum.

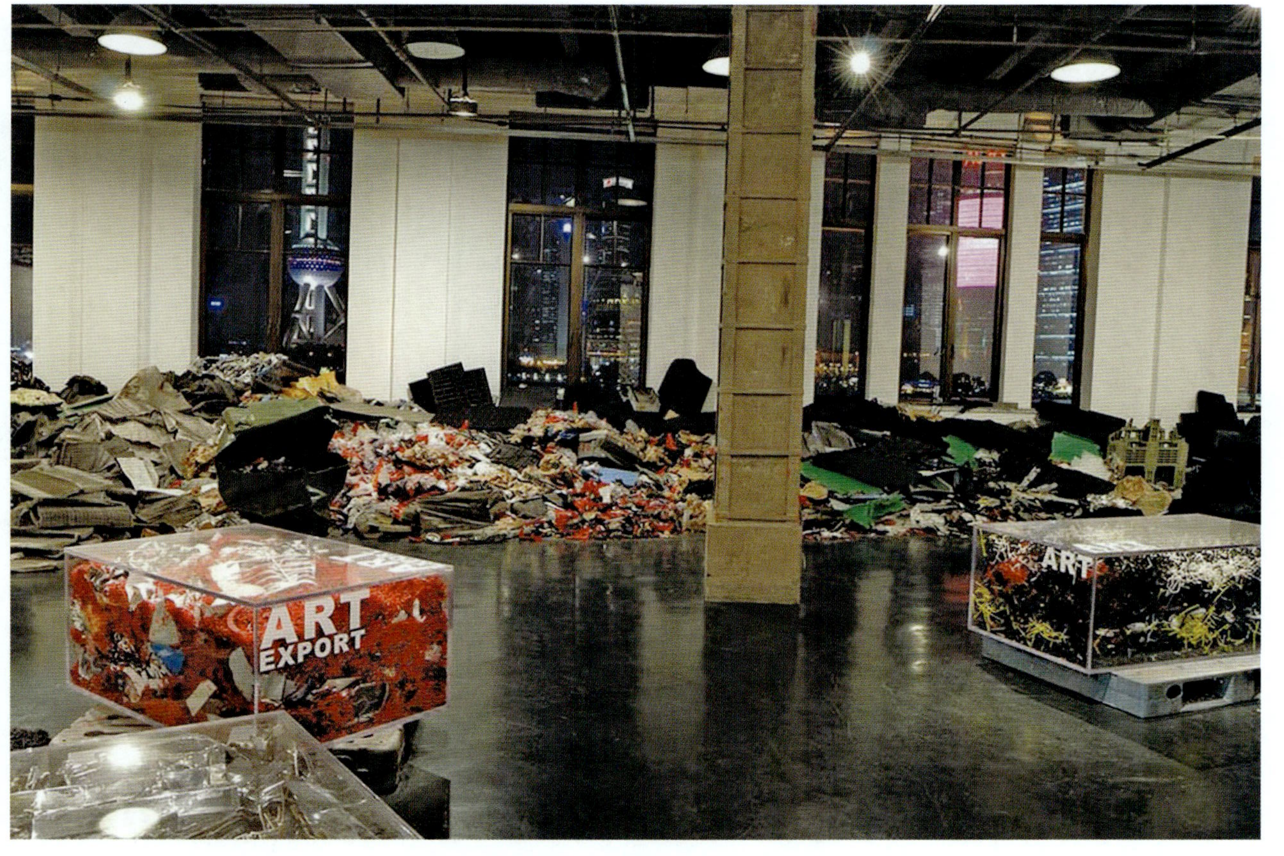

Plate 3 Liu Jianhua, *Export—Cargo Transit*, 2007. Installation view at Shanghai Gallery of Art, Shanghai, China. Image courtesy of artist.

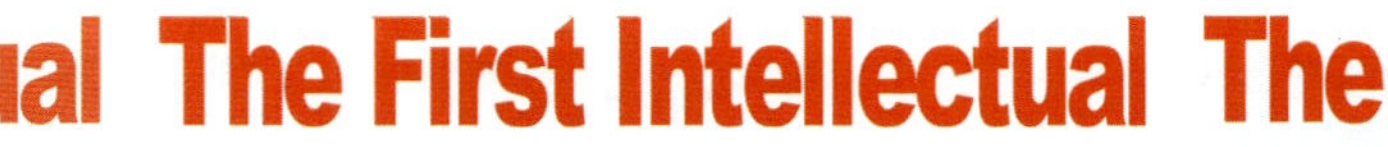
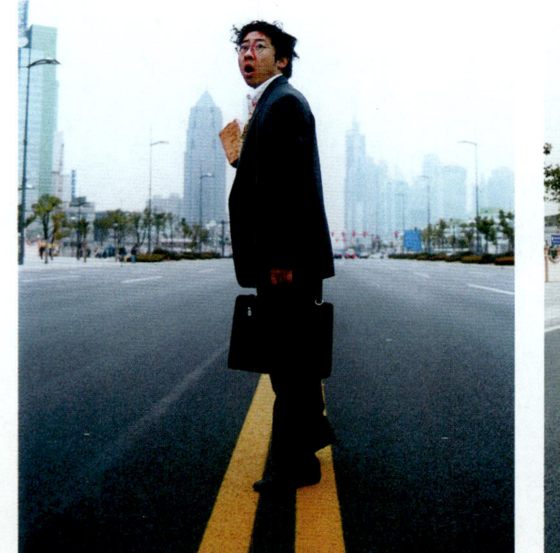
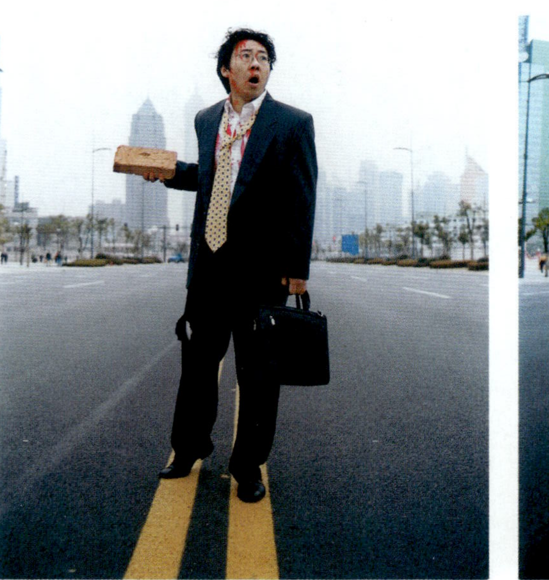

Plate 4   Yang Fudong, *The First Intellectual*, 2000. 3 color photographs. 76 × 50 inches each. Images courtesy of artist and Marian Goodman Gallery.

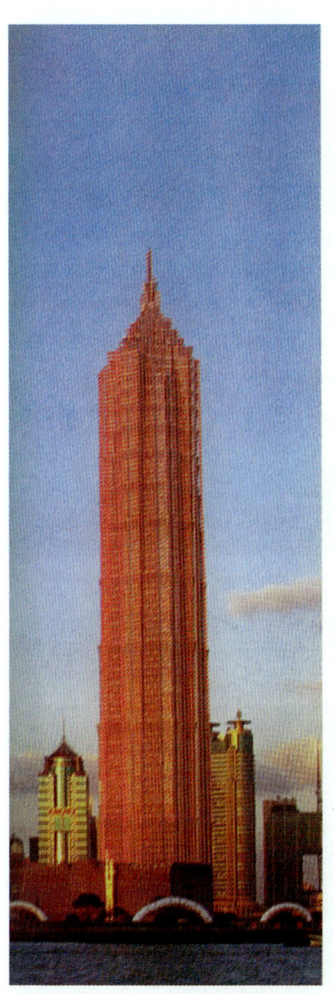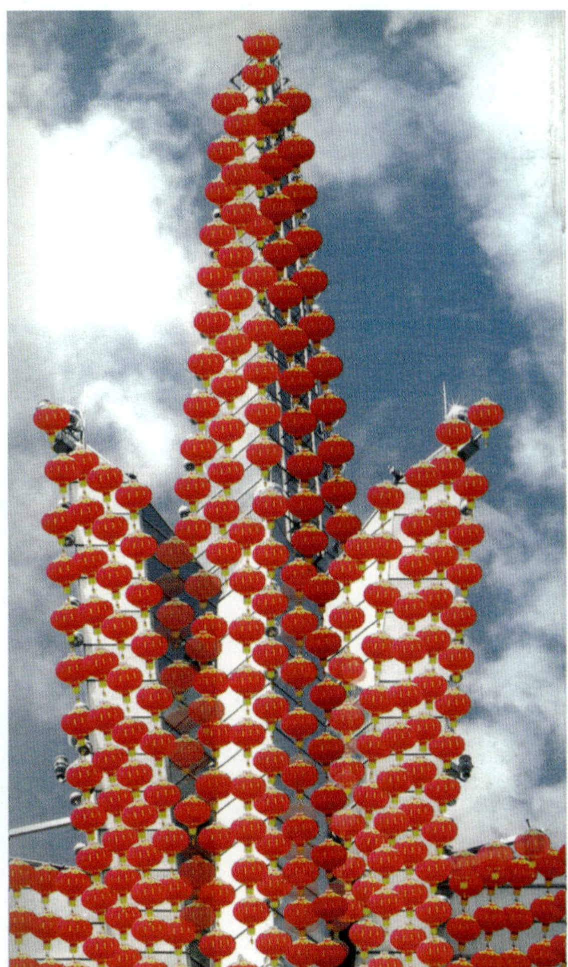

Plate 5 Gu Wenda, *Heavenly Lantern Project* for Shanghai's Jin Mao Tower, 2003. Proposed project renderings. Images courtesy of artist.

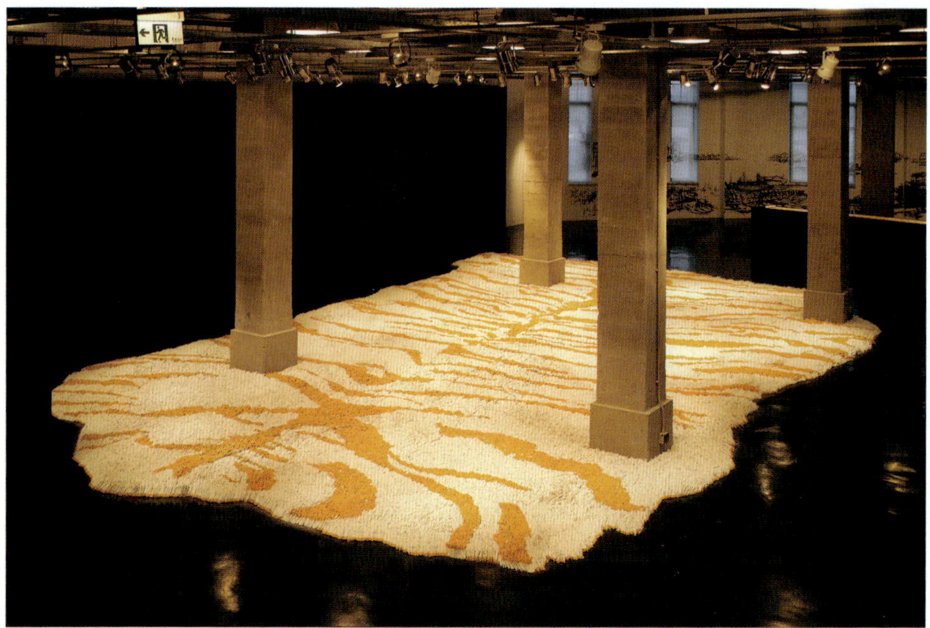

Plate 6 (a) Xu Bing, *Honor and Splendor* (Shanghai Version), 2004. 660,000 "Wealth" brand cigarettes, spray adhesive, cardboard. Approx. 354 × 275 inches. Installation view at Shanghai Gallery of Art, Shanghai, China, 2004. © Xu Bing Studio.

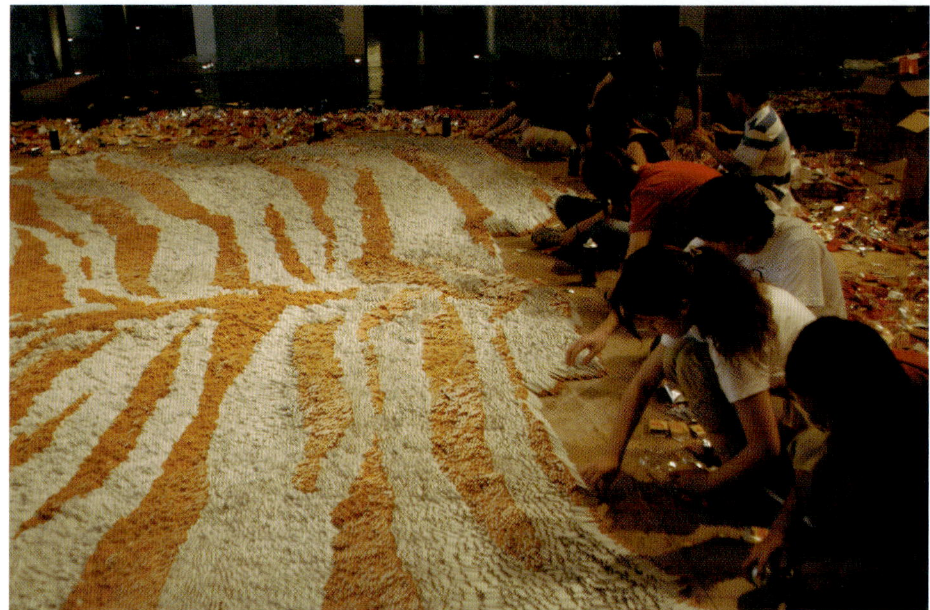

Plate 6 (b) Xu Bing, *Honor and Splendor* (Shanghai Version), 2004. 660,000 "Wealth" brand cigarettes, spray adhesive, cardboard. Approx. 354 × 275 inches. View of assistants assembling cigarettes at Shanghai Gallery of Art, Shanghai, China, 2004. © Xu Bing Studio. Images courtesy of artist.

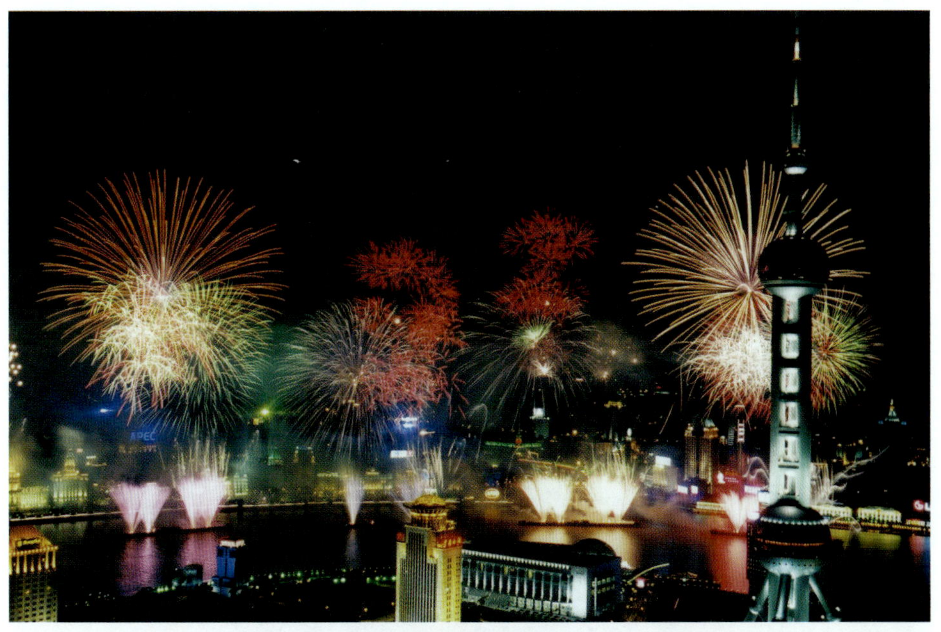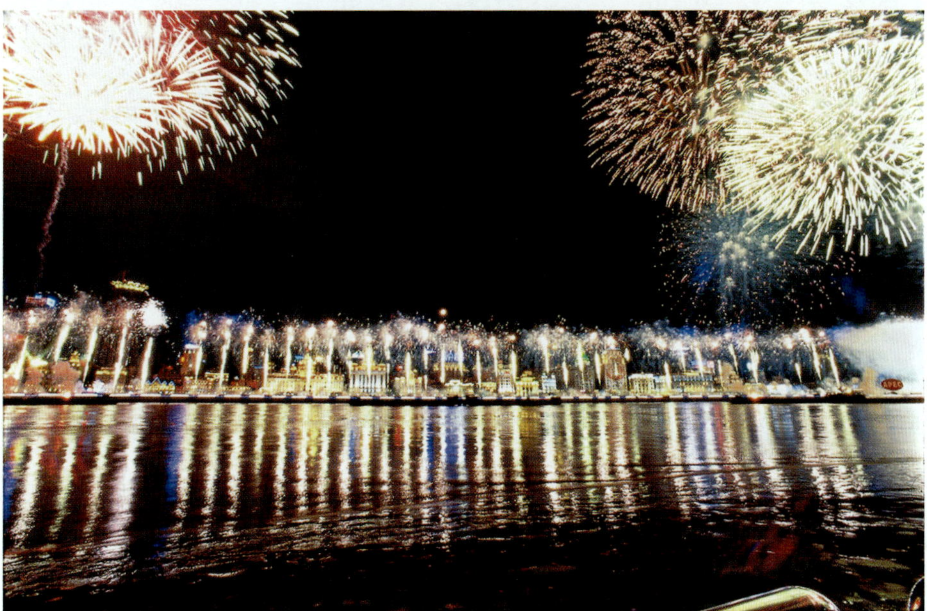

Plate 7 Cai Guo-Qiang, *Asia-Pacific Economic Cooperation (APEC) Cityscape Fireworks*, realized at the Bund, Lujiazui, and Huangpu River, Shanghai, China, on October 20, 2001. Images courtesy Cai Studio.

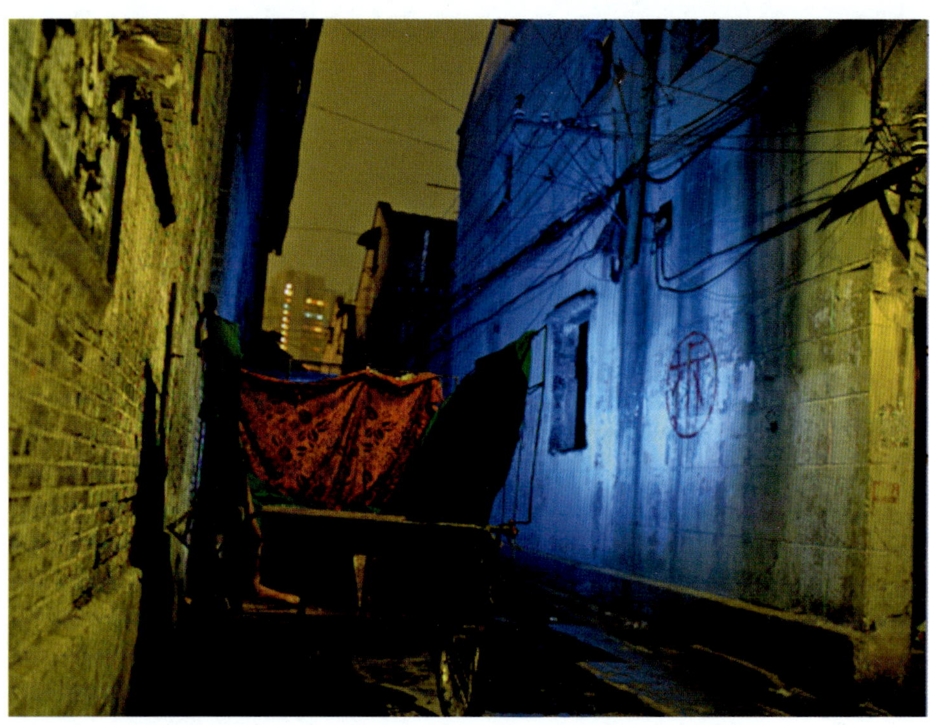

Plate 8 Liu Jiajia, *Pedicab in an old longtang alley*, from series *The Forgotten Corner of the City was Quiet at Last*, 2006. Color photograph. (This photograph was taken in a neighborhood slated for demolition, apparent in the wall marking: 拆/*chai*.) Image courtesy of artist.

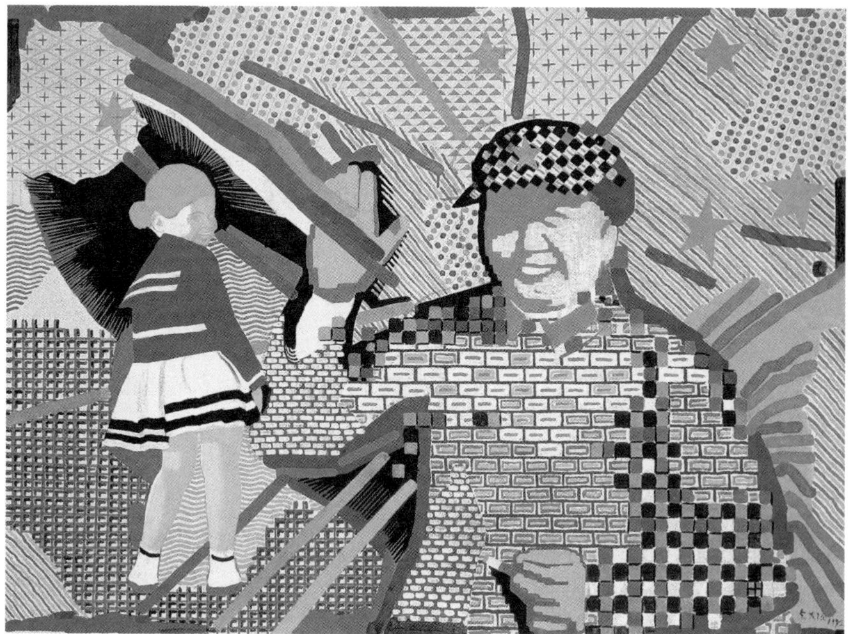

Yu Youhan, *Waving to the World*, 1992. Acrylic on canvas. 86 × 115 cm.   **2.6**

quantities of silk-screen prints, including portraits of Mao during the years of the Cultural Revolution.

While most non-Chinese viewers tend to read Yu Youhan and Wang Ziwei's paintings as disparaging deconstructions of the cult of Mao, the artists themselves publicly maintain more ambivalent, and even admiring, relationships to their subject. Wang Ziwei, for instance, writes of Mao in this positive light:

> I prefer reading books by Mao Zedong to philosophy books. Mao's understanding of freedom is much more profound than that of an intellectual. Sometimes, cultural issues become too complicated. Images of red flags seem very warm. Mao cares for the masses and communicates with them. This is quite a Pop attitude.[23]

Whatever these "Political Pop" paintings transmit, messages that necessarily vary depending on viewers' own subject positions, the works contribute to the establishment of a relatively fixed system of symbolization and aesthetic references commonly found within the mainstream pantheon of contemporary Chinese art. The collapsing together of specifically Chinese content, especially imagery from the Cultural Revolution (e.g., portraits of Mao, heroic portrayals of peasants, workers, and soldiers), and foreign-influenced styles (e.g., Warhol-like pop art) was one of the most salient features of the contemporary Chinese art exhibited abroad during the 1990s–2000s and seen throughout Shanghai's newly minted contemporary art galleries and museums. This "Political Pop" model of East-meets-West hybridity, while synthesizing cultural differences at an aesthetic level, ignores the violent conflicts that accompanied Mao's rise as a totalitarian icon. By reproducing Mao's authoritative picturing, made more benign through the addition of flowers and pastel colors, such paintings project an appearance of cultural cohesion that neglects to account for the neo-colonialist undertones of imposing French and US styles on stereotypically Chinese content.

Somewhat of an anomaly in the pantheon of contemporary Chinese painting, Shanghai-based artist Ding Yi, also included in "China's New Art, Post-1989," offers a more abstract approach to his hybridizing of Chinese and foreign references. Ding Yi's ongoing series, *Appearance of Crosses* (1992–Present), is comprised of geometric oil paintings all deriving from the appearance, duplication, and juxtaposition of the symbol of the cross, which, in Chinese, is the written character for ten (十/*shi*) (Figure 2.7). Ding Yi's paintings rely on the basic horizontal and vertical strokes of Chinese calligraphy and the monastic repetition demanded by the medium's study, while also owing much, as the artist readily acknowledges, to Western European paintings of the early twentieth century, especially works by Dutch artist Piet Mondrian.[24] In contrast to the intentionally flattened surfaces of Yu Youhan and Wang Ziwei's "Political Pop" paintings of Mao, Ding Yi's experiments with crosses/tens and selection of colors based on

potential for striking optical effects result in intricately layered compositions that offer an illusory sense of depth. Unlike many of his peers, Ding Yi insists on painting his canvases himself, rather than using assistants or outsourcing the work to painting production facilities. He works methodically at a consistently slow pace, producing about one painting per month, or a total of twelve per year. While some critics have read this deacceleration as a resistance to Shanghai's, and China's, fast-paced development, Ding Yi sees his artistic methods as forging a connection to his own lived experience. In an interview with curator Hans Ulrich Obrist, Ding Yi stated, "Unlike those artists with a team of assistants I want to keep painting my paintings by myself from the beginning until the end. This is how I make them resemble the outside world."[25]

In terms of influence, Ding Yi cites the urban surrounds of Shanghai as a particularly motivating force:

> I'm thinking critically about what it's like living in a city like Shanghai, where everything is a bit bright and loud. A lot of things here are really superficial—the lights, the appearance of the city as a whole. … In Shanghai, the colors around you—on the street, in advertisements—are fighting all the time. It's not a peaceful city. There's shouting everywhere, and that gives rise to excitement. I want my work to express this kind of reality.[26]

The artist also identifies Shanghai's modern art and design history as a source of inspiration. Rather than resort to pastiche or aestheticized appropriation, Ding Yi's art structurally aligns with *haipai* as developed by artists like Pang Xunqin (discussed in Chapter 1) in the 1930s. Educated at the Shanghai Arts & Crafts School, Ding Yi's training in product design and advertising has clearly impacted his aesthetic concerns, apparent in the serial and machinic qualities of his meticulously hand-painted canvases. While primarily situated in the realm of fine art since the 1990s, Ding Yi's practice is also more broadly conceived as one that blurs the boundaries between art and design, both in terms of how his paintings function formally and also through recent experiments with and future plans for projects that mesh art, architecture, and public sculpture.[27] Demonstrating his commitment to public art, in 2002, Ding Yi made *Cross Bridge*, an eight-meter-long bridge using his signature cross motif, which was installed in Shanghai's Pudong district (Figure 2.8). In discussing the bridge project, Ding Yi states, "It was both sculptural and architectural. … For me, this bridge project is very important, part of a much larger scheme for which I've proposed many ideas. The ones I've realized have had a functional quality, such as bus stops and structures for an electrical plant. Otherwise, it's very difficult for art to enter this sort of environment."[28] Ding Yi conceptualizes his efforts to bring art into the everyday environment of urban Shanghai as linked to the city's Republican-era past and utopian *haipai* experiments that

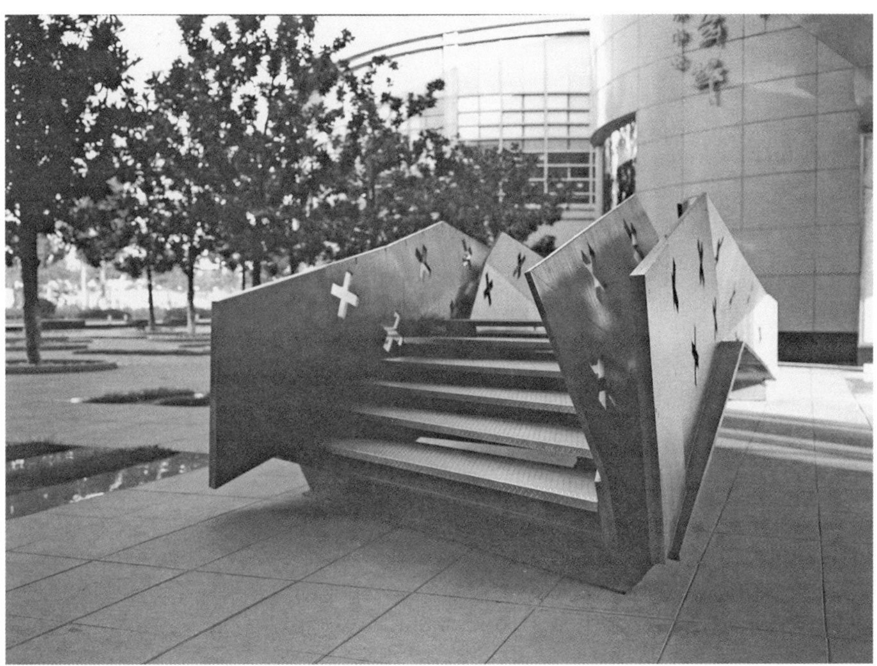

2.8   Ding Yi, *Cross Bridge*, 2001. Site-specific Lianyang Community Project.

aimed to bridge art and design. In an interview with me, he proclaimed with hopeful enthusiasm, "Today, in Shanghai, there is a little bit of the flavor of 1930s Shanghai."[29]

Old-fashioned Shanghai

Propagating superficial, romanticized visions of *old Shanghai* has become a major marketing tool within Shanghai's sites of multinational capitalist consumption. Shanghai Tang, through its founder's promotion of contemporary Chinese art, has also helped construct an art/fashion system in which multinational fashion brands and local art become increasingly intertwined. In the case of Shanghai, it is no coincidence that overseas fashion companies began forging collaborations with local artists and constructing marketing campaigns in China's booming financial and fashion capital just as the appetite for foreign luxury goods was growing increasingly voracious. Consider Christian Dior, which, like Shanghai Tang, is today owned by a multinational umbrella company—LVMH Moët Hennessy Louis Vuitton SE—the world's largest luxury-goods conglomerate run by French businessman Bernard Jean Étienne Arnault, himself a prominent art collector. In 2013, Christian Dior held "Esprit Dior," an exhibition at Shanghai MOCA, displaying Dior garments from 1947 to the present, arranged thematically and alongside artworks by eight contemporary Chinese artists.[30]

The "Esprit Dior" exhibition followed an advertising campaign revolving around *Lady Blue Shanghai* (2010), a sixteen-minute film made by US director David Lynch (Figure 2.9).[31] The short film featured prominent Shanghai locations, including the Huangpu River and its opposing waterfronts: the Bund, the former heart of the US and British-run International Settlement, lined in colonial architecture built up in the 1920s–30s with foreign capital; and Liujiazui, Shanghai's flashy financial district of the Pudong New Development Zone (east of the Huangpu River), whose development was fueled by CCP investment and post-Mao policies of economic liberalization.[32] *Lady Blue Shanghai* stars French movie star Marion Cotillard as a foreigner visiting Shanghai on business. Following the opening credits, which appear over a still shot of the Lujiazui skyline, the camera pans the facade of Shanghai's Hotel Metropole—an iconic Art Deco building commissioned by Shanghai's wealthiest foreign industrialist, Victor Sassoon, and built in 1934 by the British architectural firm Palmer and Turner.[33] Viewers see Cotillard enter the hotel lobby, ascend the elevator, and walk the long narrow hallway toward her room. As she nears her door, she hears 1920s tango music. She enters her room and

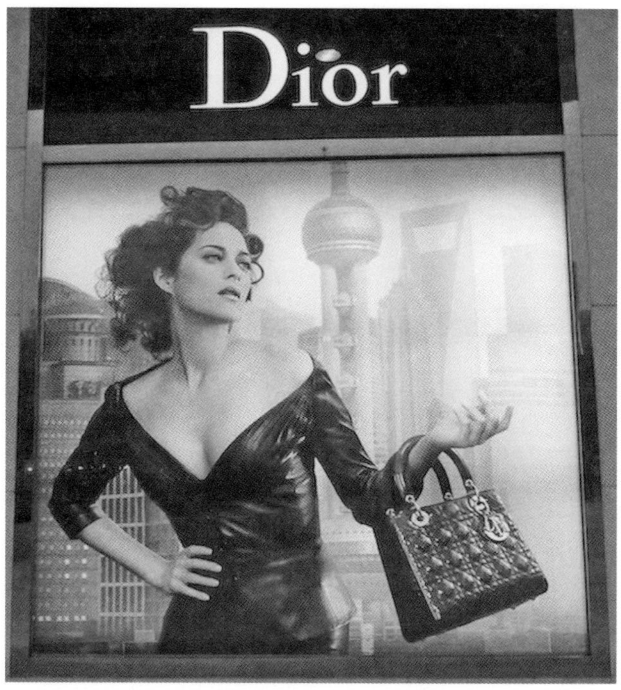

Christian Dior Advertisement featuring Marion Cotillard and Shanghai's Lujiazui Skyline, 2010.   **2.9**

realizes the music is coming from a record player inside. She stops the record. Suddenly, lights flash and a large cloud of smoke appears, dissipating to reveal a Lady Dior handbag, illuminated on a small gold footstool. Terrified, Cotillard calls the front desk. "Someone is here," she tells the guard, "someone is in my room."[34] The clerk sends up two security guards dressed in black suits. Cotillard recounts to the guards her uncanny experience that day, explaining that, while it was her first visit to Shanghai, she had the distinct sense that she had been there before. The feeling came over her when she visited Lujiazui's Oriental Pearl Radio and Television Tower. The film flashes to a blurry shot of the top of the tower, illuminated by colorful lights and a full moon. Cotillard explains, "I had learned [the tower] was inspired by a poem … about different sized pearls falling on jade. … I thought I heard the sound. As I looked up at the tower I felt … I had been here before in Shanghai. This feeling came over me as I heard the pearls falling and hitting the jade. … It seemed as if suddenly I was in the old Shanghai."[35] The 1920s tango music plays again over footage of *shikumen* homes, winding alleys, and narrow stairways, filmed in soft focus. Cotillard enters a room of *old Shanghai*, lavishly decorated in red drapes, wallpaper, carpets, lamps, furniture, and knickknacks.[36] A tall Chinese man in a suit enters the room, putting his finger over his lips and whispering hush. He approaches Cotillard and they kiss passionately. Then they run out and down an alley, past a rickshaw and 1920s model car, on stone roads and under porticos. They cross the Waibaidu Bridge, a steel structure near the Bund, which brings them back to the present, marked by footage of Shanghai's LED-soaked cityscape, elevated roads, and modern buildings made of glass and concrete. "I can't be here," the man says as the camera swirls around leaving trails of lingering light. The pair run up to a rooftop above the Huangpu River. Cotillard's lover pulls back. "I can't be here. I wish I could. … It's all very beautiful, so beautiful," he exclaims looking at the towers of Lujiazui and the neoclassical buildings on the Bund, one of which appears with a superimposed digital billboard projecting Cotillard dancing with the mysterious Dior handbag. "I have to leave," the man repeats. "But please, I love you," she says. "And I love you." He walks backward, as if pulled by some invisible force. He holds out a bouquet of blue roses before fading away. The film then returns to Cotillard and the security guards in her hotel room. Shaken, she walks over to the handbag and opens it to find a blue rose in full bloom. She takes the flower and sniffs it longingly before clutching the bag in a powerful embrace. In this blatant instance of commodity fetishism, cultural and temporal hybridity function to promote multinational capitalist consumption. *Old Shanghai*, classical Chinese culture, and post-socialist Shanghai are collapsed together as Cotillard suspects she has lived a past life in Republican Shanghai while visiting the Oriental Pearl Television and Radio Tower, Lujiazui's most iconic building erected in 1994, and learning that the architectural design references

Bai Juyi's Tang Dynasty poem *Song of Pipa* ("Pearls, big and small, fall into a jade tray").[37] Conspicuously, Lynch's short film positions Cotillard's Chinese lover as stuck in *old Shanghai*, while the French actress, blue rose, and Lady Dior handbag are able to transcend time and become contemporary.

Broken social sculptures

Even in the face of such an unabashedly exoticizing advertisement, fashion brands like Christian Dior and contemporary Chinese artists have, in recent years, collaborated in a more mutually beneficial terrain than the acknowledgement of Orientalism and corporate cooptation would suggest. However counterintuitively, fashion brand commissions and exhibitions in retail spaces sometimes afford artists the chance to work without the market demands fueling Shanghai's private art museums, many of which resort to leasing exhibition space to the highest bidder, often doubling as venues for corporate events. Furthermore, fashion houses can offer alternatives for artists striving to make work outside of the CCP's particular programs and agendas that drive many of Shanghai's state-supported museums. For instance, Fudan University professor, curator, photographer, and art critic Gu Zheng recently organized a series of exhibitions in a second-floor gallery located in Shanghai's Bottega Veneta retail space near the Bund, featuring some of China's most experimental contemporary artists, including Shanghai-based sculptor Liu Jianhua.[38]

Like the previously mentioned painters Yu Youhan and Wang Ziwei, Liu Jianhua has been collected and promoted by David Tang.[39] In addition to this patronage, Liu Jianhua has teamed up with Christian Dior. In 2008, Christian Dior held an exhibition at Beijing's Ullens Center for Contemporary Art, "Christian Dior and Chinese Artists," featuring over 100 couture pieces and Dior-inspired artworks by twenty contemporary Chinese artists.[40] For the Beijing exhibition, Liu Jianhua displayed *Regular/Fragile: Starlight* (Figure 2.10), an installation of dozens of rows of porcelain replicas of handbags, shoes, and perfume bottles, situated under golden *D*s, *i*s, *o*s, and *r*s hanging like a sparkling mobile. In the aforementioned "Esprit Dior" exhibition held eight years later at Shanghai MOCA, Liu Jianhua hung 3,000 ceramic Dior perfume bottles from the ceiling. While acknowledging Liu Jianhua's embeddedness in a contemporary Chinese art/fashion system, it is also important to recognize that his ceramic installations did not start or end with these Dior commissions. As such, Dior's sponsorship of these brand-oriented iterations should be further considered as a form of financial support that extends to the artist's wider practice.

Liu Jianhua began the *Regular/Fragile* series in 2000. The original version was presented at the China Pavilion of the 2003 Venice Biennial, and comprised thousands of handmade porcelain objects resembling commodities

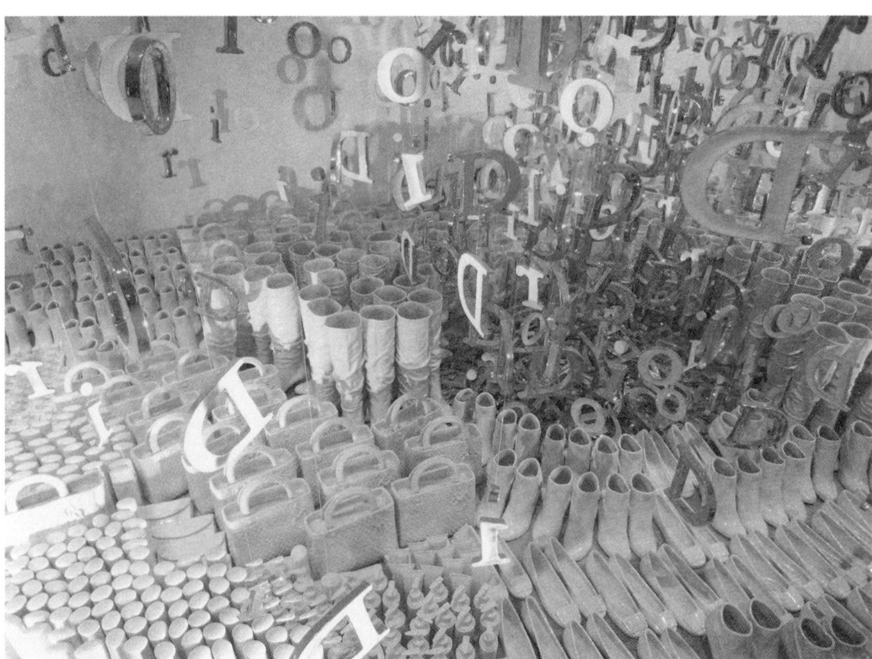

2.10   Liu Jianhua, *Regular/Fragile: Starlight*, installation at "Christian Dior and Chinese Artists," Ullens Center for Contemporary Art, Beijing, China, 2008.

such as hammers, milk cartons, handbags, high-heeled boots, baseball caps, soda bottles, toy airplanes, and thermoses. Since then, Liu Jianhua has continued to exhibit versions of *Regular/Fragile* in large-scale installations both in China and internationally, covering entire gallery floors or outdoor spaces with his porcelain commodity-lookalikes that sometimes creep up onto furniture and walls. Conjuring mainland China's seemingly incessant flows of mass-produced goods, the uniformly bluish-white porcelain objects, devoid of use value, appear like the ghostly residue of commodity culture and late-capitalist production, capable of churning out more and more things at ever increasing rates by utilizing low-paid labor in developing nations. The title, *Regular/Fragile*, remarks on the fragility of porcelain, which in similar works Liu Jianhua further accentuates by smashing objects to pieces. *Regular/Fragile* also registers the illusory nature of the values we assign to commodities (e.g., stability, permanence, undying pleasure) and the fragility of the globalized networks supporting capitalist manufacturing.[41]

As with many contemporary Chinese, and especially Shanghai-based, artists, the work of Liu Jianhua has been primarily framed in terms of Chinese content and cross-cultural meanings. Look, for instance, to the literature surrounding his early series from 1999–2001, *Obsessive Memories* and *Merriment*, which depict Ming Dynasty–style porcelain plates, sofas, and headless, armless women's bodies clothed in *qipaos*, dresses oft associated with *old Shanghai*. A gallery-sponsored catalogue of the artist's work describes *Obsessive Memories* in relation to Chinese and Western aesthetic motifs and symbols:

> Qipao has been the most symbolic representation of Chinese women, which would … arouse [viewers'] mysterious fantasy and desire for control. The sofa often brings to mind words like modern, power, money, sexy, comfort, the West, etc. The combination of these two visualized and totally different models brings a seemingly endless impact to one's imagination.[42]

The key to the series' meaning, readers are told, lies in Liu Jianhua's juxtaposition of seemingly incongruous cultural elements, especially Chinese *qipaos* and Western sofas. In the description of Liu Jianhua's *Obsessive Memories*, "China" is symbolized by a traditional woman's dress that conjures mystery, fantasy, desire, and patriarchal control, while "the West" is symbolized by a modern sofa conveying the presumably Western values of power, money, sex, and comfort. Here, the symbolic norms of the contemporary Chinese art/fashion system are maintained, as cultural categories are reductively defined and set in simplistic binary oppositions. Yet, while these juxtapositions of "traditional China" and "modern West" are evaluated primarily at the levels of form and subject matter, elsewhere the catalogue hints at different, more material ways in which these categories intersect and become complicated.

Readers are told that Liu Jianhua produces many of his projects, including *Regular/Fragile*, in the artist's hometown of Jingdezhen, China's historic capital of porcelain production since the Han Dynasty (206 BCE–220 CE).[43] From the late 1970s through the mid-1980s, in the aftermath of the Cultural Revolution, Liu Jianhua learned the craft of porcelain production while working in the manufacturing section of the Jingdezhen Pottery and Porcelain Sculpting Factory. He later studied sculpture in the Fine Arts Department of the Jingdezhen Pottery and Porcelain College. In the ensuring years, Liu Jianhua utilized his practical training in porcelain production to confront social and environmental issues related to China's fast-paced development. In *Transformation of Memories* (2003), for instance, Liu Jianhua created a series of porcelain casts of fallen trees in his hometown. The porcelain figures stood like broken memorials to the old trees that were cut down during a massive urbanization project undertaken to celebrate Jingdezhen's 1000th birthday. For the artist, the fallen trees were like corpses dotting the increasingly unfamiliar landscape of his hometown, which he hardly recognized after having been away through the 1990s and early 2000s. A catalogue writer explained:

> Before, Liu Jianhua had been proud to live in a country that respected and cherished its own tradition. But with … economic development and …

accelerating transformation towards the so-called "international metropolis," people have become apathetic and neglectful of traditional culture and (the) living environment, leaving them with a sense of emptiness. … (As) cities get more homogenous … people (grow) apathetic and "cold" towards each other.[44]

Liu Jianhua's art addresses environmental degradation while lamenting the social relations he sees as languishing amid China's post-Mao era modernization.

Simultaneously, the artist creates new social exchanges by employing modes of production that operate somewhat in parallel to the mechanics of globalization that projects such as *Transformation of Memories* seek to critique. Since the early 2000s, Liu Jianhua has cultivated a career as an internationally recognized contemporary artist, eventually settling in Shanghai, where he currently works as a professor in the Sculpture Department of the Fine Arts School of Shanghai University. He maintains a massive studio in Shanghai's recently built Taopu Arts District with multiple full-time assistants, and also a production workshop in Jingdezhen that employs local artisans on a project-to-project basis. Jingdezhen, historically a town of artisans in which generation after generation master the art of porcelain production, has been largely left out of the sweeping development that engulfed China's eastern coastal cities when Deng Xiaoping opened them as New Development and Special Economic Zones, paving the way for foreign investment and enormous factory complexes that manufacture massive quantities of goods at low cost.

Liu Jianhua is one of many artists to utilize porcelain producers and facilities in Jingdezhen. Most internationally known among numerous others is Ai Weiwei, who employed some 1,600 residents of Jingdezhen to produce one hundred million painstakingly produced, hand-painted porcelain sunflower seeds for a large-scale installation designed for the Tate Modern's Turbine Hall in London in 2010. Unintentionally, Ai Weiwei's *Sunflower Seeds* also raised environmental issues. The project originally filled the grand Turbine Hall; viewers were invited to frolic through the seeds, even pick them up and play with them. By feeling the seeds' individualized textures and seeing up close their hand-painted, hand-crafted qualities, Tate-goers in London might grasp a connection between the imported objects and their labor-intensive, highly skilled production, a connection long lost under the conditions of globalized, mass-produced manufacturing. However, soon after the exhibition opened, the seeds, which emitted dust particles when handled and walked upon, were deemed hazardous and relegated to a roped-off side room, where viewers could only gaze upon them from a distance.[45] Unexpectedly, this failed interactive reception highlighted the disconnect between consumption and production under globalization, as well as the discrepancies between what counts as toxic in developing versus developed nations.

Ai Weiwei and Liu Jianhua's methods might initially appear to follow Chairman Mao's order to artists to "go among the masses of workers,"[46] or else to mimic the more recent outsourcing operations of multinational corporations, such as Christian Dior and Shanghai Tang. But by insisting on highly skilled artisanship and working with porcelain, a craft Liu Jianhua honed through decades of study, he reverses the logic of mass production, reinvigorating Jingdezhen's artisan-based economy that has suffered both under the extremism of the Cultural Revolution and in the face of the PRC's subsequent rise as the world's factory. Liu Jianhua's ongoing work in Jingdezhen engages mainland China's and the world's dramatically changing society through the use of decentralized, industrialized, and pre-industrialized—handmade and craft-based—modes of production, while fostering collaborations with local artisans whose unique skills have been all but rendered obsolete by the forces of globalization and the so-called Made-in-China phenomenon. By maintaining a workshop in Jingdezhen, a place whose inhabitants continue to learn and pass down a specialized craft, Liu Jianhua contributes to an economy that has been isolated from the financial growth concentrated in China's large cities like Shanghai. Art projects like these fashion new economic opportunities and social configurations, and as such they should be understood as a kind of social sculpture of global proportions, in which social meanings are found not only in the art objects' aesthetics and symbols but also in the differing responses they provoke in a variety of cultural contexts, and in their travels from Jingdezhen to Shanghai to cities across the world, as well as in the hands that crafted these objects, reminding us of the many hands that make and transnationally transport most of the things we use daily.[47]

For his inclusion in the 2006 Shanghai Biennial, Liu Jianhua presented *Yiwu Survey*, an installation made from part of a shipping cargo container affixed to a wall to appear as if it were jutting through the gallery. Out of the open container spilled a mountain of small objects, including inflatable toys, clocks, plastic wastebaskets, calculators, and bicycle helmets—the same kinds of objects that Liu Jianhua casts in porcelain in *Regular/Fragile*. He had purchased the objects from Yiwu, a relatively small southeastern Chinese city of 1.2 million people in Zhejiang Province and the world's capital of small commodity wholesales. The onslaught of objects spilling out of the cargo container served as a relatively small reminder of the magnitude of China's export industry. At the time of the Shanghai Biennial, in the city of Yiwu alone, more than 1,000 cargo containers filled with labor-intensive and cheaply manufactured goods shipped out to 212 foreign countries daily.[48] The items of *Yiwu Survey*—inexpensive and made in China—are not what art or design historians generally classify as designed objects. As Matthew Turner argues in "Early Modern Design in Hong Kong," "Design literature is almost exclusively concerned with the First World," as historians of design leave much out of the canon, including both mass-produced objects and objects from developing nations.[49] And yet *Yiwu Survey*, with its hundreds of small commodities from Yiwu, appeared in the 2006 Shanghai Biennial, which was titled "Hyper Design" and promoted as "exploring the complicated, overlapping social liaison and cultural meanings hidden behind the phenomenon of 'Design.'"[50] Within this frame, Liu Jianhua transformed apparently *non-designed* objects into contemporary artworks. The project highlighted mainland China's position as the epicenter of globalized mass production, while flexing the artist's expanded role as consumer and designer.

In a photographic project completed a year prior, *The Virtual Scene* (2005), Liu Jianhua presented Shanghai's iconic Huangpu Riverfronts—the Lujiazui skyline and Bund—as blurred backdrops for poker chips stacked like unsteady skyscrapers (Figures 2.11–2.12). In *The Virtual Scene*'s sculptural iteration, the artist modeled an entire metropolis out of poker chips, some of which were stacked with dice to resemble iconic Shanghai buildings, mocking the glamorizing pretenses of China's fast-paced urbanization and speculation. As he created these photographs and models, Liu Jianhua was at work on a large-scale exhibition to be presented amid the actual settings represented in *The Virtual Scene*. Displayed at the Shanghai Gallery of Art in the upscale art/fashion complex Three on the Bund,[51] Liu Jianhua's 2007 project *Export—Cargo Transit* tackled the uneven conditions of the international art world and the environmental harm incurred by disparate global economic development (Plate 3). Overlapping with the 2006 Shanghai Biennial, *Export—Cargo Transit* consisted of a series of "sculptures" and "paintings" made out of garbage imported into mainland China from developed nations, such as the United States and

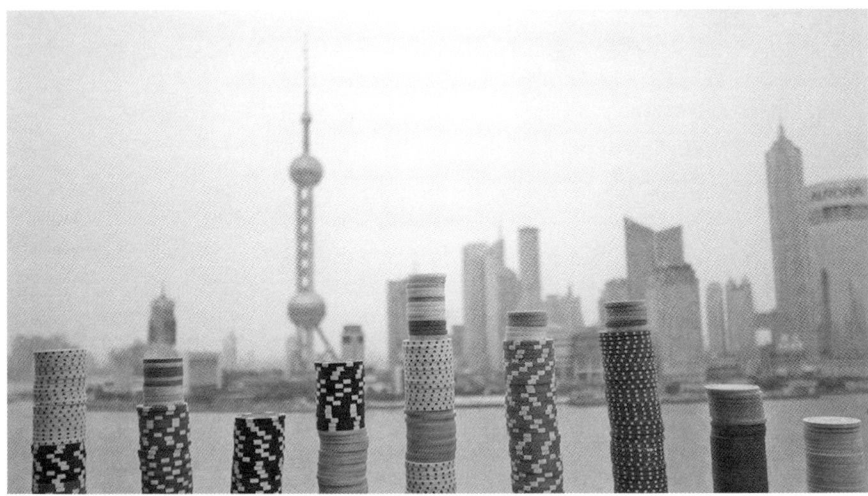

2.11   Liu Jianhua, *The Virtual Scene*, 2005. Color photograph.

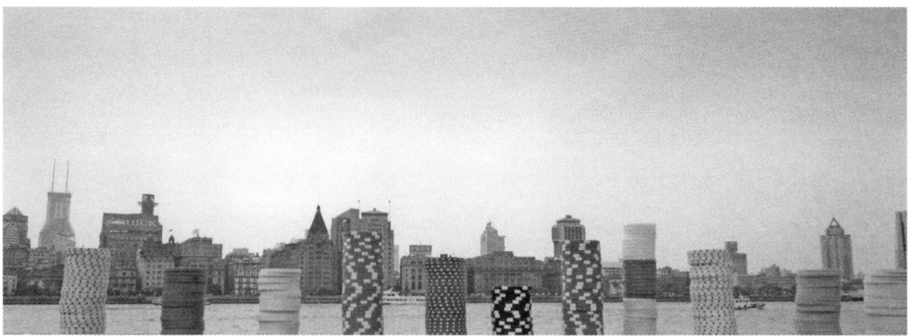

Liu Jianhua, *The Virtual Scene*, 2005. Color photograph.

Britain, encased in plexiglass and labeled "Art Export." As with *Yiwu Survey*, *Export—Cargo Transit* utilized readymade tactics that have clear ties to movements in the Western European and US-dominated canon of modern and contemporary art history, including Dada and Arte Povera. In an interview with me, Liu Jianhua recognized his appropriation of such strategies, while emphasizing above all else *Export—Cargo Transit*'s connections with the broader economic and political implications of globalization and the PRC's role as chief exporter of consumer goods and importer of consumer waste.[52]

On the gallery walls surrounding the encased detritus of *Export—Cargo Transit* appeared appalling stories, culled from both Chinese and foreign news articles, on the import of trash, like this 2007 British report of a Chinese town where trash and recycling items are sent:

> In Lianjiao's recycling plants they melt plastic down into molten lumps. It gives off fumes that can cause lung disease. Smoke stacks bellow clouds of chemicals that hang above the town. Poisonous waste pours directly into rivers, turning them to a stagnant black sludge. Entire families live amongst the filth. We visited yard after yard filled with rubbish from across Europe. We watched a container truck unloading household waste from France. Another yard specialized in German plastic. Next door we found a container-load of household rubbish just off the boat from Britain. Plastic waste is now one of Britain's biggest exports to China. Container ships arrive in Britain from China loaded with consumer goods. Many of them go back packed full of British waste.

And this report from ABC News:

> Most of the world's electronic trash, especially old computers, is dumped in China, causing severe environmental problems and illness among residents. … About 80 per cent of the world's electronic rubbish is transferred to Asia every year, 90 per cent of which ends up in China.[53]

These reports were juxtaposed against the legislation of the Basel Convention, negotiated and adopted by the United Nations Environment Program in 1989, which should have prohibited developed countries from exporting toxic waste to developing ones. As Liu Jianhua's exhibition highlights, the Basel Convention's accords have proven difficult to enforce and are in many cases explicitly ignored.[54]

Export—Cargo Transit revealed the unequal relations between the PRC and supposedly more developed Western European and North American nations, while offering a wider reflection on and critical response to urbanization, globalization, and resulting environmental hazards. Furthermore, while playing with the reimportation of foreign trash as contemporary art by foreign, non-Chinese collectors, the project self-reflectively confronted the globalization of contemporary art and Liu Jianhua's own conflicted position as a Chinese artist operating in a transnational art world. As described to me, the artist, keenly aware of how his career initially benefited from a predominantly Western European and North American art market's demand for the *new*, in this case contemporary Chinese art, encouraged foreign collectors to purchase works from *Export—Cargo Transit* while discouraging Chinese collectors. [55] Liu Jianhua thus steered his art's distribution and circulation, further contributing to the work's cross-cultural meanings. The crux of this project lay in the artist's ability to demonstrate the links between the international trade of products for mass consumption, the refuse created by bloated consumer societies, and the transnational trade of art as luxury item.[56]

Export—Cargo Transit was exhibited amid rising concerns over China's environmental problems and alarming news reports, such as subsequent reports citing outdoor air pollution as contributing to 1.2 million premature deaths in China in 2010 and the story of 16,000 dead pigs found floating in the Huangpu River, a chief water supply lining the Bund and the Shanghai Gallery of Art.[57] While sometimes taking local environmental problems as starting points, Liu Jianhua's projects also operate in critical parallel to the increasingly globalized conditions that create a fertile breeding ground for ecological trauma. Collecting commodities and trash and using artistic modes of manufacture that resemble, but ultimately depart from, the operations of multinational capitalist production, Liu Jianhua acutely represents the globalization of Shanghai and of contemporary Chinese art. His works call attention to the disconnects between bombastic state-sponsored development programs and their negative local impacts. Projects like *Export—Cargo Transit* further demonstrate the disparities between developed and developing nations, implicating the former in the ecological and social crises of the latter. Repackaging imported garbage, selling it as art, and employing seemingly outmoded artisanal labor, Liu Jianhua creates new economic microcosms, casting alternative social formations that challenge the conditions of globalization and its hazardous environmental effects.

Notes

1 See Chapter 1 for a discussion of *Xintiandi*.

2 Chen Yifei is one of the few figures whose artistic activities in mainland China successfully spanned the 1970s through the early 2000s. During the 1970s, Chen Yifei was mostly well respected as a socialist-realist oil painter. After the 1980s, he became one of the best-selling Chinese artists of his time. He was one of the first artists of his generation to study abroad in New York City, where he maintained an active gallery-based career. In the 1990s, Chen Yifei began experimenting with filmmaking while also managing a popular magazine, fashion brand, modeling agency, and the (now closed) retail store Layefe at *Xintiandi*.

3 Shanghai Tang website, http://www.shanghaitang.com/en/shanghai-tang, accessed June 1, 2011. Shanghai Tang has retail outlets around the world, including two locations in Shanghai's former French Concession.

4 The phrase I employ here, "Contemporary Chinese art/fashion system," refers to Roland Barthes' 1967 text *The Fashion System* (*Système de la Mode*) (New York: Hill and Wang, 1983), a semiotic analysis of fashion magazines that theorizes the links between fashion trends and capitalist movement.

5 The brutalities of the globalized fast-fashion industry, in particular, were highlighted by the tragic death of over 1,000 garment workers in the 2013 collapse of the Rana Plaza factory complex in Bangladesh. For an account of this event and other critical issues surrounding the fashion industry, see the documentary *The True Cost*, directed by Andrew Morgan (United States: Life is My Movie Entertainment Company, 2015). In *Gomorrah* (2006/2008), a novel-turned-film featuring poorly paid undocumented Chinese workers in Naples producing "Made in Italy" couture, we are reminded of the link between high fashion and exploited labor. See Roberto Saviano, *Gomorrah: A Personal Journey into the Violent International Empire of Naples' Organized Crime System*, trans. Virginia Jewiss (New York: Picador and Farrar, Straus and Giroux, 2006), and *Gomorrah*, directed by Matteo Garrone (Italy: Fandango and RAI Cinema, 2008), DVD.

6 Other projects by Yang Fudong and Cai Guo-Qiang are discussed in Chapters 3 and 4, respectively.

7 See, for example, many of the designs featured in the Metropolitan Museum of Art exhibition, "China: Through the Looking Glass," which is discussed in this book's final chapter.

8 Helen F. Siu, "Retuning a Provincialized Middle Class in Asia's Urban Postmodern: The Case of Hong Kong," in *Worlding Cities: Asian Experiments and the Art of Being Global*, eds. Aihwa Ong and Ananya Roy (Malden, MA: Wiley-Blackwell, 2011), 133.

9 Stella, "Shanghai Tang Café, Modern Chinese Cuisine," in *Zing* (February 2010): 5.

10 Shanghai Tang website.

11 John Colmey, "Everything You Wanted To Know About The Handover (But Were Afraid to Ask)," in *TIME* (Special Issue: Hong Kong 1997), 115.

12 Gong Li was made internationally famous for her leading role in director Zhang Yimou's *Raise the Red Lantern* (1991).

13 For a study of Mao suits, see Valery Garrett, *Chinese Dress: From the Qing Dynasty to the Present* (Rutland, Vermont: Tuttle Publishing, 2008), 218–222.

14 Anna May Wong's cosmopolitan identity stirred great interest within China, the United States, and Western Europe. In July 1928, shortly before *The Young Companion* published Wong on its cover, the German philosopher Walter Benjamin published a short article on the actress, whom he had interviewed while she was in Berlin. See Walter Benjamin, "Gespräch mit Anna May Wong: Eine Chinoiserie aus dem Alten Westen," ["Interview with Anna May Wong: A Chinoiserie from the Old West"] in *Die Literarische Welt* [*The Literary World*] 4, no. 27 (July 6, 1928): 213.

15 "Guided by Mao Tse-tung's Thought," 18.

16 美术战报/*Meishu zhanbao* [Fine Arts War News], like much of the era's newspapers and magazines, was published in Beijing as opposed to Shanghai. During the Cultural Revolution, Shanghai continued producing a great amount of visual materials, especially posters, but by the 1960s, the publishing industry that had flourished in Republican-era Shanghai was largely replaced by state-controlled publishing houses in Beijing, the PRC's political capital. This particular publication was published out of the China Industrial Art Institute (中央工艺美术学院/*Zhongyang gongyi meishu xueyuan*), founded by the artist Pang Xunqin (discussed in Chapter 1) before he was denounced and removed from his post. The white text printed on the cover's upper right corner reads: "向江青同志学习,向江青同志致敬!"/"*Xiang Jiang Qing tongzhi xuexi, xiang Jiangqing tongzhi zhijing!*" ["To learn from Comrade Jiang Qing, To Pay Respect to Comrade Jiang Qing!"]. Jiang Qing's hat, bearing the revolutionary communist star, conceals her hair, which would have been cut in a short, unisex style, as was the expectation for married women. Younger women typically wore their hair in braids. Mao badges, in addition to other Mao memorabilia, such as posters, figurines, lighters, and dishware, proliferated throughout mainland China during the years of the Cultural Revolution. Worn or displayed as talismans, such objects revealed reverence for Chairman Mao, establishing what has come to be called *the cult of Mao*.

17 The text on the cover is written in Chinese. Translation is taken from McDougall, trans. and ed., *Mao Zedong's Talks at the Yan'an Conference on Literature and Art*, 299.

18 David Tang, *Chink in the Armour* (Hong Kong: Enrich Publishing, 2010), 208–209.

19 Ibid.

20 Among numerous similar comments, artist Ding Yi told me, "I think it's a good thing to be an artist in Shanghai. We all drive Audis," Ding Yi, interview by author, April 29, 2010, audio recording, Ding Yi's Studio, Shanghai, China.

21 China Club's Long March Bar (named after the historic military retreat of the Red Army) houses art and cultural relics from the Cultural Revolution, including woodcut prints of Mao Zedong, workers, peasants, and soldiers; propaganda posters; and pro-CCP figurines. The Club's main stairwell and atrium features artworks by some of China's most well-known contemporary artists, including oil paintings by Wang Guangyi and Zhang Xiaogang.

22 Additional venues included Hong Kong Arts Centre (Hong Kong S.A.R.), Hong Kong City Hall (Hong Kong S.A.R.), Melbourne Arts Festival (Melbourne, Australia), Vancouver Art Gallery (Vancouver, Canada), University of Oregon Art Museum (Eugene, United States), Fort Wayne Museum of Art (Fort Wayne, United States), Salina Arts Centre (Salina, United States), Chicago Cultural Centre (Chicago, United States), and San Jose Museum of Art (San Jose, United States).

23 Wang Ziwei, *China's New Art, Post-1989*, ed. Valerie C. Doran (Hong Kong: Hanart TZ Gallery, 1993), 34.

24 Ding Yi, interview by author.

25 Ding Yi, interview in Hans Ulrich Obrist, *Hans Ulrich Obrist: The China Interviews* (Hong Kong and Beijing: Office for Discourse Engineering, 2009), 152.

26 Ibid., 150.

27 Ibid.

28 Ibid.

29 Ding Yi, interview by author.

30 The artists featured in "Esprit Dior" included Shanghai-based artists Liu Jianhua (discussed in the following section) and Zhang Huan (whose work for the Shanghai World Expo is described in Chapter 4).

31 This was the third installment of a series of short noir films commissioned by Christian Dior, which launched on the company's website in May 2009. The first two films were *Lady Noire*, directed by Olivier Dahan; and *Lady Rouge*, directed by Jonas Akerlund.

32 See further reflection on the Bund and Lujiazui in Chapter 4.

33 See reference to this building in Chapter 1's discussion of the montage sequence in Yuan Muzhi's *Street Angel*.

34 David Lynch, *Lady Blue Shanghai* (Shanghai: Christian Dior, 2010), Christian Dior website.

35 Ibid.

36 The room appears like a chamber in the Shikumen Open House Museum at Xintiandi discussed in Chapter 1.

37 Designed by Shanghai Modern Architectural Design Company Ltd., the Oriental Pearl Television and Radio Tower (东方明珠塔/*Dongfang mingzhuta*), built from 1991 to 1994, stands as Lujiazui's most iconic building. Composed of eleven large and small spheres, the biggest of which house a revolving restaurant and observatories clad in bright pink glass, the Pearl Tower resembles Western European counterparts such as the Belgian Atomium, made for the 1958 Brussels World's Fair, while making allusion, as Cotillard remarks, to the classical Tang Dynasty poem written by poet Bai Juyi (772–846).

38 Gu Zheng's writings are cited in the Introduction and in Chapter 4.

39 A sculpture from the artist's *Obsessive Memories* series, for instance, is on display in Tang's exclusive China Club in Hong Kong.

40 The artists featured in "Christian Dior and Chinese Artists" included Wang Du, Zhang Huan, Huang Rui, Li Songsong, Zhang Dali, Xu Zhongmin, Liu Jianhua, Lu Hao, Wang Qingsong, Yan Lei, Zhang Xiaogang, Wen Fang, Shi Jingsong, Wang Gongxin, Shi Xiaofan, Liu Wei, Rong Rong & Inri, Tim Yip, Qiu Zhijie and Ma Yangsong.

41 In other works, such as *Dream*, which responded to the 2003 crash of the Space Shuttle Columbia, Liu Jianhua literally smashes to pieces the porcelain objects comprising his installations, exhibiting their broken shards. See Liu Jianhua, *Dialectical Views on Social Spectacle* (Beijing and Seoul: Arario Gallery and Beijing Jinge Printing Co., 2007), 84–95.

42 Ibid., 151.

43 "He [Liu Jianhua] has gone back to Jingdezhen and to the factory where he had been working, carrying a well-defined idea in his mind, that of juxtaposing traditional patterns from different backgrounds (pottery and tailoring, for instance) combining them to express very powerful concepts." Ibid., 62.

44 Ibid., 15. Other works by Liu Jianhua directly confront urbanization throughout China, the expanded scale of our present-day commodity culture, and China's role as the world's primary manufacturer of cheap goods. *Shadow in the Water*, for instance (2002–03) presents a theatrically lit porcelain tableau of skewed architectural forms referencing soaring towers from various Chinese cities, which cast sharp and mutated shadows.

45 For a thoughtful overview of Ai Weiwei's *Sunflower Seeds* project, see John Jervis, "Sunflower Seeds: Ai Weiwei," in *ArtAsiaPacific* 72 (March/April 2011), http://artasiapacific.com/Magazine/72/SunflowerSeedsAiWeiwei, accessed September 1, 2015.

46 Mao Zedong quoted in Yoshihisa Higasa, "We Follow Chairman Mao's Revolutionary Line on Art and Literature," in *China Reconstructs* XVII, no. 4 (April 19, 1968): 32.

47 I am borrowing this term from German artist Joseph Beuys, who, in 1981, wrote of the need for a "social sculpture" amid the contemporary ecological crisis. See Joseph Beuys, "An Appeal for an Alternative" (1981), in *Documents of Contemporary Art: A Sourcebook of Artists' Writings and Theories*, eds. Kristine Stiles and Peter Selz (Berkeley and Los Angeles: University of California Press, 1996), 636–638. As a critic writes of Liu Jianhua's porcelain sculptures: "This art gives spectators profound insights into the reality of the society that surrounds us. They also make us think about the relation between art and politics. … In China … art is often inseparable from political or moral ideas. … That is why it is necessary to consider the relationship between daily life and … art, questions about an ideal society, and social commentary in art," Liu Jianhua, *Dialectical Views on Social Spectacle*, 45.

48 Liu Jianhua, *Dialectical Views on Social Spectacle*, 68.

49 Matthew Turner, "Early Modern Design in Hong Kong," *Design Issues* 6, no. 1 (Autumn 1989): 79.

50 Description of 2006 Shanghai Biennial, "World Events," Asia Art Archive website, http://www.aaa.org.hk/WorldEvents/Details/5983, accessed April 20, 2017.

51 See Chapter 4 for further discussion of Three on the Bund.

52 Liu Jianhua, interview and translation by author, Shanghai, China, September 18, 2011.
53 "Press clippings about imported trash," in Liu Jianhua, *Export—Cargo Transit* (Shanghai: Shanghai Gallery of Art, 2008), 32–33.
54 "Importing toxic waste into China is illegal, but waste dumping continues despite the convention. The China Quality News estimates that approximately 36 million metric tonnes of global e-waste ends up in China on an annual basis," Ibid.
55 Liu Jianhua, interview by author.
56 For Shanghai-based art critic and curator Mathieu Borysevicz, the most important thing about Liu Jianhua's garbage, displayed at the elegant Shanghai Gallery of Art, is "its newly contextualized status as consumable luxury item … [that] this foreign refuse re-enters the global market as a Chinese high-art commodity," Mathieu Borysevicz, "Export—Cargo Transit," in Liu Jianhua, *Export—Cargo Transit*, 47.
57 This amount is nearly 40 percent of the global total. These statistics come from a summary of data from the 2010 Global Burden of Disease Study, which was published in December 2012 in *The Lancet*, a British medical journal. See, among others, Edward Wang, "Air Pollution Linked to 1.2 Million Premature Deaths in China," *New York Times* (April 1, 2013), http://www.nytimes.com/2013/04/02/world/asia/air-pollution-linked-to-1–2-million-deaths-in-china.html, accessed April 1, 2013.

3 Biennialization-as-banalization, promotion, and resistance

The post-socialist period of the People's Republic of China (PRC) ushered in strong foreign and subsequent domestic interest in contemporary Chinese art. In Shanghai, on the heels of large-scale international exhibitions such as "China's New Art, Post-1989," dozens of new modern and contemporary art museums and galleries opened. Shanghai now houses, among other cultural institutions, the gargantuan state-run China Art Palace and Power Station of Art, the bank-owned Minsheng Art Museum, and the privately funded Rockbund Museum, Long Museum, Shanghai Gallery of Art, and ShanghART Gallery. The PRC's central and local governments have invested heavily in Shanghai's urban creative zones, including Red Town Sculpture Park, Taopu Arts District, and Moganshan/M50, while promoting the city's contemporary art to international audiences. This chapter analyzes the vying agendas of such cultural investments and expansions in the context of the Chinese Communist Party (CCP)-sponsored 2000 Shanghai Biennial, mainland China's premier international contemporary art event. I examine the 2000 Shanghai Biennial as a case of *biennialization-as-banalization*, in which the curators' hopes of harnessing the local spirit of Shanghai and 1920s–30s *haipai* (*Shanghai style*) were ultimately supplanted by a generic brand of CCP-approved global contemporary art that neglected to account for the city's unique historical features and current concerns. This chapter then discusses critiques of biennialization as seen in the partially censored counter-exhibition "Fuck Off," and in artworks by Zhou Tiehai and Yang Fudong, which problematize the globalization of Shanghai's contemporary art by offering multifaceted images of the city that resist idealized projections.

Artists and art historians have increasingly expressed doubt over the ability of international contemporary art biennials to adequately expand the field's narrow confines. Criticizing contemporary art's globalization and what she deems the resulting "McGuggenheim Effect," art historian and anthropologist

Saloni Mathur aptly summarizes the issues at stake in the proliferation of non-Western biennials:

> At their best, these "other" biennials were conceived through the vision for social justice of the international left; they were formulated in the wake of non-western anti-colonial struggles and third world revolutionary movements, and provided an alternative space of display for artists excluded from the Euro-Western establishment. At their worst, the biennials … have been criticized for mimicking modernist abstraction, plagued by the systemic corruption of their countries, co-opted by city promoters and the tourism industries of the host site, or have stiffened into their own centers of power involving new gestures of inclusion and exclusion.[1]

Indeed, over the past two decades, in biennials from Shanghai to Buenos Aires, globe-trotting art aficionados have often found themselves looking at many of the same sorts of formalist artworks selected by the same small group of curators.

Within mainland China, the 2008 Guangzhou Triennial stood as a self-reflective response to biennialization-as-banalization. Under the provocative title "Farewell to Post-Colonialism," the Guangzhou Triennial's curators—Sarat Maharaj, Gao Shiming, and Johnson Chang Tsong-Zung (host of "China's New Art, Post-1989")—announced their lofty goal: to free post-colonialism from ossified institutionalization and overly academic or token political correctness.[2] Scholars should be skeptical of the ability of a triennial (or biennial, or any other large-scale spectacular art-world event) to liberate a radical intellectual discourse such as post-colonialism. Nonetheless, the Guangzhou Triennial, which incorporated numerous artworks that unsettled fixed notions of identity and place, raised a set of provocative issues related to post-colonialism and art's globalization within the context of the PRC. In a publication produced in conjunction with the Triennial, curator Sarat Maharaj offers a telling indication of the differing views on post-colonialism held by the Triennial's participants and spectators. Opinions diverge widely, Maharaj writes,

> On whether China had colonized itself first with communism and then with global capitalism. On whether this made [China] unlike other colonial subjects of Empire. On whether China was simply swapping roles from underdog to top dog. On whether unease with the "other" and the unlike was about the incapacity to recognize difference without assimilating it to "our norms."[3]

These issues, along with the promising goals and troubling limitations of the CCP's turn-of-the-twenty-first-century promotion of contemporary Chinese art, had already crystallized in the 2000 Shanghai Biennial. The first iteration of mainland China's most high-profile international contemporary art event, the 2000 Shanghai Biennial was held at the state-operated Shanghai Art Museum (上海美术馆/*Shanghai meishu guan*), an institution the Biennial's curators upheld as being "at the forefront of China's open policy of engagement with the world, open to the principles of diversity and hybridity through the promotion of innovative art and ideas."[4] While the Shanghai Biennial had occurred twice (in 1996 and 1998), 2000 marked the first year the event was overseen by both local and international curators, including Shanghai Art Museum head Fang Zengxian, chief curator Li Xu, and director Zhang Qing, together with Japanese curator Toshio Shimizu and Hou Hanru, a mainland Chinese-born and educated curator who relocated from Beijing to Paris in 1990. The 2000 Shanghai Biennial also included for the first time non-Chinese figures, including well-known artists Anselm Kiefer, Matthew Barney, and Anish Kapoor and architect Tadao Ando, and it prompted many Western European and North American art professionals to travel to mainland China for the first time.

While the artworks included in the prior two biennials were mostly all either traditional Chinese ink paintings or oil paintings influenced by socialist realism or impressionist and post-impressionist styles, the 2000 Shanghai Biennial included artworks across media that would be considered more contemporary by Western standards, including photography, video, installation, and even architecture.[5] These works were purposefully juxtaposed against art by "native" and "aboriginal" artists as a way to, according to Hou Hanru, "go beyond the constraints of 'Western-centricism' by emphasizing a more global vision of contemporary art."[6] The more liberal embrace of media did not extend to content; curators ruled out artworks they presumed would be rejected by Beijing's Cultural Ministry, such as those critical of the government or with sexually explicit themes.[7] Still, the major shift away from paintings made exclusively by Chinese artists to multimedia artworks by Chinese and non-Chinese figures signaled to many the CCP's increased tolerance for nontraditional art. As Shanghai-based video and conceptual artist Xu Zhen stated in an interview with the *New York Times*, "We're now more optimistic about the state of Chinese art because the biennial turned out as it did. It was the first time a government exhibition featured video and installation art."[8] Conversely, the Biennial's shift from painting toward less traditional media was for some critics a sign of increased homogeneity, with video and installation art becoming increasingly conventional in a still Western-dominated art world deceptively labeled as global.

Attuned to concurrent debates surrounding biennialization, the curators of the 2000 Shanghai Biennial acknowledged that the problem of globalized contemporary art as Westernized contemporary art was especially thorny given the context of Shanghai, the city in mainland China that had been most historically affected by colonialism. Curators framed the exhibition as an exploratory laboratory for new cultural developments that would negotiate local (e.g., Shanghainese) and global concerns and complicate traditional East-meets-West discourses. Curator Zhang Qing hoped that the 2000 Shanghai Biennial would re-orient a supposedly global contemporary art discourse that had, up until then, been mostly dominated by Western critics and exhibitions. He writes:

> Shanghai Biennale has come to a crossroads. It has to face both cultural tradition and foreign influence. On one hand, it is firmly opposed to new conservatism and rigid adhesion to tradition, while calling for renovating and absorbing the traditional heritage to make it compatible with contemporary art and culture. On the other, it is strongly against following the West blindly and pursuing fame and profit at the cost of national dignity. At the same time, it encourages borrowing, fusing effectively humanistic spirit and other valuable elements in foreign cultures to enrich Chinese contemporary art. Shanghai Biennale is making an effort to show the active role China plays on the Asian cultural stage. Moreover, its curatorial ideal, distinguished from Western ones, is a moving testament to the uniqueness and independence of Chinese contemporary culture. In the spirit of "facing modernization, the world and the future," the exhibition provides an open space for developing theoretical frameworks and fostering critical attitudes and approaches. In this sense, the significance of the Shanghai Biennale lies, probably, beyond the show itself, even beyond tradition and modernity, beyond East and West, Left and Right.[9]

Zhang Qing called on mainland Chinese curators and artists to draw from foreign models without simply following the West. His statement also intimates negative connections between Westernization and commercialization, while advocating an expansion of China's previously inward-looking art on the nation's own terms (Chinese and Asian versus Western terms). This stance, frequently reiterated in the literature surrounding the Biennial, echoes the political rhetoric surrounding the PRC's repositioning on a global stage in the post-Mao era.

The international aims and non-Western curatorial ideals of the 2000 Shanghai Biennial were supposedly directly tied to Shanghai's local context and long-standing reputation as mainland China's most foreign-influenced, cosmopolitan metropolis. Outlining the Biennial's goals and pontificating on the relations between Shanghai's semicolonial past and globalized present, curator Hou Hanru writes:

> Inviting artists from all around the world to exhibit together with their Chinese colleagues under the banner of "Shanghai Spirit," the organisers and curators wish to examine the particular issues that affect contemporary art development in Shanghai, China's most cosmopolitan metropolis. … Shanghai's modernity

is shaped by the complex amalgamation of both Eastern and Western perspectives. … The crossroad between the East and the West is meeting in Shanghai once again, and profound lessons are being drawn and affected on both sides of the hemispheric divide. It is natural that issues of confrontation, collision, exchange and mixture between Eastern and Western cultures have become the central themes under examination. Shanghai, under the banner of "Haipai" had produced an important number of works, that collated high art discourse with popular entertainment motifs. Again, hybridity marks the fundamental character.[10]

Hou Hanru recognizes the city's semicolonial history as a shameful, but nonetheless relevant, precursor to present-day Shanghai. Insinuating that Shanghai has a rightful and collectively imagined claim to its current cosmopolitan status through its semicolonial past, the curator dismisses the city's more immediate history as an unfortunate rupture: "Depleted by long years of war of immense suffering, Shanghai's years of glory on the world stage were abated. However, Shanghai's image in the collective imaginations of the citizens of the world continued to resonate."[11] This commonplace skipping over of Shanghai's Maoist past in order to link the city's semicolonial period with its post-1989 present charts a falsely linear history of the city's global position and hybrid art. The most unique qualities of Shanghai, which bridge the city's past and present and define the "Shanghai Spirit," Hou Hanru writes, are "cultural openness, multiplicity, hybridity and radical attitude of innovation."[12] These optimistic descriptions present a simplistic account that glosses over Shanghai's many instances of closure (e.g., closures of borders between foreign and Chinese districts throughout the mid-nineteenth to mid-twentieth centuries, closures of Chinese-owned businesses, schools, and art institutions during the Cultural Revolution). However painful to recount, Shanghai's Maoist past, and especially the Cultural Revolution, when the CCP's nationalist artistic policy came to a head, should not be excluded from Shanghai's urban and art histories. The absence of reference to Shanghai's Mao-era milieu was especially glaring within the 2000 Shanghai Biennial, as the Cultural Revolution made an indelible impression on an entire generation of Chinese artists, including many of the exhibition's participants.

The Biennial's curators emphasized their inclusion of "foreign artists (from Europe, America, Australia, Africa, Asia)" and "native artists (including those from mainland China, Taiwan, and Hong Kong)."[13] Out of sixty-seven artists, thirty-two were from mainland China, two from Taiwan, and two from Hong Kong. The remaining artists were from a variety of countries, including Japan, Indonesia, South Korea, Australia, Canada, the United States, the United Kingdom, Holland, France, South Africa, Congo, and Tanzania. This eclectic representation of nations appeared to support the Biennial's global/local aims. However, national categorizations can be deceptive, neglecting to account for the fluid identities that many contemporary artists and art professionals inhabit.

For instance, some artists from Hong Kong (a British colony until 1997, and then a uniquely defined Special Administrative Region of the PRC) claim to share more cultural references with foreign artists than mainland Chinese artists. The Biennial also included numerous overseas Chinese artists (ethnically Chinese people who were born abroad or had emigrated from the PRC, like curator Hou Hanru), who resist neat categorization as "native" or "foreign."

Finally, the Biennial's strikingly low numbers of Shanghai-based artists and lack of Shanghai-oriented artworks failed to support the curators' local side of their dual global/local commitment. Aside from Hou Hanru's catalogue essay and the Biennial's venue and subtitle, "Shanghai Spirit," the exhibition demonstrated very little connection with the city or its history. One of the Biennial's few participants with a direct link to Shanghai, overseas Chinese artist Cai Guo-Qiang, who was born in Fujian Province and educated at the Shanghai Theater Academy, was designated under the national label of the United States, where he immigrated after having lived in Japan. For his contribution to the 2000 Shanghai Biennial, Cai Guo-Qiang produced one of the only works to directly interact with the local cityscape: *Self Promotion for the People*, a series of digital photographs of people and places around Shanghai displayed outside the exhibition venue (Figure 3.1). Cai Guo-Qiang's art and popularity overseas provoked hostile responses from some local critics. In his paper delivered at the Biennial, "The Shanghai Biennial Should Not Become a

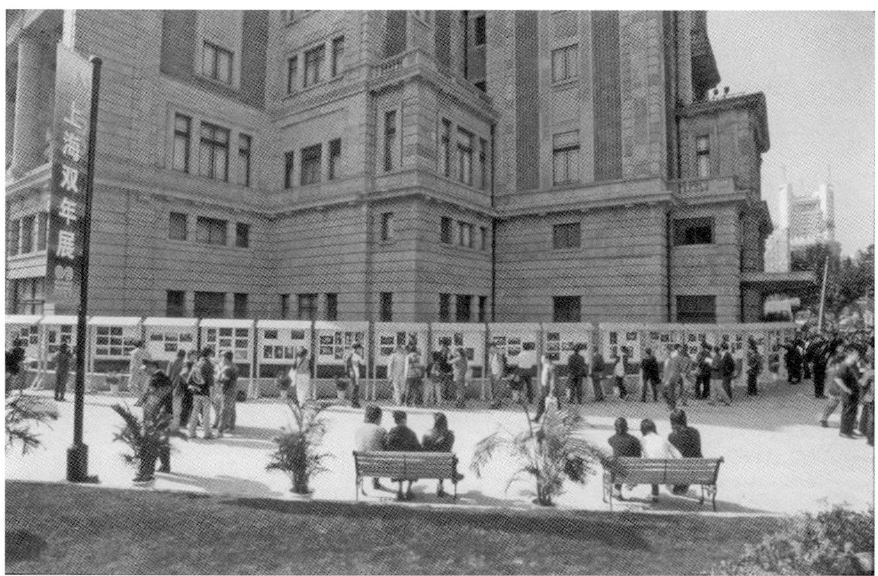

Cai Guo-Qiang, *Self Promotion for the People*, installation at the "Shanghai Biennial," Shanghai Art Museum, 2000.

3.1

Market Stall in China for Western Hegemony," critic Wang Nanming chastised Cai Guo-Qiang for manufacturing what he calls a "Chinatown Culture," an artistic tendency, especially on the part of overseas Chinese artists, to "appropriate simple motifs or symbols left behind by tradition … formulating these motifs into some 'essential' markers of Chineseness."[14] In a cutting jab, Wang Nanming argues, "These … art projects are at best only on par with mass recreational activities in China's tourist industry, the culture of street stalls and ethnic performances made for tourists."[15] Wang Nanming denounces artists like Cai Guo-Qiang for exploiting Chinese tradition toward the creation of art that panders to foreigners' expectations of what contemporary Chinese art should be. He further laments art's globalization as dependent on Westernization and commercialization. Such comments call out purportedly global contemporary artists for instilling banal cultural essentialisms, while also demonstrating that the 2000 Shanghai Biennial's promises of openness and East/West harmony concealed persistent tensions between local, foreign, and overseas artists, curators, and critics.

This means war

In 1996, the first year the Shanghai Biennial was held, Shanghai-based artist Zhou Tiehai satirized the growing globalization of the city's contemporary art, which would climax with the 2000 Shanghai Biennial, in his ten-minute-long video *Will* and accompanying sketches (Figure 3.2). Referencing

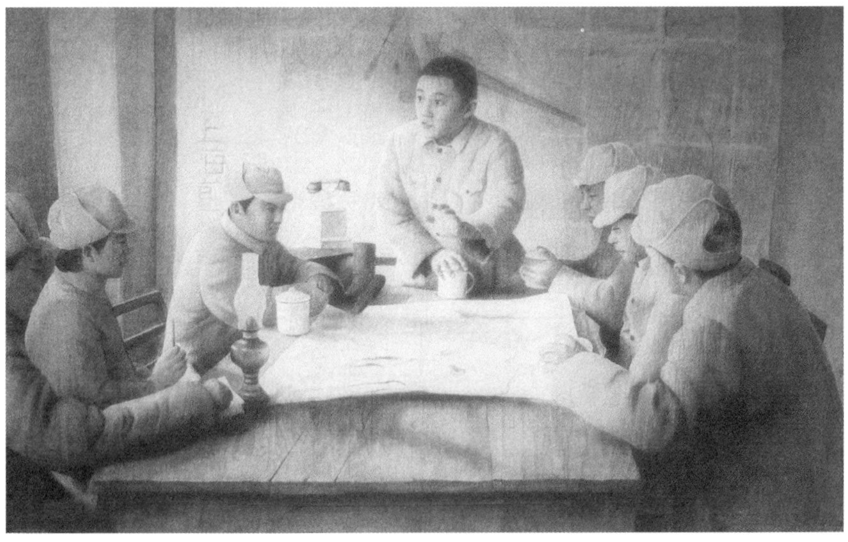

3.2   Zhou Tiehai, *Will*, 1996. 35 mm black-and-white film.

Shanghai's distinct semicolonial past and also the city's widely overlooked but more immediate and deeply formative Maoist history, *Will* complicates the staid tropes of East-meets-West and Old-meets-New proliferating throughout Shanghai and in the field of contemporary Chinese art. The video foregrounds cross-cultural conflicts between Shanghai's local artists and foreign curators. First exhibited in the Western European venue of the 1999 Italian Venice Biennial, *Will* mocks the desperation of artists seeking international acclaim and the random ways clueless Western art curators, critics, and gallerists visit Shanghai-based artists' studios and select works for exhibition inclusion. Set in present-day Shanghai, the film integrates a spate of historical references, including its black-and-white, silent format (Chinese and English subtitles relay pertinent information and dialogue) and comedic timing—elements reminiscent of Shanghai's Republican-era cinema. Meanwhile, period costumes, including Mao suits and Soviet-style hats with earflaps, along with militaristic language, distinctly reference China's Mao era. This hybridization of temporal references, along with *Will*'s content, suggests that the uneven relations between Chinese artists and Western critics, curators, and gallerists are akin to cultural inequalities and tensions rampant during both China's semicolonial period and the Cold War.

The video begins with a discussion of how to put Shanghai's art community on a global art-world map. In "Act One—The Military Meeting," a military officer explains the situation in front of a map belonging to the Shanghai Avant-garde Business Association.[16] A group of men huddle around the map, to which the officer points. The film's subtitles read:

> This is a military airport to secretly welcome museum presidents, critics and gallery owners. In order to smash their blockade against us forever, we must take action immediately to build our own airport. … Comrades, we must remember that we will have nothing without our own airport.[17]

This opening scene draws parallels between avant-garde art and business, as suggested by the Shanghai Avant-garde Business Association's name; and between art and war, as the military officer announces strategies for establishing the position of Shanghai-based art in an international art world. The Association's scramble to build an airport and secure foreign investments highlights the need for Shanghai's artists to claim territory and limited resources. Likely referencing Beijing, which by the mid-1990s had already established mainland China's largest contemporary art scene, frequented by foreign curators, critics, and gallerists, the military officer cites another city's monopoly in welcoming art professionals, declaring that Shanghai must have its own secret military airport. The scene not only references military strategizing, but also specifically that of China's socialist era, as the Mao suit–clad men refer to one another as "comrades". Mixing Maoist references with business buzzwords like "monopoly," the video insinuates that Cold War–era tensions continue to characterize current art-world relations while suggesting that these tensions are now dominated by economic versus ideological concerns.

Will then unfolds in a series of eight acts. In "Act Two—The Cafeteria," Chinese artists discuss their need to "establish close relationships with critics and journalists." In "Act Three—In the Hospital," a long line of Chinese patients wait to meet with a Western doctor, who briefly checks each patient's X-rays and vitals. Here, Zhou Tiehai equates artists waiting for quick face time with foreign curators with patients waiting for a doctor's check-up, insinuating that these meetings are both necessarily rushed because of the vast number of others scrambling to get appointments. "Act Four—Art Tour Guide" satirizes the arbitrary ways foreign art professionals visit Chinese artists' studios, portraying discussions between a local art tour guide/translator and a group of Western curators. "I've heard that Z is an outstanding artist, shall we go and see his work as well?" asks a curator. The guide hastily concludes, "Z lives far from here, we don't have enough time."[18] In "Act Five—Heartfelt Calls," an artist makes desperate calls from a payphone, pleading with those on the other line, "I'll take part in any exhibition you have," and in "Act Six—You Betrayed Me," an artist meets with a rival critic, causing the critic he originally worked with to accuse him of betrayal. Act Six again conjures the metaphor of war, revealing that artists are forced to choose sides and demonstrate loyalty to vying factions within the art world. "Act Seven—You Only Have Traditional Chinese Medicine and Witchcraft" speaks most directly to conflicts between foreign and local expectations in regard to contemporary Chinese art. A group of four Chinese men dressed in dynastic robes and hats are gathered around a table with a Western curator. The curator says, "You only have traditional Chinese medicine and witchcraft, but no art." A fifth Chinese person enters the room and exclaims, "Nonsense! We do have art. … Must our art live up to your standards?" This act raises the problem of the imposition of non-Chinese criteria in evaluating contemporary Chinese art, while critiquing how foreign art professionals expect and seek out traditional Chinese motifs in art from the PRC.

Will's final two acts paint a dismal fate of contemporary Chinese art. In "Act Eight—The Godfather," a weeping old man, presumably an older Chinese artist, laments, "There are so few outstanding new artists. I'm worried about the next generation. … (The godfather holds the hands of two people) … You're still quarreling. That makes me uneasy." Here, Zhou Tiehai suggests that the fierce competition between artists to secure international recognition has stymied art's development, leaving little hope for the next generation of artists. "Act Nine—The Raft of the Medusa" is a filmic re-enactment of French artist Théodore Géricault's *The Raft of the Medusa* (1818–19), an iconic painting of

French Romanticism depicting the tragic, violent, and cannibalistic aftermath of a capsized naval ship. *Will*'s script reads:

> Panorama: Ten or so people are huddled on a raft floating in the sea.
> Close shot: Someone has died.
> Close shot: Someone is struggling.
> Close shot: Someone is thinking.
> Subtitle: We can't go forward. We can't go back either.
> Panorama: They are all desperate and shout into the distance.
> Subtitle: FAREWELL ART!

The reference to a classical Western painting subverts the expectation often held by foreign critics and curators (as implied in Act Seven) that contemporary art from China should contain only traditional Chinese motifs. By enacting *The Raft of the Medusa*, which features a French frigate wrecked on its way to a Senegalese port that had been handed from British to French rule, *Will* recalls a tragedy linked to the supposedly heroic expeditions of Western colonialism. Act Nine expands the video's metaphors of artist-as-soldier and artist-as-businessman to that of artist-as-colonized victim.

Will mixes a wide range of historical references (e.g., Western imperialist expansion of the early nineteenth century, silent film from semicolonial Shanghai, Maoist isolationist policies, and Cold War politics) with its mid-1990s present, as foreign art professionals began gaining interest in contemporary Chinese art. Transgressing any simple notion of cultural hybridity or East-meet-West harmony, the video constructs a complex form of temporal hybridity and suggests that Shanghai's historic cross-cultural tensions persist in the city's rapidly globalizing art world. Zhou Tiehai illustrates the anxieties of Chinese artists wishing to take part in international exhibitions and media platforms while likening the role of the artist to that of a soldier going to war. Due to the increasingly global nature of contemporary art, the war Zhou Tiehai presents is not a civil war (though Shanghai vies with Beijing as capital of the Chinese art world) but an international one. Chinese artists/soldiers must fight for the attention of powerful foreign critics and curators who have preconceived notions of what Chinese art should be, and their intermediaries—guides and translators who capriciously visit certain studios over others.

Will reflects Zhou Tiehai's artistic philosophy, which he seriously described to me as premised on the beliefs that "Avant-garde art is a business" and "Being an artist is like being a soldier in war."[19] Zhou Tiehai introduces the additional analogy of world war in thinking through the production, reception, and circulation of avant-garde art, as *Will* demonstrates that the "business" of Chinese avant-garde art in the 1990s is based on inequitable cross-cultural tactics (e.g., Western critics promoting Chinese artists, Western curators exhibiting Chinese art, Western collectors buying Chinese artworks). In line with Zhou Tiehai's thinking of art-as-business, after the release of *Will* (for which he gained international acknowledgment at the Venice Biennial), he began purposely refusing to produce his own paintings, outsourcing the work to assistants, "like a businessman."[20] The 1999 painting series *Press Conference* furthers Zhou Tiehai's argument that cross-cultural tensions are inherent to the field of contemporary Chinese art. The series comprises a portrait of the artist standing at a podium in front of various international flags, and it includes the text: *The relations in the art world are the same as the relations between states in the post Cold War era.*

Another fucking exhibition

Zhou Tiehai was one of many local Shanghai-based artists included in "Fuck Off," an exhibition sharing *Will*'s defiant stance. Organized by artist Ai Weiwei and curators Feng Boyi and Huan Tianxue in critical response to the perceived limitations of the Shanghai Biennial, "Fuck Off" was held concurrently with the 2000 Shanghai Biennial at Shanghai's privately run East Link Gallery. "Fuck Off" emphasized independence from the PRC's state-run institutions while exhibiting younger, local, and more experimental artists, including woman artist Cao Fei, known for her edgy photographs and new media works, whom the curators felt had been unfairly left out of the Shanghai Biennial. While male artists dominated "Fuck Off," the inclusion of women artists, even as a minority, bolstered the exhibition's subversive status. Women artists have been notoriously excluded from the PRC's mainstream art institutions and exhibitions, epitomized by their shockingly low numbers in Shanghai biennials.[21]

The introductory notes to the "Fuck Off" exhibition catalogue proclaimed:

> In today's art, the "alternative" is playing the role of revising and criticizing the power discourse and mass convention. … It aims at dealing with such themes as cultural power, art institution, art trends, communications between the East and West, exoticism, post-modernism and post-colonialism, etc. "Fuck Off" emphasizes the independent and critical stance that is basic to art existence, and its status of independence, freedom and plurality in the situation of contradictions and conflicts. It tries to provoke artists' responsibility and self-discipline, search for the way in which art lives as "wildlife," and raise questions about some issues of contemporary Chinese art. Allegory, direct questioning, resistance, alienation, dissolution, endurance, boredom, bias, absurdity, cynicism and self-entertainment are aspects of culture as well as features of existence. Such issues are re-presented here by the artists with unprecedented frankness and intelligence, which leaves behind fresh and stimulating information and traces of existence.[22]

"Fuck Off" encompassed a host of provocative works. The exhibition included photographs from Ai Weiwei's *Perspective* series (1995–2003)—distance shots of national political monuments, including the White House and Tiananmen Square, dwarfed by the artist's middle finger; and *Eating People* (2000), the photographic documentation of a performance in which artist Zhu Yu purportedly ate an aborted fetus.[23] Surprisingly, amid "Fuck Off"'s plethora of explicitly subversive and disturbingly abject works, the Chinese Cultural Inspection Bureau singled out Shanghai-based artist Yang Fudong's photographic triptych, *The First Intellectual* (2000) (Plate 4), for official removal from the exhibition.[24]

The *First Intellectual* portrays a young man dressed in a business suit, carrying a briefcase in one hand and a brick, which has been hurled at and wounded him, in the other. He stands in the middle of the road in Shanghai's Pudong District, modern high-rises framing his agitated body. Only through the work's title and accompanying caption can we identify this figure as an intellectual, hinting at Yang Fudong's ambiguous definition of the term: "The spirit of intellectuals is the dream you have for yourself and the sensation of chasing a dream in dreams. In other words, being an intellectual means imposing the status of being an intellectual upon oneself."[25] Shocked and bloodied, this intellectual, the first to emerge in post-socialist China, finds himself in a state of crisis. He is ready to direct his pain and frustrations at anyone or anything by smashing them with the brick that was thrown at him. But no one person or thing emerges as the intellectual's primary target.

When choosing to remove *The First Intellectual*, officials may have recognized that this work, perhaps more than any of the others included in "Fuck Off," threatened to debunk the myths surrounding the urbanization and globalization of Shanghai—myths that had been persistently constructed by events like the 2000 Shanghai Biennial, which promoted a generic and benignly positive image of the city both at home and abroad. For Yang Fudong, life in Shanghai is informed not by a harmonious, collective globalism but by an increasingly privatized and alienated existence shrouded in delusion:

> A hundred million people live in this city, and these hundred million people basically live in solitude. … In a city, very few people carelessly lift their heads and look up, and everybody basically has this flat visual angle, even though there are high buildings on either side. … So in terms of visual experience, city people are narrow and limited.[26]

Artists and intellectuals in crisis

The fraught role of Shanghai's new class of artists and intellectuals plays a central role in Yang Fudong's subsequent project, *Seven Intellectuals in a Bamboo*

Forest, an epic 35-millimeter black-and-white film. Divided into five lengthy parts ranging from 29 to 90 minutes, *Seven Intellectuals* was exhibited in a multichannel installation at the 2007 Venice Biennial and again at the Asia Society in New York City in 2009. Yang Fudong shot *Seven Intellectuals* slowly over the course of four years, with each segment taking roughly one year to create. The artist told me in an interview that the slowness of this production reflects his desires to merge his own art and life and provide a counterpoint to the fast pace of life in consumerist Shanghai.[27] *Seven Intellectuals* draws from Shanghai's Republican-era imagery and genealogy of cross-cultural hybridity while reflecting on the artist's role in post-socialist China.

The film draws its title and thematic concept from *Seven Sages of the Bamboo Grove*, a Chinese legend of a group of seven scholars said to have lived during the third dynasty CE under the tumult of the early Six Dynasties period.[28] This period and those following it were marked by war, civil strife, and political chaos, and it is believed that many of the era's artists and intellectuals exiled themselves, rejecting civilization by retreating into secluded mountains and forests. Among such figures, the Seven Sages were said to have retreated to a bamboo grove to carry out their various intellectual pursuits—drunkenly engaging in Daoist-influenced philosophical discourse, creating poetry, and making music—all in a natural environment far from the political and social turmoil of the day. Yang Fudong's reference to the *Seven Sages* illuminates the crises facing intellectuals in China's post-1989 milieu, a period characterized by tremendous urbanization, the rise of state-sponsored capitalism, the aggressive solidification of one-party rule, and increasing restraints placed on personal liberties.

Seven Intellectuals follows a group of five young men and two young women (the seven intellectuals) as they move back and forth between China's countryside, notably Huangshan (Yellow Mountain) in Anhui Province and urban Shanghai, where the film concludes. Whether these intellectuals are talking (though dialogue is minimal), bathing, kissing, eating, reading, watching a cabaret performance, or playing baseball on a rooftop in Shanghai, they are almost always depicted as bored and listless (Figures 3.3–3.4). Ennui appears as a symptom of the young intellectuals' spiritual detachment and disillusionment with China's preceding sociopolitical movements and ideologies, such as the Republican era's New Culture Movement and Maoist communism. In contemplating the social shifts reflected in *Seven Intellectuals*, Yang Fudong remarks:

> To me, the great change that is happening today in society can be seen and perceived in various forms. This transformation relates to people's mental attitude, the many changes in their way of thinking and their ideology. Numerous factors come into play, which concern the loss of traditional values and even the concept of tradition. In this sense, there is a loss. At the same time, the arrival and assertion of the new sometimes creates a sort of selfish existence, an existence that doesn't have much meaning. What is lost is the idea of living together, a collective

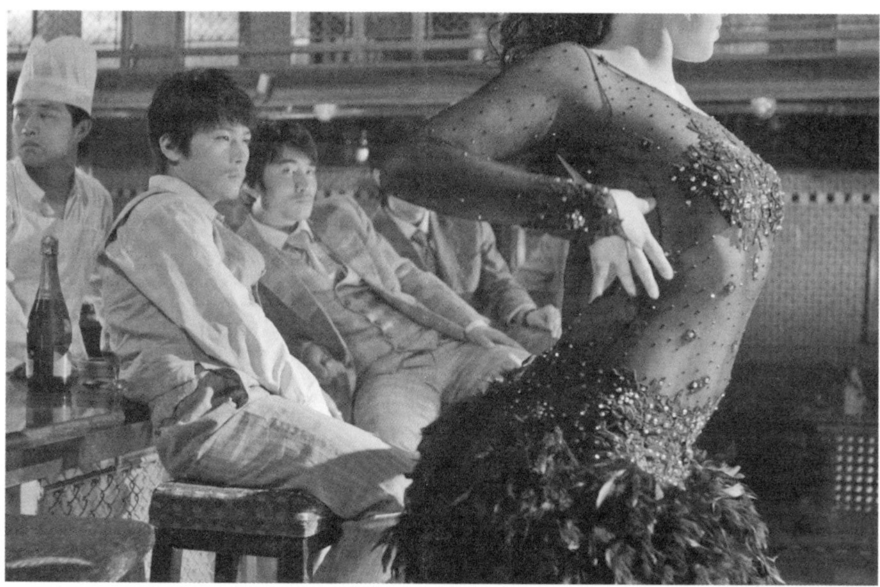

Yang Fudong, *Seven Intellectuals in a Bamboo Forest*, Part V of V, 2007. 35 mm black-and-white film.   **3.3**

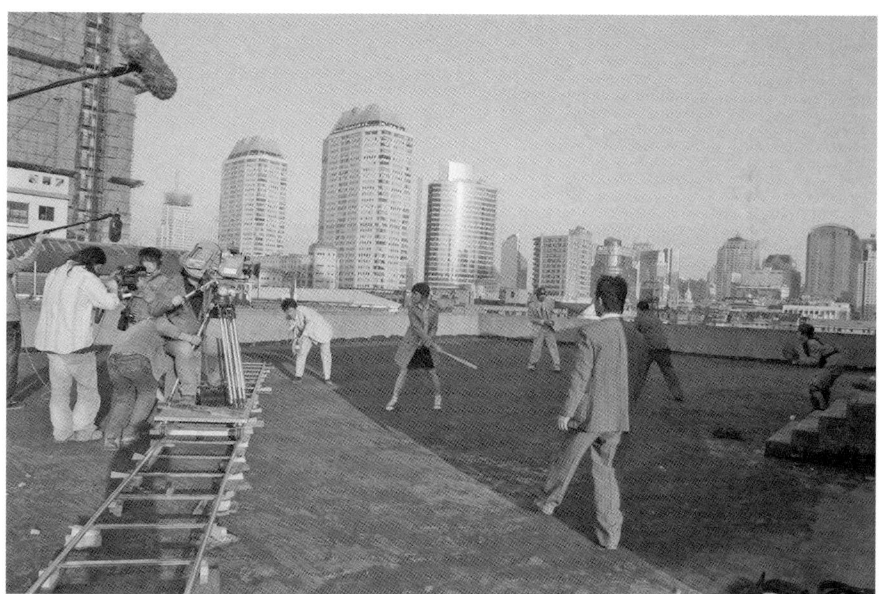

Yang Fudong, *Seven Intellectuals in a Bamboo Forest*, Part V of V, 2007. 35 mm black-and-white film.   **3.4**

search for a better way of life. … Many young people—I'm referring above all to the generation subsequent to mine—don't take the past into consideration at all. They don't even need to forget it, since they didn't know it in the first place.[29]

Part Two of *Seven Intellectuals* is set in Shanghai's former French Concession and occurs almost entirely inside an early-twentieth-century semicolonial *shikumen* home, where the intellectuals reside.[30] Throughout the film's Shanghai segments, the characters spend extensive time indoors, suggesting that urban individuals have become estranged from their rapidly developing environment and that intellectual life has become increasingly privatized.[31] In Part Two, the camera frequently fixates on the intellectuals' blanks stares as they nonchalantly engage in idle chitchat or discuss sex (one man tells another of his predilection for older women) and existential concerns (e.g., growing old). Their detached communication betrays both indifference and longing.

One of the part's earliest scenes is a close-up sequence featuring a young man caressing and erotically licking a young woman's chest. She writhes in pleasure. "What are you writing?" she asks, as the man uses his tongue to write Chinese characters. He replies, "美术/*Meishu [Art]*." "I know … Anyway, I know," the woman whispers. The brief exchange offers a moment of sensual intimacy rarely found among the young intellectuals, while the act of writing and art making are exposed as attached to fleeting desire and ultimately ephemeral; *art* disappears as the saliva fades from the young woman's chest. Even when the intellectuals are pictured together—having sex, dancing, eating, singing, and playing guitar—they appear as if in isolation, communicating with verbal and bodily restraint. Through these scenes, Yang Fudong argues that the collective political action and ideological commitment that characterized Shanghai's intellectual climate since the Republican era had, by the turn of the twenty-first century, given way to individuals living detached lives in quiet upper-class interiors.

In Part Five, the *Seven Intellectuals'* final section, the protagonists return to Shanghai after spending time in a rural landscape and on a desolate island, roaming about aimlessly over the fields and rocky seaside terrain. The intellectuals' return to Shanghai signals their failure to communally connect both with nature and each other and their inability to live peacefully in hermetic exile like their namesake predecessors, the *Seven Sages*. Back in Shanghai, the seven intellectuals proceed to get drunk in lavishly decorated bars, hang out on a rooftop surrounded by imposing skyscrapers, and take up odd jobs, such as working at a demolition site or cooking in a restaurant. This final part includes scenes of the intellectuals swimming with oxygen tanks amid fish and coral underwater, drifting through and half-heartedly noticing the oddities in an antique shop, riding horses across the path of an oncoming steam engine, and playing pool outside amid the rubble of a demolished building. The men and women, incessantly plagued by ennui, wander aimlessly throughout the nonsensical city, suggesting that a sense of purposelessness pervades the life of China's young urban intellectuals.

Seven Intellectuals is presumably set in the present day, although incongruous and overlapping historical details confuse this. The men, for instance, wear 1940s Western-style suits along with contemporary accessories like small hoop earrings. The film contains a far-reaching mixture of references: Shanghai's silent-era cinema; Jim Jarmusch's films; classical Chinese scroll paintings; Maoist emphases on collective rural training. When strung together, *Seven Intellectuals'* surreal scenes and images make viewers feel as if they are slipping from one dream sequence into the next, crafting a picture of Shanghai as a fantasy world of bewitching consumer culture, full of what Yang Fudong calls "false luxuries."[32] These multiple stylistic and temporal references produce a palimpsestic portrait of contemporary life in China and of Shanghai in particular, which, like Pang Xunqin's 1931 watercolor *Such is Shanghai* (discussed in Chapter 1), refuses to add up to any coherent whole.[33] Unlike the mutual embrace of pastiche and nostalgia seen in *Xintiandi* and Shanghai Tang (discussed in Chapters 1 and 2), *Seven Intellectuals'* echoes of *old Shanghai* serve as haunting reminders that the city's cosmopolitan facades mask deep-seated tensions, demystifying the city's long-standing East-meets-West reputation.

The film's final segment concludes in Shanghai's Xian Qian Fang, a Republican-era Art Deco theater that has been transformed into a swanky restaurant, where some of the male intellectuals take up cooking jobs (Figure 3.5). As in the Shanghai Tang advertisement featuring Gong Li, the figure of the cook is used in *Seven Intellectuals* to symbolize the reemergence of a class-based society and the redevelopment of a service economy in post-socialist Shanghai. In *Seven Intellectuals*, however, the cook is not juxtaposed with a successful, superior urbanite (Shanghai Tang's movie starlet); rather, the intellectual urbanites, unable to find any position in society, are left to join Shanghai's recently reemerged under-class. While this hybridization of the intellectual and worker was state-imposed during the Cultural Revolution (when artists, for example, were forced to collaborate with workers), in 1990s–2000s Shanghai, this hybridization emerges as a consequence of an increasingly materialistic society in which cultural capital falls subservient to economic capital, casting the artist/intellectual in a state of estranged exile.

In *Seven Intellectuals'* final scene, the camera travels down a dark wood-paneled corridor, softly illuminated by dozens of small lamps fixed to the walls, and into the grand ballroom of Xian Qian Fang. The ballroom is outfitted with half a dozen large round tables, mirrored panels, a diamond-patterned carpet, white drapes decoratively strewn around rectangular columns, chandeliers, and smaller lights hanging from the ceiling. The camera hovers in to reveal the seven intellectuals, joined by a few other men, sitting around the room's center table, eating and drinking in silence. There is no one else in the restaurant. Two screens in the background play identical footage, seemingly from other parts of *Seven Intellectuals*: those set in the countryside, where the

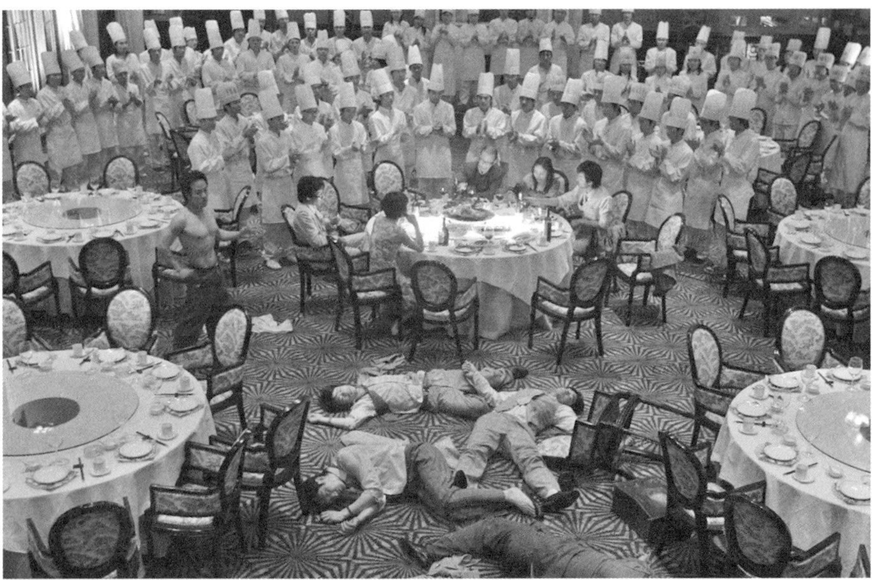

3.5   Yang Fudong, *Seven Intellectuals in a Bamboo Forest*, Part V of V, 2007. 35 mm black-and-white film.

struggling intellectuals tried but failed to find fulfillment. This stage-like setting in a former theater calls viewers' attention to the artificiality of the lives of these cosmopolitan urban dwellers.

Two of the intellectuals, a young man and a young woman, silently get up from the table and begin to dance—an odd combination of ballroom, tango, and contemporary movements. Two other male intellectuals rise from the table and begin wrestling with one another, knocking into the couple, and bringing the dancing man into their rumble. A fourth intellectual joins in, so that two pairs of twisted fighters tumble about violently on the ground, while the female intellectual retreats to the table, dropping a napkin into the fray in a bullfighting-like gesture. The last intellectual, meanwhile, arises from the table and dances by himself, stripping off his clothes. Simultaneously, nearly a hundred men wearing cooks' uniforms and tall white hats enter in single file and form a semicircle around the periphery of the room. The men who were fighting separate, each lying sprawled out on the floor as if dead. The cooks clap in unison. Their clapping provides a rhythm to which the last intellectual, now shirtless, continues to dance. This scene, in which the intellectuals turn on each other in violence and end up in isolation, evidenced by the single dancer, reiterates that Shanghai, with its luxurious, revamped Art Deco surfaces, is in reality a lonely empty dream world. Material consumption, which has replaced the poverty of China's socialist years, offers false promises of contentment and spiritual fulfillment. *Seven Intellectuals* aims to reveal that the city's materialism generates an intellectually vapid environment, leaving alienated individuals to dance only with themselves.

Local delusions

In thinking through what he describes as the "false luxuries" of Shanghai, Yang Fudong remarks:

> Everyone imagines that things are happening in some place where they have never been. … I think that the city has a lot of this kind of thing: descriptive delusions. … A lot of people can give an extravagant description of Shanghai. … Let someone start talking, and the place comes to life. You ask, has he been up there? Maybe he hasn't been anywhere. In other words, there's a kind of rumor in cities that produces fantasies, and those rumors create delight. This delight is false, but it influences a lot of people. Saying this brings us to a topic that I've been especially interested in: the capacity of rumors—and here's the main point—delusion. Image also has this power, like the power of rumors to delude.[34]

The artist critiques the mythologizing of Shanghai, arguing that hyperbolic descriptions and striking images, such as those surrounding the 2000 Shanghai Biennial, delude people by projecting a delightful fantasy of the city as a unified entity. Projects like *Seven Intellectuals*, *Will*, and "Fuck Off" reveal that contemporary life in Shanghai is characterized not by cohesion but by a collision of realities and temporalities that ultimately obscure, rather than clarify, young denizens' conceptions of the past. In rapidly urbanizing and homogenizing Shanghai, as in a globalizing art world characterized by biennialization-as-banalization, individual subject positions, and especially the role of the artist/intellectual, are thrown into deep-seated crisis.

Notes

1 Saloni Mathur, "Museums and Globalization," *Anthropological Quarterly* 78, no. 3 (Summer 2005): 701–702.

2 Wang Huangsheng, director of the Guangdong Museum of Art, the Triennial's primary host, introduced the curatorial theme as such: "'Farewell to Post-colonialism' is not a superficial denial of the importance … of this intellectual tradition. … The severe political conditions under post-colonialism have not receded, but in many ways are even further entrenched under the machinery of globalization. However, as a leading discourse in curatorial practice and criticism, post-colonialism is showing its limitations in being increasingly institutionalized as an ideological concept. Not only is it losing its edge as a critical tool, it has generated its own restrictions that hinder the emergence of artistic creativity and fresh theoretical interface," Wang Huangsheng, "Preface to the Third Guangzhou

Triennial," in *Farewell to Post-Colonialism: The Third Guangzhou Triennial*, eds. Johnson Chang Tsong-Zung, Gao Shiming, and Sarat Maharaj (Guangzhou: Guangdong Museum of Art, 2008), 30–31.

3 Sarat Maharaj, "Counter Creed: Quizzing the Guangzhou Triennial 2008 According to James Joyce's 'Catechetical Interrogation,'" *Printed Project: 'Farewell to Post-Colonialism,' Querying the Guangzhou Triennial* 11 (2008): 8.

4 Hou Hanru, "Shanghai Spirit: A Special Modernity," in 上海双年展/*Shanghai shuangnian/Shanghai Biennale* 2000, ed. Chen Long (Shanghai: Shanghai Art Museum, 2000), n.p.

5 The 1996 Shanghai Biennial, under the theme "Open Space," included twenty-six local oil painters and three overseas Chinese installation artists, including Gu Wenda (discussed in Chapter 4). The 1998 Shanghai Biennial focused on the development of Chinese ink painting and solely exhibited Chinese ink painters.

6 Hou Hanru, "Shanghai Spirit," n.p. The presence of "native" artworks, such as traditional Chinese ink paintings, was notably marginal; out of the sixty-seven artists included in the exhibition, just four made ink paintings.

7 Citing curator Li Xu, *New York Times* reporter Lily Tung explains that "works that the [Beijing Cultural] Ministry deemed overly political or pornographic were ruled out," Lily Tung, "Arts Abroad; Spreading Openness With a 3rd Shanghai Biennale," *New York Times* (May 30, 2001), http://www.nytimes.com/2001/05/30/arts/arts-abroad-spreading-openness-with-a-3rd-shanghai-biennale.html, accessed May 1, 2015.

8 Xu Zhen quoted in Lily Tung, "Arts Abroad."

9 Zhang Qing, "Beyond Left and Right: Transformation of the Shanghai Biennial," in *Shanghai Biennial 2000*, n.p.

10 Hou Hanru, *Shanghai Biennale 2000*, n.p.

11 Ibid.

12 Ibid.

13 Fang Zengxian, Preface to *Shanghai Biennial 2000*, n.p. As scholar of contemporary art Chin-tao Wu has observed, the pretenses of a de-territorialized, borderless art world are often debunked by looking at the nationalities of artists in contemporary art biennials, including those in non-Western locations, wherein Westerners tend to far outweigh non-Westerners. In the case of the 2000 Shanghai Biennial, the numbers were actually fairly evenly geographically dispersed. Chin-tao Wu, "Biennials without Borders," in *Theory in Contemporary Art since 1985*, 2nd edition, eds. Simon Leung and Zoya Kocur (Malden, MA and Oxford, UK: Blackwell Publishing, 2012), 56–63.

14 Wang Nanming, "The Shanghai Art Museum Should Not Become A Market Stall in China for Western Hegemony—A Paper Delivered at the 2000 Shanghai Biennale," in *Contemporary Chinese Art: Primary Documents*, ed. Wu Hung with Peggy Wang (New York: The Museum of Modern Art), 353.

15 Ibid.

16 Zhou Tiehai, 必须/*Bixu/Will* (1996), script reprinted in *The Art of Zhou Tiehai* (Shanghai: Shanghai Art Museum, 2006), n.p.

17 Ibid.

18 Ibid. The artists are called by letters (A, B, C, D, E, X, Y, and Z), which speaks to their relative anonymity while further mocking the fact that non-Chinese art-world professionals are often unable to properly pronounce or remember Chinese artists' names.

19 Zhou Tiehai, interview by author, August 18, 2008, audio recording, Zhou Tiehai's studio, Shanghai, China.

20 Ibid. Zhou Tiehai has long claimed that his well-known *Joe the Camel* painting series, which features the Camel cigarette brand's cartoon spokesman in a number of classical Western art-historical backdrops, subverts foreign curators' expectations of contemporary Chinese art by integrating Western corporate and art imagery and excluding traditional Chinese art references. Further testament to his own navigation of the combined worlds of business and art, in 2010, Zhou Tiehai was appointed deputy director of Shanghai's Minsheng Art Museum, a contemporary Chinese art museum founded and funded by the China Minsheng Banking Corporation.

21 As Chin-tao Wu has observed, "It is clear that the Shanghai Biennale … falls a long way short of what is already an unfavourable ratio as far as women artists are concerned. In the two series held in 1996 and 1998, women artists were in single digits, while the first two Shanghai Biennials in the new millennium, in 2000 and 2002, had only about 15 percent of women artists. Only in the edition of 2008 did the percentage reach a somewhat more respectable—or slightly less scandalous—31.3 percent. But in its two latest editions figures fell again to 24.5 percent in 2012 and 28.9 percent in 2014," Chin-tao Wu, "Missing in Action: Women Artists and Biennials" (unpublished conference paper), presented at National Taiwan Normal University Graduate Institute of Art History, May 26, 2017. Despite adverse conditions, a number of important women artists emerged in the PRC in the 1990s–2000s, such as Yin Xiuzhen, Lin Tianmiao, Xiao Lu, and Inri. Most of these artists are Beijing-based and produce works that unfortunately do not fall within the purview of this book's study. There is the exception of Yin Xiuzhen's Shanghai-related mixed-media sculpture *Portable City—Shanghai*, a minor iteration of her larger *Portable Cities* series. Yin Xiuzhen was also included in the 2008 Shanghai Biennial as one of very few women artists to appear in any Shanghai biennial.

22 Ai Weiwei, Feng Boyi, and Hua Tianxue, 不合作方式/*Bu hezuo fangshi*/*Fuck Off* (Shanghai: East Link Gallery, 2000), n.p.

23 See Meiling Cheng's discussion of "Fuck Off" and Zhu Yu's performance in *Beijing Xingwei: Contemporary Chinese Time-Based Art* (London, New York, and Calcutta: Seagull Books, 2013).

24 Melissa Chiu, Preface to *Yang Fudong: Seven Intellectuals in a Bamboo Forest*, eds. Melissa Chiu and Miwako Tezuka (New York: Asia Society, 2009), 8.

25 Yang Fudong cited in Molly Nisbet, "Wild Shanghai Grass," in Nisbet and Zhang Yaxuan, *Yang Fudong: Seven Intellectuals in a Bamboo Forest*, ed. Angie Baecker (Beijing: Office for Discourse Engineering, 2008), 40.

26 Yang Fudong, "Interview: The Power Behind," interview by Zhang Yaxuan, in *Yang Fudong: Seven Intellectuals in a Bamboo Forest*, ed. Angie Baecker, 119.

27 Yang Fudong, interview by author, September 13, 2008, audio recording, Shanghai, China.

28 As detailed in an essay on the Seven Sages published in a catalogue of Yang Fudong's *Seven Intellectuals*, "For generations in China, there have been men who served or should have served in public office but faced moral dilemmas that caused them to turn away from official service. This rejection was a way to respond to the corruption that developed after the Confucian bureaucratic system of government was institutionalized in China during the Han Dynasty (206 BCE–220 CE). Withdrawal from public life was interpreted as a rejection and condemnation of the corrupt system," Adriana Proser, "Seven Sages of the Bamboo Grove: Chinese Models of the Unconventional," in *Yang Fudong: Seven Intellectuals in a Bamboo Forest*, ed. Melissa Chiu and Miwako Tezuka, 25.

29 Yang Fudong, "Wild Shanghai Grass," 40.

30 See Chapter 1 for a discussion of Shanghai's *shikumen* vis-à-vis the shopping mall/cultural complex *Xintiandi*.

31 In describing Part 2 of *Seven Intellectuals*, Yang Fudong explains, "No matter what city you inhabit, you understand nothing better than your own family, your home, those private spaces that truly belong to you. … A lot of times, the things in an individual's residence have nothing to do, in fact, with bustling. … Everybody is quietly living in some corner of this city," Yang Fudong, "Interview: The Power Behind," 119.

32 Ibid., 175.

33 See Chapter 1 for a discussion of *Such is Shanghai*.

34 Yang Fudong, "Interview: The Power Behind," 175.

<h1>Installing a world city   **4**</h1>

The art of worlding

At the turn of the twenty-first century, a number of Chinese artists and curators living abroad accepted official invitations to return to the People's Republic of China (PRC) to help develop the country's contemporary art programs. Others elected to return, sensing more artistic freedom and opportunities in their home country. Many of these returning "sea turtles" (海龟/*haigui*), as they are nicknamed in mainland China, had participated in edgy experiments of the "1985 Chinese New Wave Movement" and left the PRC after 1989 in part to avoid artistic censorship.[1] This reverse migration of artists and art professionals back into mainland China seemed to signal the government's more liberal support for the arts. Yet the promotion of contemporary art within the PRC remained somewhat restrictive. As artist Gu Wenda told me, "If you produce a large public art work or exhibition in China, it has to be politically removed. … It has to be neutral, or a good image for the country."[2] Critics have expressed concern over the discrepancies between officially approved images of the new global China as socially, culturally, and economically progressive and realities defined by growing income disparity, pollution, corruption, inflation, and tightening control over civil liberties. Since the early 2000s, many "sea turtle" artists have imagined and created large-scale art installations and exhibitions in Shanghai, the showpiece of global China. Studying the transnational production and conflicted reception of these Shanghai-based projects, and the sociopolitical issues they have raised, illuminates how artists navigate the tricky terrain of contemporary art in the PRC while confronting their own diasporic identities. This chapter examines Shanghai-rooted art projects proposed and created by three of China's most internationally renowned contemporary artists, all of whom have had extensive experience living and working in and out of mainland China: Gu Wenda, Xu Bing, and Cai Guo-Qiang.[3] Each project tackles globalization in the context of the PRC, and specifically Shanghai, by utilizing cross-cultural content, aesthetic motifs, and conceptual tropes. My analyses aim to disrupt a clichéd assumption underlying recent discussions of contemporary Chinese art and urban Shanghai: that both category and city effortlessly encapsulate harmonious East-meets-West encounters. Later in the chapter, I examine a more recent project by Cai Guo-Qiang, which subtly critiques the concurrent officially lauded 2010 Shanghai World Expo; and Ai Weiwei's subsequent impromptu performance staged in protest at the demolition of his Shanghai studio. I argue that the celebratory and critical art projects presented here speak less to the seamless integration of diverse cultures and fluid insertion of Chinese art into the Western-dominated canon of contemporary art and more to the mistranslations, social inequities, and hybridizing of art and commodity culture that belie Shanghai's worlding.

In the anthology *Worlding Cities: Asian Experiments and the Art of Being Global,* cultural anthropologist Aihwa Ong and urban theorist Ananya Roy define *worlding* as the promotion of Asian cities, over the past two decades, as vanguard international capitals, defined in both global and local (e.g., Asian, Chinese, Shanghainese) terms. Ong and Roy redeploy worlding as articulated by postcolonial theorist Gayatri Spivak, who used the term to describe how Western European and North American imperialism produces "Third World" cultures imagined as pure, exploited, and rich in heritage.[4] Springing from Spivak's argument, which recuperates subaltern subjects in the face of the imperialist worlding of foreign nations and peoples, Ong and Roy account for the nationalism and authoritarian power foisted on Asian urbanites by their own countries, governments, and even themselves. The authors identify a myriad of worlding forces, including private investments, intercity rivalries, flashy buildings designed by "starchitects," and autocratic state power, such as that wielded by the Chinese Communist Party (CCP), all of which effectively publicize Asian cities as economic and cultural centers of international import.

Within contemporary art discourse, art historian Pamela Lee has recently conjured the notion of worlding in her book *Forgetting the Art World,* which addresses late twentieth and early twenty-first-century art amid globalization. Lee argues convincingly for abandoning the ideal of a definitive art world, positing "the work of art's world" as a worlding process in which economic and political forces crystallize to reflect and construct the tenets of globalization while perpetuating the myth of a borderless society.[5] Even in their disparate theorizations, Spivak, Ong, Roy, and Lee all suggest that worlding, be it the worlding of foreign cultures, Asian cities, or contemporary art, functions as a *creative* (which, in all cases, insinuates *market*) force with the power to plot that which has not yet come into being. Simultaneously, these scholars warn that worlding often results in the construction of glimmering facades that mask bleak contemporary realities plagued by rising economic disparities and the eclipsing of individual freedoms. In Shanghai, worlding's deceptive powers often come to the fore as contemporary art is harnessed toward figuring the city's global identity.

Global celebration

In 2003, internationally acclaimed artist and Shanghai native Gu Wenda instigated a series of plans for *Heavenly Lantern Project for Shanghai* (Plate 5), one
proposal in a larger series aimed at covering architectural monuments around
the world in red Chinese lanterns. In a corresponding publication, Gu Wenda
described the goals of *Heavenly Lantern Project*:

> [To] celebrate the multiple cultures in our modern society by erecting a series
> of large-scale works in a unique and grand manner full of Chinese cultural
> symbolism. … The goal of this work is not only to cover buildings with simple
> hanging lanterns, but the lanterns are intended to be the mouthpieces of a civi-
> lization and an ethnic herald in this series. Famous architecture and historic
> icons all over the world represent different civilizations and periods in world
> history. Draping and covering these monuments is not the traditional visual
> concept of contemporary art, but is a symbol of a civilization's dialogue with a
> symbol of another civilization in a unique manner, as well as one civilization's
> understanding and exposition of another. Understanding civilization from
> another point of view is what the *Heavenly Lantern* project intends to promote
> while making the decorated building more splendid and meaningful; intend-
> ing, like an ancient adage in China: "to make perfection still more perfect."[6]

Gu Wenda's stated intention for the Shanghai iteration was to create an East-
meets-West installation by covering the city's soaring Jin Mao Tower in red
paper lanterns as a celebration of the fusion of international architecture,
modern progress, and national tradition. One of Shanghai's tallest skyscrapers, the Jin Mao Tower, designed by US firm Skidmore, Owings, and Merrill,
is located in the city's chief economic hub: Lujiazui Financial District in the
Pudong New Development Zone.[7] The tower houses international corporate
offices, entertainment facilities, and the Grand Hyatt Hotel. Featured in popular films such as James Bond's *Skyfall* (2012), the Jin Mao Tower, along with the
Lujiazui skyline, has become a worldwide signifier of Shanghai's cosmopolitan
status and financial prowess.[8] Rather than merely emulate the skyscrapers of
Chicago, New York, and Tokyo, the Jin Mao Tower is known for integrating
specifically Chinese design elements, such as a pagoda-like setback design,
eighty-eight floors (eight being an auspicious number in traditional Chinese
culture), and proportions that revolve around the number eight.[9] Like the
building it proposed to cover, *Heavenly Lantern* stylistically drew from stereotypically Chinese motifs, including red lanterns and Chinese calligraphy (Gu
Wenda's well-known pseudo-Chinese characters were planned to be printed
on each lantern), while also referencing land art, installation art, and public
projects by artists working primarily in Western Europe and North America,
like Christo and Jeanne-Claude.

Yet, in addition to its proclaimed East/West cultural hybridity, *Heavenly Lantern* also blended fine art, design, architecture, advertising, and civic and national marketing. Toward the visualization of *Heavenly Lantern*, Gu Wenda employed a lobbying team (including museum directors and corporate CEOs) to negotiate with civic administrations and governmental bodies, assistants trained in architecture to produce mock-ups and blueprints, a contractor to design the assembly of the installation and the fabric for the lanterns, a construction group to physically install the work, mainland Chinese factory workers to produce the lanterns, and bilingual assistants to translate the promotional material from Chinese into English, the *lingua franca* of the art world.[10] Like many successful Chinese artists, Gu Wenda has long employed numerous women as assistants, who serve as a crucial, but vastly under-acknowledged, component of the PRC's contemporary art workforce (Figure 4.1). In regard to his production methods, Gu Wenda, who trained as a painter in Hangzhou's China Academy of Art, commented:

> Traditionally, if you practice painting, you just need a canvas and paint. … Now you really have to conduct your work as a director … you have to consider all the elements. … I still believe, if you want to go to other levels, if you want to do a public project, you need to collaborate with the government and corporations, financial aids … museums … transportation departments … city governments … central governments.[11]

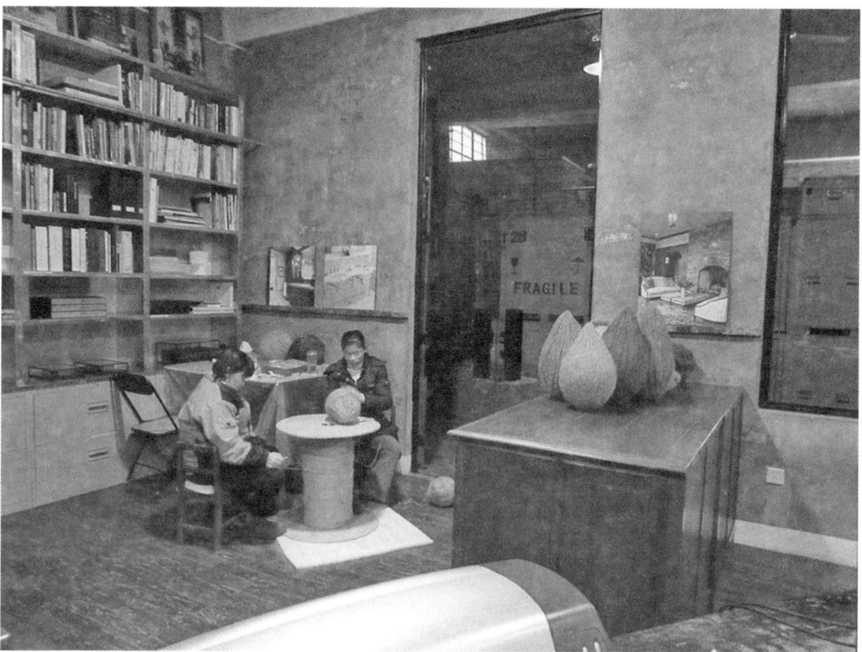

4.1   Assistants working in Gu Wenda's studio, 2010.

As an artist/director, Gu Wenda oversees various aspects of an art installation's production and runs an enterprise that relies on increased division of labor and various bureaucratic and institutional collaborations. These methods are not unlike those developed as early as the 1960s, when Andy Warhol set up his factory in New York City to produce silk-screen prints. What is markedly different in Gu Wenda's practice, however, is its transnational fluidity, which is defined by the artist's maintenance of studios both within mainland China (Shanghai and Beijing) and in the United States (New York City), as well as his dual mainland Chinese and overseas Chinese identities.

The artist sees himself as functioning like a cultural ambassador, spreading a positive image of Chinese culture abroad and a positive image of Western culture within China, while touting his installations as cultural bridges. In the case of *Heavenly Lantern*, the artist also emphasized the work's potential marketing power and ability to bolster cultural tourism and promote Shanghai and, by extension, China, worldwide:

> The *Heavenly Lantern* project would take the possibilities of advertising to newer heights and become a magnet for the world's media. ... Besides creating a glorious image for the society, politics and culture of the country and for Shanghai in particular, the project would create a charming focus for the Shanghai travel industry, and create a market for many commemorative products ... while contributing to help shape Shanghai as an international metropolis.[12]

Gu Wenda expressed a desire to contribute to Shanghai's worlding, or the city's ability to shine on a world stage, as both distinctly cosmopolitan (evident in the project's engagement with global contemporary art trends and modern architecture) and particularly Chinese (signaled by the use of red lanterns as national symbols).[13]

As with all of his large-scale installation projects, Gu Wenda hopes *Heavenly Lantern* will travel internationally, championing Chinese culture and "grand symbolism" abroad. To this end, he designed proposals for *Heavenly Lantern Hong Kong*, *Singapore*, and *Davos*. Testament to his overriding interest in the economics of art, Gu Wenda prioritized exhibiting the project in cities that are financial capitals and/or hold particular significance within the late-capitalist economy. *Heavenly Lantern Davos* (2003), for example, was designed specifically for the World Economic Forum, held annually in Davos, Switzerland, and which in 2003 coincided with Chinese New Year. For this installation, Gu Wenda proposed to cover the Hotel Belvedere, where forum guests stay, in red Chinese lanterns in order to extend Chinese New Year's celebrations of the "happiness of life [and] the joy of harvest" by "celebrating the good will of the world, which is concentrated in Davos during the World Economic Forum."[14] Gu Wenda sought to utilize Chinese cultural symbolism to celebrate transnational free-market capitalism, as promoted during the World Economic Forum; and transnational free-market capitalism to celebrate Chinese cultural symbolism, exemplified by Chinese New Year and festive red lanterns.

Heavenly Lantern's proposed combination of cosmopolitan and national symbols does more than simply promote the PRC, and specifically Shanghai, on a global stage; it generates an image of the country's newly hybridized political and economic circumstances, in which the CCP's power combines with multinational capitalism. While foreign-designed buildings like Shanghai's Jin Mao Tower might appear to herald the spread of Western-dominated capitalism and corporate power, *Heavenly Lantern*, if successful in covering these buildings with symbols of Chinese nationhood, would produce a multilayered portrait of China's free-market capitalism combined with state power. The project thus indexed what Aihwa Ong proposed as a "theory of sovereign exception."[15] This theory poses an alternative to the notion, generally accepted by urban and cultural studies theorists, that the development of modern contemporary architecture around the world is "merely the reflex of the expansion of capitalism or corporate power," by recognizing that recent urbanization in Asia and the corresponding race for Asian cities to unveil the tallest, most cutting-edge skyscrapers is fueled not only by corporate expansion and the proliferation of Western-dominated capitalism but also by the command of authoritarian regimes, exemplified by China's one-party rule.[16]

While aiming to smooth over cultural tensions resulting from the globalization of China's economy, *Heavenly Lantern*'s circulation or, more appropriately, its lack thereof, ultimately highlighted such tensions. In the early 2000s, as Gu Wenda began drafting the Davos proposal, mainland China's position within the world economy was soaring. For the first time, the PRC's state-sanctioned economic model, referred to as "socialism with Chinese characteristics," posed a viable threat to the North American and Western European model of democratic capitalism that had dominated international political and economic arenas since the second half of the twentieth century. Considering the suspicion and fear with which many political leaders have regarded mainland China's economic ascension, it is not surprising that projects such as *Heavenly Lantern Davos* were never realized. Conceived of as a celebration of the integration of multiple cultures, *Heavenly Lantern* has been continuously derailed by uneasy sentiments attached to Chinese cultural symbols. As Gu Wenda recounted to me, his plan to install the work at the Dutch Cathedral of Groningen, after years of planning, was ultimately rejected by the city council when some of its members voiced concerns over China being a communist state.[17] In such cases, *Heavenly Lantern* has revealed more about cross-cultural conflicts than the harmonious cultural unions Gu Wenda purported to highlight.

Such cross-cultural conflicts further define Gu Wenda's professionalization as an artist. He has narrated his own development this way:

> In the '80s [in China], it was totally about Western contemporary art and philosophy, so there was the danger of losing your own cultural identity. So I had a slogan in the early '80s: I want to use Chinese tradition to go against Western contemporary, but use Western contemporary to criticize Chinese tradition … to go both ways, so that I wouldn't lose my own cultural identity.[18]

Here, Gu Wenda foregrounds the uniqueness of his educational background—he studied traditional Chinese ink painting in Hangzhou (and emphasizes that the majority of his prominent artist peers studied Western-style oil painting or alternative media)—and his personal experiences with contemporary Western art gained by living in New York City, where he moved in 1987.[19]

Yet the artist's formative experiences in New York extend beyond a familiarization with dominant Western art trends. Gu Wenda's early encounters with the art market and capitalism more generally were intensely revelatory:

> When I went to the States, I was totally non-informed about capitalism. At the time I left China, there was no single commercial gallery. My generation … was all about Marxist ideology, socialism, communist ideology. In a sense, it was very naïve, very romantic, very idealistic—nothing really related to reality. I never had a bank account before I left China. I got my first bank account in New York. So New York gave me actually a physical education … just being there, to be trained [about] capitalistic property, the art market … everything. So, I had these kind-of two extremes, existing in me.[20]

The artist believed these new encounters with the art market and Western capitalism (what was in the late 1980s swiftly transforming into an increasingly globalized economic system in which the PRC and the United States would emerge as the two most prominent powers) opened his eyes to the future of contemporary art and made him better equipped to confront the inevitable changes that art would undergo in post-socialist China:

> By the time of the turn of the [21st] century, Chinese artists are mostly not focused on social issues anymore, or political issues. The younger generation is more focused on the market, self-promotion; it's more capitalistic than the older generation, like my generation, which had more social criticism. … I better understand the younger generation, because of being in New York, so I think in the future, the market will be the centerpiece.[21]

This statement reveals the drastic ways in which ideas about art have changed from China's socialist to post-socialist eras. Gu Wenda accurately predicted early on that, in opposition to Maoist privileging of artistic collectivity and art as a revolutionary political tool, Chinese artists of the younger generation would be more interested in selling their art and establishing their own careers.

The decade leading up to the 2008 financial crisis marked a watershed period for contemporary Chinese art, ushering in a strong overseas market and a burgeoning local one. CCP officials began vocally proclaiming support for contemporary Chinese art. In 2008, Gu Wenda commented:

> Chinese artists are benefiting so much from political, social, and economic developments in China. … Ten years ago, you only saw the promotion of traditional landscape painting or calligraphy that was safe from politics, but now you can see more contemporary culture being promoted.[22]

Contemporary Chinese art is today upheld for both its commercial viability and its ability to promote abroad a positive image of the new China. Gu Wenda has aligned his practice with these new expectations, formulating artworks like *Heavenly Lantern Project for Shanghai*, which, if realized, would stand as a worlding project that celebrates the hybridization of art, architecture, urban development, governmental sponsorship, and multinational capitalism. While Gu Wenda continues to promote *Heavenly Lantern* for its ability to blend tradition and modernization and Chinese and Western cultures, the project's failures, such as its ultimate rejection by politicians in Groningen, also reveal the persistence of cross-cultural tensions informed by lingering Cold War ideological divisions, even as communist China embraces free-market reforms.

Critical world view

Also acknowledging the recent expansion of governmental support for contemporary art and the growing ties between art and development in China, famed artist Xu Bing commented, "The old concept about art and government being at odds has changed. Now artists and the government are basically the same. All the artists and the government are both running with development."[23] In 1999, amid China's rapid state-sponsored economic growth and globalization, Xu Bing embarked on *Tobacco Project*, an ambitious multipart installation and transnational exhibition. The project foregrounded the social and political tensions accompanying Shanghai's worlding by commenting on the city's past as China's primary importer of foreign-brand cigarettes and its present as a capital of consumer luxury goods. Although Xu Bing is more closely connected with Beijing and New York, two cities in which the artist currently maintains studios, *Tobacco Project* focused on Shanghai and its status, both past and present, as a center of international exchange and capitalist/communist collisions. First exhibited at Duke University in Durham, North Carolina (2000), later at the Shanghai Gallery of Art (2004), and more recently at the Virginia Museum of Fine Arts (2011) and the Contemporary Art

Museum in Ridgefield, Connecticut (2012), *Tobacco Project* has in each iteration confronted issues surrounding globalization and US-Chinese economic relations through the lens of urban and transnational histories. The project stemmed from Xu Bing's artist's residency at Duke University and revolved around the Durham-Shanghai tobacco trade of the early twentieth century, originally dominated by the British American Tobacco (BAT) Company, which was financed in large part with money from Duke. *Tobacco Project* engaged 1920s–30s *haipai* (*Shanghai style*) by exhibiting BAT's Republican-era advertisements, such as the company's annual decorative calendars, while also including the artist's own mock advertisements and smoking paraphernalia, including multistemmed tobacco pipes and matchbooks printed with satirical slogans such as "Even Communists are Free to Smoke." These objects were juxtaposed with archival documents and statistical reports exposing the lucrative tobacco trade between Duke University, BAT, and Shanghai (where BAT located its headquarters and chief manufacturing plant); and medical records related to the smoking-related death of Xu Bing's father.[24]

The primary location of *Tobacco Project*'s Shanghai exhibition was the Shanghai Gallery of Art at Three on the Bund—an upscale cultural complex in a revamped colonial building on Shanghai's Huangpu Riverfront, formerly the heart of the British and American-run International Settlement.[25] In 2004, Three on the Bund, originally built as the Union Assurance Building (1916) by British architectural firm Palmer and Turner, was readapted by US architect Michael Graves, well known for his postmodern buildings, such as the Portland Building (1982), that draw from a myriad of historical referents; and his belief that design should be accessible to everyone, exemplified in his popular line for Target. Graves left the exterior of the building intact, transforming Three on the Bund's interior into an open-plan, multi-floor "concept space" initially housing China's first Armani flagship store, an Evian spa, gourmet restaurants and bars, and the Shanghai Gallery of Art. At the time of *Tobacco Project*'s exhibition, held just after Three on the Bund's opening, the Shanghai Gallery of Art had already become known as the city's most elite contemporary art gallery. Xu Bing's comment regarding the project's site— "the Shanghai Gallery of Art at Three on the Bund is very fitting because it is the base of American presence in Shanghai"—hints at the artist's ruminations on Shanghai's semicolonial past toward a rethinking of present-day US-China trade relations.[26]

The main exhibition at the Shanghai Gallery of Art consisted of five primary installations: *Traveling Down the River* (a replica of a classical Chinese landscape painting burned by a giant uncut cigarette), *Tobacco Book* (an oversized book handmade from tobacco leaves),[27] *Honor and Splendor* (comprised of hundreds of thousands of cigarettes arranged on the gallery floor to resemble a giant tiger skin rug), *Window Facing Pudong* (an ink drawing on the gallery's interior wall and windows representing the waterfront as an early twentieth-century tobacco trading port), and *Match Flower* (a vase containing a bouquet-like arrangement of long matches). *Match Flower* was exhibited with a number of smaller sculptural works, such as a ceramic ashtray painted with a *No Smoking* logo and a work entitled *Rounding Up/Rounding Down*, made of packets of 555-brand cigarettes decorated with ink drawings of an abacus. Like many of *Tobacco Project*'s individual works, *Rounding Up/ Rounding Down* reflected the collision of the local Chinese economy (symbolized by the abacus, a traditional Chinese counting tool) with foreign business expansion (evident in 555, a British cigarette brand). Not long before *Tobacco Project*'s Shanghai exhibition, 555, a popular brand in Republican Shanghai, announced plans to reestablish a large tobacco production and supply base in mainland China. Details like these intimate how aspects of Shanghai's semicolonial past, such as the imposition of foreign products on a local population, continue to resonate in the city's current climate.

Wu Hung, art historian and curator of *Tobacco Project*'s Shanghai exhibition, emphasized the parallels between the history this project presented and Shanghai's contemporary socioeconomic situation as the city emerged as a world center of finance, reliant on investment by multinational corporations, who, in turn, depended on China as a low-cost producer and giant consumer of goods:

> Because of the *Tobacco Project*'s relocation to Shanghai, its central concepts subtly shifted to the Sino-American relationship and China's globalization process. In this way, the movement of the project from Durham to Shanghai came to mirror the global expansion of the American tobacco industry in general and its rapid development in China specifically. … Viewing the show, no one could fail to hear a loud echo between the past and the present: once again there was the huge investment of foreign money, technology, and management, and once again China provided the world with cheap labor as well as an oversized market.[28]

The Shanghai display of *Tobacco Project* raised parallels between foreign-brand cigarettes in early twentieth-century Shanghai and contemporary art at the turn of the twenty-first century. The small sculptural works surrounding *Match Flower* were arranged in a series of illuminated glass cases that strikingly resembled those found in high-end jewelry stores (Figure 4.2). These cases were set in the Shanghai Gallery of Art's most luxurious space—a marble-clad atrium with an open plan that provided glimpses of the elite goods and services offered on the floors above and below the gallery. In what the artist claimed was an unintentional outcome, this arrangement framed *Tobacco Project*'s small sculptures as pristine luxury items in one of Shanghai's most exclusive retail spaces. Xu Bing's production of a local history was hence itself

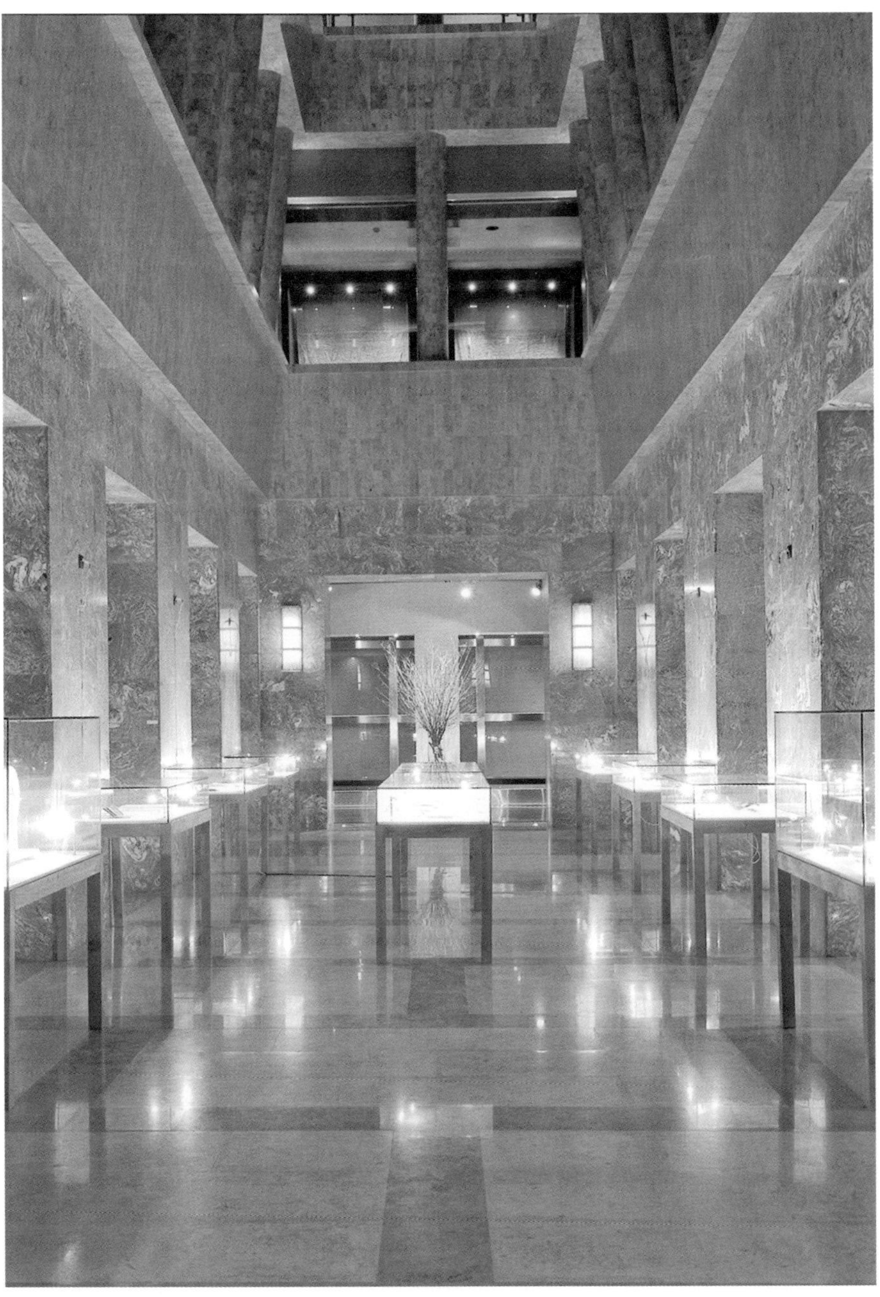

Xu Bing, *Match Flower* (Shanghai Version), 2004. Branches, red match-head paste, vase. Approx. 70 inches high. Installation view at Shanghai Gallery of Art, Shanghai, China, 2004. **4.2**

impacted by globalization, which made the development of the cosmopolitan luxury complex of Three on the Bund possible.

During a conference held in conjunction with *Tobacco Project*'s Shanghai exhibition, Beijing-based art historian Yin Jinan made the following remarks regarding *Match Flower*'s surrounding installation:

> In Shanghai, one views art as one views jewelry, one views jewelry as one views art. This would not likely be the case in Beijing. This environment is demonstrative of Shanghai's development. Shanghai becomes a very big city; it develops into the financial center. This is just one symptom of Shanghai's sudden explosion. When I look at these works, I grasp a sense of irony.[29]

Such comments hint at the ways in which Shanghai's contemporary art, mocked by some intellectuals as crass and commercial, still gets contrasted with the supposedly more cultured art of Beijing. As within Republican-era *haipai* versus *jingpai* (*Shanghai style* versus *Beijing style*) debates, Shanghai, as China's primary financial center, continued to be described as a place in which market-driven aspirations trump pure artistic pursuits.

Li Xu, then chief curator at the Shanghai Art Museum, described *Tobacco Project*'s jewelry-like display vis-à-vis museological issues, which he in turn related to breaks with Chinese tradition and the import of foreign cultural paradigms:

> I see so many delicate and beautiful things arranged in the display cabinets. It doesn't matter if you describe this display using the concept of the library, or the jewelry store. … Most of all, this exhibition uses the methods of museum display. … It's not Chinese. Historically, China didn't have a museum system, or an art gallery system, or an exhibition system. Imperial court art held a monopoly over the museum system. … Nowadays, art has become more populist—that's why everyone can get involved in this discussion.[30]

Li Xu's comments voiced an ambivalent position held by many art critics within mainland China. As he suggested, the foreign-influenced institutionalization and marketization of Chinese art problematically undermined Chinese tradition while simultaneously affording the possibilities of more populist receptions and a more open discursive terrain.

The curator also drew connections between existing cross-cultural tensions in contemporary Shanghai and those that existed during the city's semicolonial period. As *Tobacco Project* reminded viewers, such tensions had abounded in Shanghai ever since Britain's 1842 victory in the First Opium War, still considered today as the primary marker of China's century of deepest humiliation. Li Xu theorized:

> Tobacco replaces opium, and … we also use contemporary art to replace tobacco. This is to say these things are all fashionable … all fashionable

addictions. Now, we are addicted to contemporary art. … This is the outcome of globalization—making Chinese culture contemporary. … Today we are holding this conference in this building—this is a result of the combination of economic capital and cultural capital. This method of combining these two is an international style. This exhibition in Shanghai shows that there is no distinction between cultural capital and economic capital. Three on the Bund's Armani store and famous restaurants all show distinguished, international styles—does this capitalistic movement and its understanding and expression of cultural capital share much in common? Of course.[31]

Drawing analogies between opium, tobacco, and contemporary art, all considered as foreign and thus fashionable products, Li Xu argued that the localized addiction to contemporary art was a symptom of Shanghai's participation in a global economy, which, as during the semicolonial period, spawned hybrids of economic and cultural capital. Here, the craze for the new, which at the beginning of both the twentieth and twenty-first centuries in Shanghai was intimately linked to foreign influences, is likened to an addiction or a desire that will never be fulfilled. Li Xu saw in the combination of economic and cultural capital the emergence of an international style, which again echoed early theories of *haipai*, as supported by and supporting commercial business and the city's foreign-run districts. Yet by the early 2000s, economic capital was being produced *as* cultural capital and vice versa, through the media's relentless promotion of new commodities as new culture and by multinational corporate brands and venues like Three on the Bund, which strove to perpetually promote new art and fashions.

Xu Bing's *Tobacco Project* intervened in this conflation of economic and cultural capital. Rather than simply creating new artworks, the project demanded that viewers think historically about Shanghai's semicolonial period while suggesting that this past continued to haunt the city's globalized present. By displaying archival documents and found imagery, along with a wall of drawings that reference the former colonial waterfront, *Tobacco Project* presented traces of the early twentieth-century export of cigarettes by Western imperialist powers and their import by a local Chinese population eager to consume these harmful products because their foreignness made them fashionable. However unwittingly, *Tobacco Project*'s jewelry-like displays further highlighted the artificiality of this fashionable allure.

In another *Tobacco Project* installation, Xu Bing mocked the preciousness of art. *Traveling Down the River* (Figure 4.3), one of *Tobacco Project*'s largest installations and the piece that generated the greatest debate, consisted of a 30-foot-long cigarette, which was laid upon and burned over a reproduction of the famous Song Dynasty Chinese painting *Along the River During the Qingming Festival* by Zhang Zeduan.[32] Yin Jinan again revealed a bias toward Chinese traditional art over contemporary art when he argued that the rest of

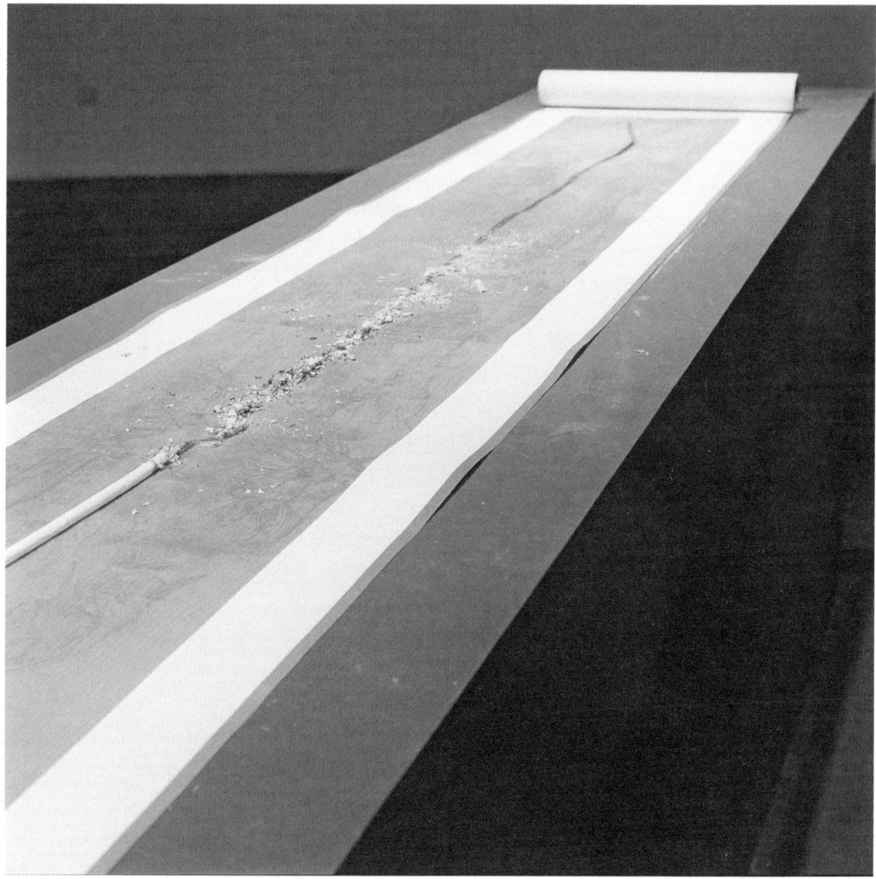

4.3   Xu Bing, *Traveling Down the River* (Shanghai Version), 2004. Long uncut cigarette, burned on a reproduction of *Along the River during the Qingming Festival* by Zhang Zeduan. Approx. 315 inches long. Installation view at Shanghai Gallery of Art, Shanghai, China, 2004.

Tobacco Project could not begin to compare to *Traveling Down the River*, since the landscape painting this work appropriated has long been recognized as the most important painting in Chinese art history.[33] He concluded that the cigarette burns in Xu Bing's reproduction symbolized how foreign imperialism and modern capitalism have sliced through traditional China.[34] While Yin Jinan's comments hinted at the complicity of overseas Chinese artists, like Xu Bing, in this slicing process, his main insinuation was that Shanghai (once a bastion of foreign imperialism and today mainland China's financial center) has set the stage for the commercialization and corruption of traditional Chinese culture.

Jokingly citing a scolding he received from a gallery assistant when he leaned on *Traveling Down the River*'s pedestal, Shanghai-based art historian, curator, and photographer Gu Zheng remarked that the low-cost reproduction of *Traveling Down the River* was "converted into gold" through the pedestal on which it was placed, the upscale space of the Shanghai Gallery of Art, and Xu Bing's international fame.[35] Referencing a telling comment made by the gallery's art director, "*Once artworks enter this space, they become like holy scriptures,*"[36] Gu Zheng highlighted how an artist's cosmopolitan identity and gallery's commercial cachet inform the reception of contemporary art, transforming simple objects, such as an inexpensive reproduction of a classical painting, into luxury items. This is a point Dada artist Marcel Duchamp famously raised when submitting a urinal to the Society of Independent Artists in New York in 1917 and when doodling on a reproduction of the Mona Lisa in 1919. *Tobacco Project* further complicated the blurring of boundaries between low commodity culture and high art by calling attention to the ways foreign products, including imported cigarettes and contemporary art made by overseas artists, were transformed into luxury items, establishing a high commodity culture in a postcolonial, post-socialist country.

Tobacco Project visually transformed cigarettes into luxury items, which in turn stood as contemporary artworks. In the installation *Honor and Splendor*, Xu Bing used 660,000 cigarettes to create the illusion of a fashionable luxury commodity—an oversized tiger-skin rug—which took up almost the entire floor of the gallery's main exhibition hall (Plate 6a). The cigarettes were arranged with their heads and filters alternating, so that they produced the appearance of an orange and white striped carpet. In an attempt to comment on the use of labor during the early twentieth century when foreign companies like BAT employed poorly trained Chinese laborers, Xu Bing hired old migrant workers to open the hundreds of cigarette packages, and students to assemble the cigarettes (Plate 6b). By acting as a director, overseeing this labor-intensive assembly (which was photographed and published in subsequent *Tobacco Project* publications), Xu Bing did more than merely represent the parallels between semicolonial and early twenty-first-century Shanghai; he actively engaged the dynamics of globalization.

Xu Bing explicitly acknowledged his own position as a transnational figure within a globalized trading network, prominently displaying a check from a US collector who purchased works from *Tobacco Project*'s Durham exhibition, along with financial statements from Duke University, who helped fund the project. These inclusions rendered transparent the private and institutional support that financed the project from overseas, while revealing the artist's own role as a multinational trader in luxury items, namely contemporary artworks. Together with *Honor and Splendor*, Xu Bing's inclusion of financial documents underlined two crucial ways in which Shanghai's current global economic circumstances differed from those of the city's past. Whereas in the early twentieth century, Shanghai was a major importer of foreign-made goods, by the turn of the twenty-first century, the city (and China more broadly) had become a major exporter of Chinese-manufactured goods, including Chinese art eagerly bought by foreign collectors. Furthermore, cultural and economic exchanges in Shanghai were no longer dominated by Westerners but were largely steered by overseas and transnational Chinese figures like Xu Bing and Gu Wenda, professional artists able to move fluidly in and out of mainland China. When I asked Xu Bing in an interview about *Tobacco Project*'s reference to US-China economic relations, he remarked, "*Tobacco Project* looks like it's talking about history, but it's still applicable to the relationship today."[37] Yet rather than simply compare Shanghai's past and present, *Tobacco Project* revealed conflicts between the desire to preserve local identities and achieve global aspirations that extended beyond the long-standing East-meets-West cliché. The project's critical reception at the Shanghai Gallery of Art, wherein curators criticized the merits of *haipai* and increasing parallels between art and luxury commodities, illuminated the historically rooted debates—over Shanghai's embrace of an initially foreign-propagated capitalism—at the heart of the city's worlding and the promotion of global contemporary art.

Explosive borders

At the dawn of the twenty-first century, Chinese-born and currently US-based artist Cai Guo-Qiang produced a work heralding the international rise of Asian economic powers, as well as the PRC's, and specifically Shanghai's, leading role in this ascent. Commissioned by Asia-Pacific Economic Cooperation (APEC), a multi-government–led economic forum devoted to free trade and accelerated business growth across the Pacific Rim region, Cai Guo-Qiang created *APEC Cityscape Fireworks*, an ostentatious, dazzling display of fireworks celebrating the close of APEC's 2001 conference held in Shanghai (Plate 7). Showcasing Shanghai's historic and present-day landmarks of world city status, the fireworks show straddled the Huangpu River and the adjacent respective sites of Xu Bing's *Tobacco Project* and Gu Wenda's *Heavenly Lantern*: the Bund, historical marker of Shanghai's semicolonial past; and the Lujiazui skyline, current symbol of the PRC's exponential post-socialist economic growth.

Cai Guo-Qiang's *APEC Cityscape Fireworks* exemplified the increasingly common, albeit sometimes strained, collaborations between CCP officials and contemporary Chinese artists. Cai Guo-Qiang subsequently designed fireworks displays for a second APEC Conference (the 2014 meeting in Beijing) and the 2008 Beijing Olympics. Ai Weiwei, in another instance, collaborated with architects Herzog and De Meuron on the National Stadium for the Beijing Olympics, before deciding to boycott and denounce the event as propaganda. In discussing such collaborations, film director Zhang Yimou, who served as artistic director of the opening ceremonies of both the Beijing Olympics and the 2014 APEC Conference, stated:

> Art needs to be free, but these projects have political requirements, and no one can do anything about it. This is China's current situation. I personally am very familiar with these circumstances. So when you talk about creative work on these projects, those artists who grew up in free Western countries are not able to understand this. We really envy them, but there is nothing we can do about it.[38]

APEC Cityscape Fireworks erupted at night when the Lujiazui Financial District's flashy, postmodern towers were illuminated by giant LED signs featuring advertisements for foreign and Chinese corporations, as well as governmental slogans proclaiming a healthy communist state. To many foreign observers, this combining of contemporary art, multinational capitalism, and communist propaganda marked a striking irony. But we should note art's participation within the terrain of global capitalism described by Chinese studies scholars Arif Dirlik and Xudong Zhang: "Under conditions of global capitalism, Chinese states and populations are no longer merely the 'objects' of forces emanating from Euro-America but are themselves significant contributors to the operations of capitalism."[39] When considered in the context of the PRC's economic expansions, Cai Guo-Qiang's *APEC Cityscape Fireworks* revealed much more than superficial East-meets-West tropes and encounters; the spectacle offered an explosive view of state power combined with economic liberalization and the intensified implications of border crossing.

APEC Cityscape Fireworks comprised nearly 20 minutes of fireworks, which erupted from numerous launching points, including ten barges, eighteen yachts, and twenty-three buildings on and along the Huangpu River.[40] The spectacular display featured a myriad of references, including cosmic forms, such as constellation and UFO-shaped fireworks; and various signifiers of traditional Chinese culture: red lanterns, boats adorned with fire-breathing dragons, and the fireworks themselves, the artist's signature medium and a seventh-century Chinese invention.[41] The artist's promoters have frequently pointed to Cai Guo-Qiang's incorporation of these motifs and use of fireworks as a medium in celebrating his ability to blend Chinese mythologies with individualistic creation, and Eastern tradition with Western art styles such as conceptual art and land art. The catalogue for "Cai Guo Qiang: I Want to Believe," the artist's 2008 solo exhibition at New York City's Guggenheim Museum, described *APEC Cityscape Fireworks* as "incorporating iconic symbols from both traditional Chinese culture and Cai's personal vision of the cosmos."[42] In summarizing Cai Guo-Qiang's larger oeuvre, the exhibition's curator, Alexandra Munroe, wrote: "Arising from the epic geopolitical shifts of the post-Cold War, his work transgresses cultural boundaries as the ultimate creative force of our borderless age."[43]

This focus on Cai Guo-Qiang's ability to transcend borders through cross-cultural aesthetic motifs elided the significance of APEC's telling command of a massive cultural explosion over mainland China's key financial metropolis. Shared cultural references in *APEC Cityscape Fireworks* existed more deeply in the artwork's engagement with mainland China's state-sponsored multinational capitalism, apparent in its sponsorship by APEC, a primary engine of free trade comprised of various nations devoted to economic liberalization, including the world's most powerful economic powers and long-standing allies/competitors: the United States (joined in 1989) and the PRC (joined in 1991). Beyond simply celebrating cultural diversity and harmonious international cooperation, *APEC Cityscape Fireworks* heralded Shanghai's and the PRC's rising status in a global economy that overcomes East/West binaries through transnational market forces.[44]

Staged on October 20, just over a month after the terrorist attack on New York City's World Trade Center on September 11, 2001, *APEC Cityscape Fireworks* constituted an unexpectedly timely and uncanny projection of the PRC's rising economic might in the face of US collapse. The work's grand finale consisted of a simulated eruption of contemporary Shanghai's most iconic tower, Lujiazui's Oriental Pearl Radio and Television Tower (Figure 4.4).[45] In light of the attack on the World Trade Center, Cai Guo-Qiang's orchestrated explosion from the Pearl Tower created a haunting sight that marked the start of a new era through comet-like fireworks extending from the building's

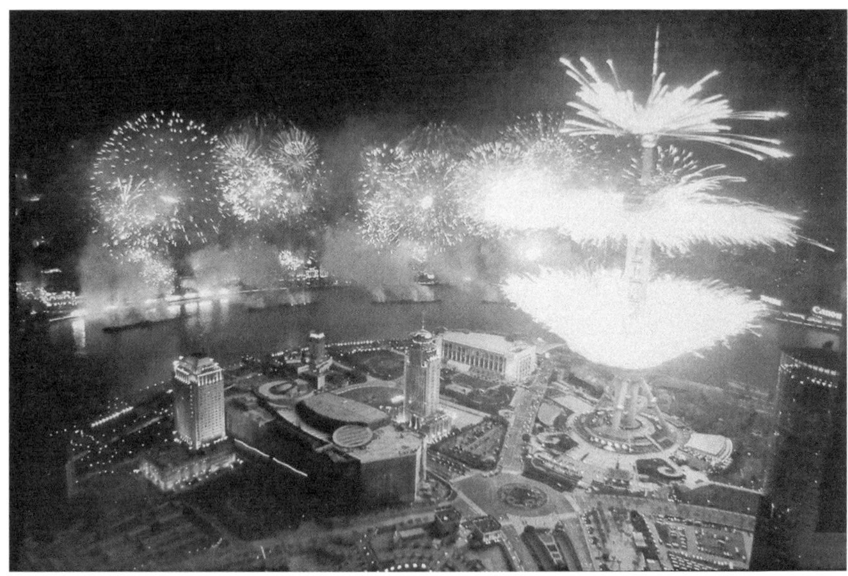

4.4 Cai Guo-Qiang, *Asia-Pacific Economic Cooperation (APEC) Cityscape Fireworks* finale, realized at Oriental Pearl TV tower, Shanghai, China, on October 20, 2001.

futuristic orbs. Shanghai's 2001 APEC Conference was considered especially significant because of its occurrence in the immediate aftermath of 9/11 and the subsequent slowdown of the US-led global economy—a glimmer of crises to come. Government-approved Chinese reports announced that Shanghai's convening of the APEC Conference was an appropriate signal of the PRC's economic development despite widespread economic downturn: "For the host … the only country in the Asia-Pacific region to enjoy rapid economic growth, the success of APEC 2001 in Shanghai signifies the further integration of China into globalization and its increasingly important role in the world."[46] This statement aligned with other CCP-generated news stories emphasizing that Shanghai's reopening to international trade in the 1990s was orchestrated by the Chinese state on its own terms and highlighting how fast the PRC had modernized in comparison to Western nations.

Shanghai's current economic situation marks a clear departure from that of the mid-nineteenth to mid-twentieth centuries, when Western European, US, and Japanese powers imposed their own financial systems and institutions on the city. That colonial-capitalist history was monumentalized on the Bund, which comprises neoclassical landmarks, such as the old British Customs House, built by foreign capital and architectural firms.[47] After the founding of the PRC, the Bund became a site for victory parades, and its buildings were covered in long red banners with anti-imperialist, pro-communist slogans. At the outset of the Cultural Revolution in 1966, Red Guards described these transformations with vigor:

> The waterfront of the [Huangpu] River in Shanghai was, until the liberation, the centre of imperialist plunder of the Chinese people. The buildings here have still carried many reminders of the imperialists and here the Red Guards and revolutionary workers and staff have gone in for revolutionizing in a big way. They have taken down all the imperialist signs from walls and removed the bronze lions outside one of the big buildings [the formerly British-owned Hong Kong and Shanghai Banking Corporation].[48]

Today, there are few reminders of the Bund's Mao-era makeovers. Even within the United States, documentation of the anti-imperialist protests on Shanghai's riverfront has been suppressed. In 2010, Zhang Yuqing's *Waves of Anti-American anger along the Bund*, a 1961 propaganda poster, was pulled from the San Francisco Asian Art Museum exhibition "Shanghai: Art of the City." The poster portrays spirited groups of Chinese workers protesting against US imperialist capitalists, represented by two cowering figures: Uncle Sam with a dollar sign emblazoned on his chest and a US soldier pictured with a small missile. Protestors hold banners with slogans like "American Imperialism out of Taiwan!" which also line the facades of the Bund's colonial buildings, literally covering the city's semicolonial past. As explained to me by the founder of Shanghai's Propaganda Poster Art Center, Yang Peiming, who lent numerous posters (including Zhang Yuqing's) to the Asian Art Museum, *Waves of Anti-American Anger along the Bund* was pulled at the very last minute.[49] Apparently somebody felt that the poster failed to support the exhibition's aim of "celebrating the visual culture of Shanghai from its beginnings as a trade port to its current status as an economic and artistic powerhouse that has captured the world stage."[50]

In recent years, luxury goods, services, and experiences like those offered by Three on the Bund (the site of Xu Bing's *Tobacco Project* and a launching site in Cai Guo-Qiang's *APEC Cityscape Fireworks*) have largely replaced the Bund's earlier economic and state services—the British and US-run International Settlement's banks and governing institutions and, after 1949, those CCP-controlled ones. The former Union Assurance Building, which now houses Three on the Bund, is capped with a cupola. In Western Europe and the United States, banks and governmental institutions have long modeled their buildings on classical Greek and Roman architecture or, as in this case, on Renaissance cathedrals. The use of heavy stone and historical references supposedly gives these buildings an air of permanence, while religious references hint at the institutions' good moral standing. In its exterior design, Three on the Bund, like other examples of the Bund's neoclassical architecture, flexes what sociologist Max Weber defined at the turn of the twentieth century as the chief features contributing to the development of Western capitalism: man's attempt to conquer nature and a work ethic rooted in religion.[51] In turn, Weber argued that China was slower in adopting capitalism because of the country's traditional sociopolitical structure, which denigrated the merchant class (a bias that resonates in the *haipai* versus *jingpai* debates), and exalted the "cultured man," a member of China's elite literati, as the highest Confucian ideal.[52]

By the early twenty-first century, the PRC had clearly adopted a new economic system with its own brand of CCP-sponsored capitalism, in which the cultured man (or woman) plays an integral role as worlding agent. This new cultured person is well represented by the transnational contemporary Chinese art star (still most often a man), who blends traditional Chinese motifs with contemporary global trends, maintains residences and studios in China and overseas, and negotiates equally well with private investors and governmental bureaucracies while celebrating, critiquing, and/or contributing to the rise of world cities like Shanghai. This cultured man's ethos rings out in Cai Guo-Qiang's statement regarding his fireworks projects: "It is from this destructive nature of consuming such a great amount of money in a split second that the pleasure derives."[53] That is to say, the PRC's new cultured person is a cosmopolitan figure who can simultaneously produce and consume without limits.

Nearly a decade after staging *APEC Cityscape Fireworks*, Cai Guo-Qiang presented himself in a more humble light, writing: "I have been gathering peasants' dreams, and within these dreams I see myself: I am a child of this land, I am a son of peasants—no—I am a peasant."[54] This quote appeared in the pamphlet for the artist's exhibition, "Peasant Da Vincis," organized to inaugurate the Rockbund Art Museum, located not far from Three on the Bund. For "Peasant Da Vincis," Cai Guo-Qiang exhibited dozens of inventions, including robots and flying machines, made by people living in rural locations in mainland China, which the artist had collected over many years.[55] The exhibition and the establishment of the privately funded Rockbund Art Museum coincided with the 2010 Shanghai World Expo, a large-scale international event aimed at showcasing Shanghai as a world city. In "Peasant Da Vincis," Cai Guo-Qiang subtly critiqued the Shanghai World Expo, riffing off the event's slogan, "Better City, Better Life" (城市，让生活更美好/*Chengshi, rang shenghuo geng meihao*) by painting "Peasants–Making a Better City, a Better Life" (农民,让城市更美好/*Nongmin rang chengshi geng meihao*) on the wall of a construction site near the Rockbund Museum (Figure 4.5). The

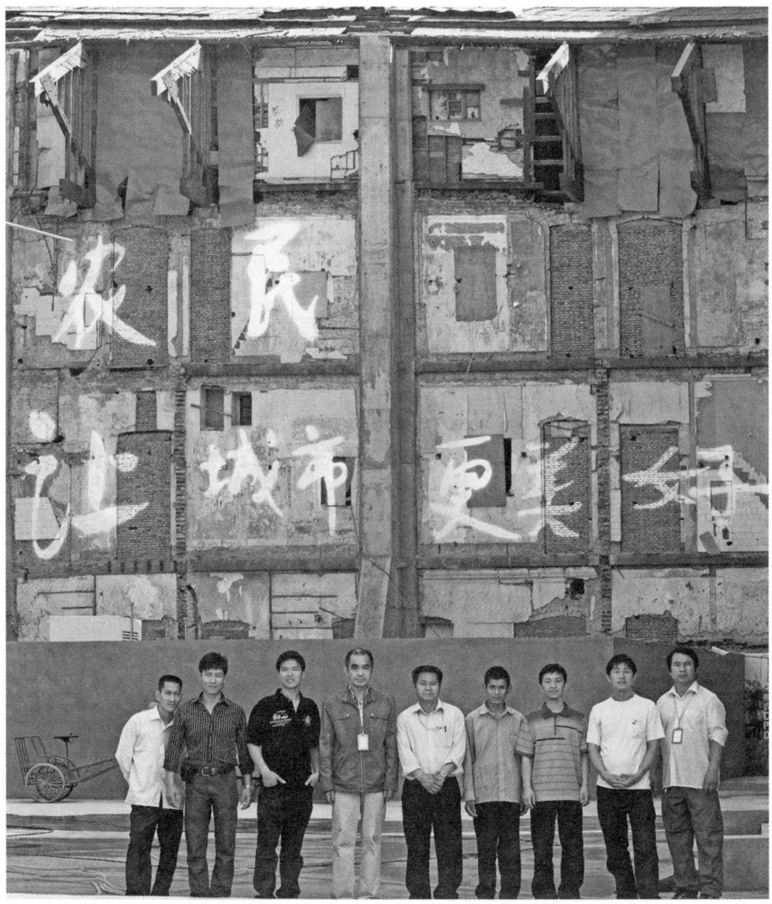

Cai Guo-Qiang, *Peasants—Making a Better City, a Better Life*, realized in conjunction with the exhibition "Peasant Da Vincis" at the Rockbund Art Museum, Shanghai, China, 2010.   **4.5**

graffiti acknowledged an overlooked aspect of the PRC's breakneck urbanization, calling attention to the devalued migrant labor that fuels Shanghai's development and makes possible flashy events like the World Expo. Cai Guo-Qiang's urban intervention functioned in part like commonly circulated photojournalistic images of Shanghai, which juxtapose impoverished migrant workers and their ramshackle, cargo container–like dormitories against the gleaming skyscrapers that these laborers build.

Outside the state-run Chinese media, criticisms of Shanghai's World Expo were ubiquitous, especially on internet blogs and among families and friends. In the months leading up to the Expo, many people I spoke with in Shanghai—from neighbors to taxi drivers to professors—lambasted the events as an extravagant waste of money and something they themselves could not afford to attend. Friends privately joked that the Expo's China Pavilion, a shiny red structure resembling an inverted pagoda with upper levels that extend beyond its lower levels, appropriately symbolized the new, post-1989 China by projecting an overblown image to the world despite its lack of a solid foundation. Throughout 2010, "Better City, Better Life" flashed steadily on the massive LED screens affixed to the Aurora Plaza and Citigroup Tower skyscrapers of Pudong's Lujiazui Financial District. Across the Huangpu River from Lujiazui's multinational corporate towers, Three on the Bund stood as a shadowy reflection of Shanghai's current financial prowess and as a reminder that the city's positioning as a financial center has been accompanied by heavy investment in cultural capital. The Bund's cultural complexes, along with Shanghai's sparkling lights and fireworks displays, act as dazzling worlding screens that cover over long-standing debates surrounding imperialism and the violent conflicts of mainland China's more immediate socialist history.

Pandas and river crabs

The 2010 Shanghai World Expo was a colossal event that signaled how, after decades of isolationism during the Mao era, government officials and private investors have today re-positioned Shanghai as the PRC's primary international center, not only of finance but also of art and design. Aihwa Ong accurately characterized Shanghai's World Expo as "the most explicit demonstration yet of a can-do determination to experiment with cutting-edge innovations in urban architecture, industry, and design."[56] While keenly acknowledging how the CCP's massively scaled design projects globally promote the PRC's expanding megacities, Ong overlooked the crucial globalizing role contemporary art has played, especially in Shanghai. Art's globalizing prowess was clearly seen in the Shanghai World Expo and its aftermath. Following the event's conclusion, two main Expo structures—the China Pavilion and Urban Future Pavilion—were converted into China Art Palace (中华艺术宫/*Zhonghua yishu gong*) and

Power Station of Art (上海当代艺术博物馆/*Shanghai dangdai yishu bowu-guan*), now the world's largest state-run museums devoted to modern and contemporary Chinese art.

Furthermore, during the Expo, numerous famous Chinese artists and designers (including Huang Jiancheng, the China Pavilion's chief designer), received commissions to produce sculptures for the Shanghai Expo Park. For his commissioned Expo Park sculpture, the currently Shanghai-based artist Zhang Huan, who got his start doing abject body performances on the depressed outskirts of Beijing in the mid-1990s, exhibited two giant stainless-steel pandas named Hehe and Xiexie, said to celebrate international peace and harmony.[57] *Hehe Xiexie* epitomized Zhang Huan's local/global artistic strategy, by which sculptures made in China integrating obvious Chinese symbols (e.g., pandas) receive international exposure. Art and cultural historian Winnie Wong has pointed to Zhang Huan's transformation from a commercial painter to underground performance artist to global art star as emblematic of recent currents in contemporary Chinese art.[58] Performance-studies scholar Meiling Cheng has characterized these shifts as "paradigmatic of the mobility, hybridity and variety of contemporary art-making under globalization."[59]

Promotional materials have hailed Zhang Huan, like many of mainland China's most internationally acclaimed contemporary artists, for bridging East/West divides. John Mack, former CEO of Morgan Stanley, who sponsored the artist's solo show at Asia Society in New York, wrote in 2007, "Residing in both Shanghai and New York, [Zhang Huan] is a true internationalist who makes connections that show us new ways of appreciating both cultures. … As a financial services pioneer in China and worldwide, Morgan Stanley is honored to partner with Asia Society in its exhibitions … that foster mutual understanding between Asia and the rest of the world."[60] This statement underscores how the recent positioning of contemporary Chinese art within a transnational culture industry has been widely predicated on what curators, collectors, and corporate sponsors identify as encounters of East-meets-West, or "Asia meets the rest."

Now, Zhang Huan employs over a hundred laborers in a factory-like studio on the outskirts of Shanghai to produce his large-scale works, including giant pandas and Buddhist-themed art that circulates internationally, such as *Three Heads Six Arms* (2008), a public sculpture installed outside of San Francisco's Asian Art Museum in conjunction with the aforementioned "Shanghai: Art of the City" exhibition and 2010 Shanghai World Expo.[61] As such, I argue that Zhang Huan's East/West encounters exist less in the artist's superficial appropriation of Chinese symbols and more in his outsourcing of labor, which he oversees like so many heads of multinational manufacturing companies utilizing inexpensive labor in China, currently known as "the world's factory." What is actually being moved between "Asia and the rest of the world"? Is it art forms, ideas, and cultural experiments or corporate identities, financial services, and nationalist political agendas? Or is it the cult of the art star personality, a manufactured symbol of *Chineseness*, artistic labor, and art as cultural capital? As I've aimed to show throughout this book, it is all of these things moving to and fro, informing, enriching, and threatening each other much in the same way that the local and foreign paradoxically intertwined toward production and destruction ever since the height of Shanghai's semicolonial occupation.

The names of Zhang Huan's Shanghai World Expo pandas reference 和谐/*hexie*, meaning *harmony*, a widely proliferated CCP buzz term used to promote a harmonious Chinese state. In recent years, the term has also been satirically co-opted by dissident Chinese artists and activists who use *harmonizing* as a euphemism for the government's censoring of the internet and other media. The year following Shanghai's World Expo, Ai Weiwei played with the *hexie* term in a public gathering-turned-impromptu performance. In 2011, Ai Weiwei received word that an originally state-condoned studio he was having constructed in an emerging arts district in Shanghai was being torn down. Officials cited improper following of planning procedures as the reason for the destruction, but Ai Weiwei and his supporters suspected that the demolition was a backlash against the artist's increasingly vocal critiques of the government. The state's initial support and subsequent wrecking of Ai Weiwei's Shanghai studio revealed how fraught relations between CCP officials and contemporary Chinese artists can become. As the PRC has invested in the nation's cultural industries, helping establish creative zones in cities like Shanghai and Beijing, officials must balance the desire to demonstrate an openness toward contemporary art with orders to silence artists who address taboo subjects, such as government corruption.[62] Artists, meanwhile, might need to compromise their ideas if they wish to undertake government-sponsored commissions (as seen in Cai Guo-Qiang's APEC projects) or maintain officially supported studios.

The announcement that Ai Weiwei's Shanghai studio was being torn down came after two years of construction, just as the US$1.1 million building was nearing completion. In playful protest, Ai Weiwei, already well established with a studio complex in Beijing, threw a river crab feast (the Chinese word for *river crab*, 河蟹/*hexie*, phonetically resembles the CCP's harmony buzz term). Hundreds of people attended Ai Weiwei's river crab party, excluding the artist, who had been placed under house arrest in his Beijing compound.[63] In defiance of the PRC's censorship of the worldwide web, Ai Weiwei harnessed a particular demolition site in Shanghai, a local delicacy, and a swiftly mobilized group of urban participants, orchestrating a performance that circulated widely through mainstream news channels outside of China, such as the *New York Times*. Ai Weiwei's antagonistic relationship with the Chinese state, highlighted by the construction and demolition of his Shanghai studio, significantly raises the artist's international profile. In recent years, numerous journalists, art critics, and art historians have pointed to the importance of Ai Weiwei as a global artist.[64] What tends to be missing from these accounts is detailed analyses of the local contexts under which the artist operates.

While Chinese officials increasingly promote Shanghai's global contemporary art, the CCP also dictates, either directly or indirectly through artists' and curators' own choices and self-censorship, what this art can be; impressive fireworks and harmonious pandas are displayed at official events, but dissident river crabs are not. Even as an art star who has lived and traveled abroad extensively and embraced the internet toward worldwide circulation, Ai Weiwei's personal freedom remains under constant threat. The fragility of the Chinese artist's cosmopolitan privilege was publicized by Ai Weiwei's 2011 arrest and imprisonment, and his selfie, taken four years later, with his passport, which had just been returned.

Worlding facades celebrating Shanghai's global status, global contemporary art, and global China abound in the city's twenty-first-century landscape. Yet even artworks intended to celebrate globalism can produce failures, as seen in Gu Wenda's inability to erect *Heavenly Lantern*. The artworks explored in this chapter generate criticisms (e.g., ambivalence toward the luxurious displays of Xu Bing's *Tobacco Project*, Cai Guo-Qiang's graffiti acknowledging the important role of migrant labor in Shanghai's urbanization, Ai Weiwei's river crab party/protest) that reveal cracks in Shanghai's worlding facades.

Notes

1 For a discussion of sea turtles/overseas returnees (海龟 / 海归, both pronounced *haigui*) versus "ground beetles" who never left mainland China, see Jiayun Zhuang, "Left Hand and Right Hand—Waving from the Past in the Post-Socialist Factory" (unpublished conference paper), presented in the panel *Bad Hauntings: Contemporary Asian Art in the Post-Era*, Association for Asian Studies (AAS) annual conference, Honolulu, Hawaii, 2011. See Gao Minglu's writings on the "1985 New Wave Movement" in the exhibition catalogue *The Wall: Reshaping Contemporary Chinese Art* (Beijing and Buffalo, NY: Millennium Art Museum and University of Buffalo, 2005).

2 Gu Wenda, interview by author.

3 Gu Wenda attended Hangzhou's China Academy of Art before moving to New York City, and he currently maintains studios and residences in New York City, Shanghai, and Beijing. Xu Bing attended Beijing's Central Academy of Fine Arts, later moved to New York City, and finally returned to Beijing, where he has served as the vice president of the Central Academy of Fine Arts. Cai Guo-Qiang studied theater production in Shanghai before moving to Tokyo and later to New York City, where he currently resides and maintains a studio. Both Gu Wenda and Xu Bing first gained international fame for their various experiments with

the deconstruction of Chinese characters and installation projects, praised by critics for their combining of traditional elements, namely Chinese calligraphy, with supposedly modern, Western frameworks for art, namely installation and postmodern linguistic deconstruction. For an insightful discussion between Gu Wenda, Xu Bing, and others, see Simon Leung, Janet A. Kaplan, Wenda Gu, Xu Bing, and Jonathan Hay, "Pseudo Languages: A Conversation with Wenda Gu, Xu Bing, and Jonathan Hay," *Art Journal* 58, no. 3 (Autumn, 1999): 86–99.

4 Referring to Gayatri Chakravorty Spivak's *A Critique of Postcolonial Reason: Toward a History of the Vanishing Present* (Cambridge, MA: Harvard University, 1999), Aihwa Ong explains, "Worlding and reworlding were articulated by Spivak in her postcolonial attempt to recuperate subaltern subjects through a rendering of the Heideggerian concept of 'being in the world,'" Ong, Introduction to *Worlding Cities: Asian Experiments and the Art of Being Global*, 11.

5 Pamela M. Lee, Introduction to *Forgetting the Art World*, 8.

6 Gu Wenda, "Heavenly Lantern: Shanghai, A Wenda Gu Art Production Proposal" (2005), trans. by David Mao, in 天堂红灯(金茂大厦, 上海)/*Tiantang hongdeng (Jinmao dasha, Shanghai)/Heavenly Lantern (Jinmao Tower, Shanghai)* (Shanghai: Gu Wenda Studio, 2005), n.p.

7 See more on Pudong in the Introduction and Chapter 2.

8 The Lujiazui skyline is also a chief marker of China's economic liberalization, which first crystallized in the country's Special Economic Zones (SEZ). Leader Deng Xiaoping established China's first SEZ in the southern coastal city of Shenzhen in 1980, more than ten years before Pudong was annexed as a New Development Zone.

9 The tradition of utilizing eight and scales of eight within design for auspicious associations used to be primarily limited to southern China, as seen in the tradition's prevalence in Hong Kong.

10 Gu Wenda, interview by author.

11 Ibid.

12 Gu Wenda, "Heavenly Lantern," n.p.

13 While Gu Wenda never actualized his proposal for the Jin Mao Tower, *Heavenly Lantern* debuted at the Europalia China Art Festival in Brussels, Belgium in 2009. In 2016, the artist realized an iteration of *Heavenly Lantern* for his solo exhibition "Gu Wenda: Journey to the West" at Shanghai Twenty-first Century Minsheng Art Museum. This version comprised an installation of colorful lanterns on the museum's facade and a large-scale participatory public art event, in which approximately 10,000 school children wrote their wishes for the future on lanterns.

14 Gu Wenda, "Heavenly Lantern," n.p.

15 Aihwa Ong, "Hyperbuilding: Spectacle, Speculation, and the Hyperspace of Sovereignty," in *Worlding Cities: Asian Experiments and the Art of Being Global*, 206.

16 Ibid.

17 Gu Wenda, interview by author.

18 Ibid.

19 Wang Dongling, a painter and one of Gu Wenda's former classmates at Hangzhou's China Academy of Art (中国美术学院/*Zhongguo meishu xueyuan*), describes

Gu Wenda as a renegade student who daringly crossed boundaries in a conservative climate, where most professors were concerned only with recuperating the basic skills and techniques of traditional Chinese painting in the aftermath of the Cultural Revolution. Wang Dongling, interview by author, April 17, 2010, Wang Dongling's studio, Hangzhou, China.

20 Gu Wenda, interview by author.

21 Ibid.

22 Ibid.

23 Xu Bing made this comment when discussing his official appointment as vice president of the China Central Academy of Fine Arts (中央美术学院/*Zhongyang meishu xueyuan*) in Beijing in 2008. Xu Bing quoted in David Barboza, "Schooling the Artist's Republic of China," *New York Times* (March 30, 2008), http://www.nytimes.com/2008/03/30/arts/design/30barb.html, accessed January 29, 2012.

24 Individual artworks and installations have been added and/or altered within each exhibition; my discussion focuses on *Tobacco Project*'s Shanghai exhibition.

25 A secondary location, an abandoned warehouse meant to conjure the site of an old tobacco warehouse, displayed a single installation, *The Invention of Tobacco*, composed of stage smoke and neon signs forming the Chinese text of a Republican-era tobacco advertisement.

26 Xu Bing, interview by author, May 13, 2010, audio recording, Beijing, China.

27 The content of the book, stamped in both English and Chinese translations, came from Sherman Cochran's book *Big Business in China: Sino-Foreign Rivalry in the Cigarette Industry 1890–1930* (Cambridge, MA: Harvard University Press, 1980), a key text for Xu Bing's research. While Cochran's book tells a two-sided story of the tobacco industry in late nineteenth and early twentieth-century China, highlighting both powerful Chinese and foreign companies, Xu Bing focuses instead on the dominance of Western companies and, in particular, BAT.

28 Wu Hung, "Xu Bing's Tobacco Project and its Context," in *Xu Bing: Tobacco Project*, ed. John B. Ravenal (Richmond, VA: Virginia Museum of Fine Arts, 2011), 37–40.

29 Yin Jinan in a panel discussion that accompanied the exhibition at Shanghai Gallery of Art, printed in "Yancao jihua · Shanghai" Xueshu Tao Hui ["Tobacco Project—Shanghai" Academic Seminar] (2005), in 徐冰 – 烟草计划/*Xu Bing—Yancao jihua* [*Xu Bing—Tobacco Project*], ed. Wu Hung (Beijing: Zhongguo Renmin Daxue Chubanshe, 2006), 152.

30 Li Xu, "Yancao jihua Shanghai," 158. Li Xu was one of the curators of the 2000 Shanghai Biennial, discussed in Chapter 3.

31 Ibid., 158–160.

32 Coincidentally, a large-scale, digitally animated version of the scroll, created for the occasion of the 2010 Shanghai World Expo, now stands as the popular centerpiece of China Art Palace's collection.

33 Yin Jinan, recalling his own inclusion of the original *Traveling Down the River* in an exhibition that he curated in Shanghai two years prior, states "[Even] in Shanghai, *Traveling Down the River* attracted the most attention. I was surprised to find that such a painting would receive such attention in Shanghai," Yin Jinan, "Yancao jihua Shanghai," 166.

34 Ibid.

35 Gu Zheng, "Yancao jihua Shanghai," 162.

36 Ibid.

37 Xu Bing, interview by author.

38 Zhang Yimou in *Sky Ladder: The Art of Cai Guo-Qiang*, directed by Kevin Macdonald (Netflix, 2016), DVD. Also in this documentary, see Cai Guo-Qiang's response to the question, "Why do you collaborate with the Chinese government on these projects?": "Everywhere in the world, artists work for their own governments. … For example, for the London Olympics, Damien Hirst designed a national flag–inspired stage set for the arena. But this sort of thing is only an issue if you are Chinese. Working for my country only becomes problematic because I was born in China." See also coverage in this documentary of the artist's work on the 2014 APEC Conference, which highlights his frustrations over how he must compromise his original vision for the project while working with CCP officials in Beijing (e.g., he has to give up his plans for a projected video and the use of environmentally friendly fireworks). "The risk is the ceremony might become a standard fireworks show," Cai Guo-Qiang says. A CCP official, addressing Cai Guo-Qiang, says, "You have to figure out something creative with all these chains on you. I'm a pragmatist. Mao taught us to be practical and realistic. So, overall, our measures are in accordance with your idea. We'll support you only when you follow the rules," *Sky Ladder: The Art of Cai Guo-Qiang*.

39 Arif Dirlik and Xudong Zhang, *Postmodernism & China*, 3–4.

40 Wang Hui, "The Dialectics of Art and the Event," trans. Rebecca Karl, in *Cai Guo-Qiang: I Want to Believe*, eds. Thomas Krens and Alexandra Munroe (New York: Guggenheim Museum, 2008), 42–48.

41 In China, it is a common point of national pride that the Chinese invented gunpowder, but it was foreigners that subverted its use from one of celebration (through fireworks) to violent destruction (through weapons). Cai Guo-Qiang, who has lived outside of his home country of China for decades and who is currently residing in New York City, played with this local-versus-foreign dichotomy. The artist connects his experiments with fireworks, which he has been working with since the 1980s, to his upbringing in Quanzhou, a major manufacturing center of fireworks.

42 *Cai Guo-Qiang: I Want to Believe*, 116.

43 Alexandra Munroe, *Cai Guo-Qiang: I Want to Believe*, 25.

44 Aihwa Ong, who described Cai Guo-Qiang as an epitomizing "cosmopolitan artist" in "What Marco Polo Forgot: Contemporary Chinese Art Reconfigures the Global," in *Current Anthropology* 53, no. 4 (August 2012): 471–483, writes elsewhere that "despite the claims of some American scholars and policy makers that the emergence of the Pacific Rim powers heralds an irreducible cultural division between East and West, these parallel narratives … disguise common civilizational references in a world where the market is absolutely transcendental," Aihwa Ong, *Flexible Citizenship: The Cultural Logics of Transnationality*, 7.

45 See Chapter 2 for a description of the Oriental Pearl Radio and Television Tower.

46 Guo Xiaohong, "Shanghai APEC 2001: Its Significance," *2001 in China* (October 22, 2001), http://www.china.org.cn/english/20989.htm, accessed March 10, 2012.

47 See Chapter 1's mention of these buildings in relation to the opening credits to Yuan Muzhi's *Street Angel*.

48 "Guided by Mao Tse-tung's Thought," 18.

49 Yang Peiming, interview by author, February 21, 2010, Propaganda Poster Art Center, Shanghai, China. Zhang Yuqing's poster still appears in the exhibition's catalogue. See Knight and Chang, *Shanghai: Art of the City*, 200–201.

50 Jay Xu, "Director's Preface," in *Shanghai: Art of the City*, ix.

51 See Max Weber, *The Protestant Ethic and the Spirit of Capitalism* (1904–1905), ed. and trans. Peter Baehr and Gordon C. Wells (New York: Penguin Books, 2002). Weber is referring to Protestantism rather than Catholicism, which is the more specific reference conjured by Three on the Bund's cupola.

52 Recent East Asian scholarship has challenged Weber's thesis, as economists and social scientists look to Confucianism as a powerful cultural factor in the rise of the so-called Asian Tigers. Economist Hung-chao Tai, for example, credits certain Confucian values such as emphases on personal relations (*guanxi*) as significant contributors to the rise of Asian economies in the latter half of the twentieth century. See, among others, Hung-chao Tai, "The Oriental Alternative: An Hypothesis on Culture and Economy," in *Confucianism and Economic Development: An Oriental Alternative?* (Washington, DC: The Washington Institute Press, 1989), 6–37.

53 David Rodriguez Caballero, "East-West-East: Interview with Cai Guo-Qiang," in *Cai Guo-Qiang: On Black Fireworks* (Valencia: Institut Valencia d'Art Moderne, 2005), 123.

54 Cai Guo-Qiang, "A Little About Me and Peasant Da Vincis," in 蔡国强：农民达芬奇/*Cai Guo-Qiang: Nongmin Dafenqi/Cai Guo-Qiang: Peasant Da Vincis* (Shanghai: Rockbund Art Museum, 2010) (exhibition pamphlet), 35.

55 See Cai Guo-Qiang, 蔡国强：农民达芬奇/*Cai Guo-Qiang: Nongmin Dafenqi/Cai Guo-Qiang: Peasant Da Vincis* (Guilin, China: Guangxi Normal University Press, 2010).

56 Aihwa Ong, Introduction to *Worlding Cities: Asian Experiments and the Art of Being Global*, 1–2.

57 Zhang Huan released this statement about his World Expo sculpture: "As harmony grows among people as well as nations, peace will flourish in the world. *Hehe Xiexie* (Harmony) is the common dream of all inhabitants worldwide. As people advocate justice, pursue peace, and oppose war, a healthier environment is created on earth, making it more equal, more free and more gratifying. By establishing a new international order and the rising of great compassion, harmony can thrive in the world, with nature and in prospering times." Zhang Huan website, http://www.zhanghuan.com/worken/info_65.aspx?itemid=1053&parent&lcid=156, accessed June 1, 2011. *HeHe Xiexie* was located between the Chinese and Taiwanese Expo Pavilions. Mainland China and Taiwan have had infamously strained relations, with a history of military aggression resulting from the island's struggle for independence. However, these relations appear to be growing better in recent years, symbolized by mainland China's 2008 gifting of two giant pandas to Taiwan. This feel-good political gesture is blatantly mirrored in Zhang Huan's sculpture, which panders to the CCP's motto of building a "harmonious society" (和谐社会/*hexie shehui*).

58 For an insightful analysis of Zhang Huan's transition from performance artist in Beijing's East Village to global artist with large-scale production facilities in Shanghai, see Winnie Wong, "Chapter Three: True Art and True Love in the Model Bohemia," in *Van Gogh on Demand: China and the Readymade* (Chicago: University of Chicago Press, 2013), 115–119.

59 See Meiling Cheng's reading of Zhang Huan's work in her vivid accounts of post-socialist Chinese performance art in Meiling Cheng, *Beijing Xingwei: Contemporary Chinese Time-Based Art*, 14.

60 John J. Mack in *Zhang Huan: Altered States*, edited by Melissa Chiu (New York: Asia Society, 2007), introductory notes, n.p.

61 For a descriptive account of Zhang Huan's studio, see Wu Hung, 張洹工作室/ *Zhang Huan gongzuo shi* [*Zhang Huan's Studio*] (Guangdong: Guangxi Normal University Press, 2009).

62 Ai Weiwei raised this politically sensitive issue when he created artworks about, and challenged officials to account for, the thousands of children who died in poorly constructed schools during the 2008 Sichuan Earthquake. Many people have argued that the construction of the affected school buildings was substandard as a result of corrupt deals between local officials and under-supervised developers and builders.

63 Commenting on the demolition and well-attended protest party, Ai Weiwei stated, "You can't imagine that in Communist history, this would happen," Ai Weiwei cited in Edward Wong, "Chinese Authorities Raze an Artist's Studio," *New York Times* (January 12, 2011), http://www.nytimes.com/2011/01/13/world/asia/13china.html, accessed September 1, 2015.

64 Pamela Lee, for instance, concludes her compelling book on contemporary art and globalization with a Tweet regarding Ai Weiwei's 2011 arrest, arguing that the artist's legal troubles and commitment to free online communication "signals … the mortal prospects of a globalized art world uncontained by, or perhaps liberated from, its historically policed borders," Lee, *Forgetting the Art World*, 190–191.

From Shanghai to New York
by way of conclusion

In writing this book, I set out to examine Shanghai's ghosts, forgotten artists, and repressed cultural histories lingering beneath the city's designer surfaces. I explored how contemporary artists have confronted and constructed projects around Shanghai's specters. Considering the prevalence of superficial emphases on *old Shanghai* seen in contemporary Shanghai-based design projects like *Xintiandi* and Shanghai Tang, I, like many of the artists I presented (e.g., Ding Yi, Yang Fudong, Xu Bing), found it necessary to look in more depth at Shanghai's romanticized Republican-era past, when the city's global mythologies took root and some of the earliest theorizations of Chinese modernity first appeared.

A key theorist of Chinese modernity, author Zhang Ailing grew up in Republican Shanghai and later relocated to Hong Kong and ultimately to Los Angeles, where she adopted the name Eileen Chang. In *Lust, Caution*—what Taiwanese director Ang Lee, who adapted the novella to film, calls Zhang Ailing's most "beautiful" and "cruel" story—a Chinese patriot betrays her country over love perceived through a diamond ring.[1] An Indian-owned jewelry store in Shanghai's French Concession, and the store's windows onto the cinematic city, set the stage for this tale's climax, wherein the heroine decides to save the Japanese sympathizer she has been seducing with the covert intention of assassinating:

> Inside she could hear only the muffled buzz of the city outside—because of the war, there were far fewer cars on the road than usual. … Though she was vaguely aware that something was about to happen, her heavy head was telling her that it must all be a dream. She examined the ring under the lamplight, turning it over in her fingers. Sitting by the balcony, she began to imagine that the bright windows and door visible behind her were a cinema screen across which an action movie was being shown.[2]

In writing on espionage, sex, and love in foreign-occupied Shanghai, Zhang Ailing defined modernity in relationship to the city's hybrid spaces (French cafés, Indian-owned jewelry stores, cinematic windows), material possessions (diamonds), and human subjectivities (Western-influenced bourgeois perspectives, wills of national traitors). As with many of the artworks examined throughout this book, such as Pang Xunqin's watercolor *Such is Shanghai*, Zhang Ailing's writings picture Shanghai as a hotbed of collisions between local and international concerns that crystalized in the city's foreign-run locales and dazzling allures. Highlighting Shanghai's cultural eclecticism as both sparkling and sinister, Zhang Ailing foreshadowed, with grave intensity, our current climate, in which transnational exchanges fuel the world's major cities and feature prominently in artistic content and production. The tragic annihilation of *Lust, Caution*'s heroine finally reveals that Shanghai's fashionable hybrids constitute explosive entanglements.

In her 1943 essay "Chinese Life and Fashions," Zhang Ailing further defined Chinese modernity as *being in fashion*, which in Republican Shanghai meant hybridizing national tradition, foreign references, and urbane cosmopolitanism, represented in her characters' outward appearances and outlooks, in the spaces they inhabit, and in *haipai*, Shanghai's unique 1920s–30s cross-cultural style.[3] Zhang Ailing's vivid descriptions of modernity relied on shifting fashions and the unique urban terrains from which they sprang, and, like most of her compatriots, she pictured her own Republican Shanghai as China's most fashionable and modern city. Her stories and theories of modernity, which position Shanghai as their primary protagonist, support the stance underlying this book: art historians' recent discussions over the integration of nation-based non-Western modernities and contemporaneities are missing an important point. While remaining inseparable from their national contexts, models of modernity and contemporaneity, conceived of in relationship to art and visual culture, are above all else, as Zhang Ailing intimated, tied to their urban specificities. Since modern and contemporary art and related theories grow from cityscapes, shouldn't one of the most pressing tasks for the historian of twentieth and twenty-first-century art be the analysis of those alternative modernities and contemporaneities vis-à-vis the specific urban environs in and on which they act?

Today, the global positioning of art and design reverberates not only in the city of Shanghai but also in major metropolises around the world. Look, for example, to New York City and the recent exhibition "China: Through the Looking Glass," hosted by the Metropolitan Museum of Art. Celebrated as creating "A Dialogue between East and West," the exhibition integrated art, fashion, and film from ancient times to the present, posing an ambitious and wildly popular model for presenting visual culture transnationally and across time and media.[4] Co-organized by the Costume Institute and Department of Asian Art and curated by Costume Institute director Andrew Bolton in collaboration with Hong Kong–based film director Wong Kar-wai, who served as artistic director, "China: Through the Looking Glass" was hailed as "a stunning, cinematic journey in which magnificent examples of the haute couture and avant-garde ready-to-wear are presented alongside masterworks of Chinese art."[5] While signaling the hopeful promises of our increasingly globalized artistic and cultural spheres, the exhibition also registered some of the major problems associated with the global turn in contemporary art: uneven representation, cultural aestheticization, and national stereotyping.

On the evening of May 4, 2015, the Metropolitan Museum hosted its highest profile and most lucrative annual event, the Met Gala, which that spring celebrated "China: Through the Looking Glass." As per tradition, guests were encouraged to dress in line with the exhibition's theme, in this case the influence of traditional Chinese culture on modern and contemporary Western fashion. Gala attendees incorporated vague references to Chinese motifs, such as ancient seals, dragons, Tang Dynasty–style headdresses, and the color red.[6] The event's most spoken about (and largely derided) item of clothing, pop singer Rihanna's bright yellow caped gown with thick faux-fur trim and a sweeping circular train, appeared to be the evening's only dress by a Chinese designer, Guo Pei, who was coincidentally the sole fashion designer from mainland China prominently featured in the exhibition.[7] Glaringly missing from both gala and exhibition were contemporary Chinese artists and designers.[8]

The exhibition's twentieth and twenty-first-century fashions displayed were almost all designed by Western European and North American figures, highlighting Christian Dior (whose contemporary Chinese art–related branding campaign I discuss in Chapter 2), Yves Saint Laurent, Ralph Lauren, Alexander McQueen, Valentino, House of Chanel, and House of Givenchy, among others.[9] The historical referents, meanwhile, were almost all Chinese, culled from vast stretches of time and genres (e.g., ancient earthenware, dynastic embroidered silk, ink painting and calligraphy, white and blue porcelain, 1920s-era Shanghai movie starlet style, Mao suits), and all collapsed under the equivocal labels of "China" and "East." The exhibition's pairing of recent Western fashions with older Chinese costumes and decorative arts betrays the underlying premise that Chinese culture is inherently historic, traditional, steeped in the country's dynastic past, and influential, whereas Western culture is inherently modern, contemporary, fashionable, and referential—an essentializing myth steeped in divisive binaries that scholars, curators, and practitioners of contemporary art and design must finally move beyond.

The introductory wall text of "China: Through the Looking Glass" asserted:

Like Alice's make believe world [in Lewis Carroll's *Through the Looking-Glass*], the China mirrored in the fashions in this exhibition is wrapped in invention and imagination. Stylistically, they belong to the practice of Orientalism, which since the publication of Edward Said's seminal treatise … has taken on negative connotations of Western supremacy and segregation. … This exhibition

> attempts to propose a less politicized and more positivistic examination of Orientalism as a site of infinite and unbridled creativity. Through careful juxtaposition of Western fashions and Chinese costumes and decorative arts, it presents a rethinking of Orientalism as an appreciative cultural response to its encounters with the East. The ensuing dialogues … encourage new aesthetic interpretations and broader cultural understandings. As if by magic, the distance between East and West … diminishes.[10]

While purporting to free audiences from the negative traps of Orientalism, the exhibition embraced a declaredly depoliticized strategy of display wherein stylistic East/West divisions remained.[11]

"China: Through the Looking Glass" presented an eclectic mixture of Chinese decorative art objects spanning thousands of years. The curators aimed to fend off inevitable critiques of exoticization and offset the unevenness of the exhibition's modern and contemporary Western fashions versus traditional Chinese art and decorative arts through the prevalent display of Chinese films arranged by Wong Kar-wai and the inclusion of some historical examples of Western European–produced *chinoiserie*.[12] Consciously acknowledging that the entire show foregrounded imaginations of China, the exhibition's catalogue essays, wall texts, and press releases emphasized that "China: Through the Looking Glass" presented a fantasy—Western fashion designers' impressions of China, which were admittedly mostly gleaned through cinema, including 1920s–30s era Hollywood films mired in stereotypes, such as Chinese American actress Anna May Wong as *Chinese Dragon Lady*.[13] The exhibition's organizers had predicted the most difficult question that would be asked by critics: "Why didn't the exhibition show more of modern and contemporary China?"[14] The simple answer was that the exhibition was not about modern and contemporary China but about Chinese history and fantastical creative inspiration. The more complicated response was that any idea of China is always a fantasy, built, like attempts at definitively classifying an entire nation's contemporary art, on the myth of unified authenticity; consider the varied case studies I've presented in this book, the paradoxes they reveal, and how many of the artists and designers creating art in and about Shanghai come from and/or work in other cities in and out of mainland China.

Visitors to "China: Through the Looking Glass" could begin to glean insight into certain facets of contemporary culture in international context that moved beyond East-meets-West aesthetics, though not necessarily through the objects on display. The exhibition relied on loaded cross-cultural collaborations—between the Metropolitan Museum's East Asian Department (regarded as one of the Western world's most prestigious custodians of Asian art) and Costume Institute (sometimes belittled as populist purveyors of the decorative versus high arts); corporate sponsor, US-owned company Yahoo, which held a large stake in the PRC's online retailer Alibaba; the PRC's state-run Palace Museum in Beijing, which loaned Emperor Puyi's robes to the show; and fashion industry insiders and celebrity VIPS who attended the Met Gala, including overseas Chinese businesswoman and exhibition collaborator Wendy Deng and movie star Gong Li. Here, we see the intertwining not only of Chinese and Western styles but also of fashion and fine arts, art institutions and entrenched curatorial departments, governmental support, private corporate sponsorship, and celebrity culture.

The exhibition's wider invisible social phenomena, such as the prominent role Chinese garment workers play within the globalized fashion industry, still need to be more fully explored, especially amid the widespread promotion and consumption of luxury commodities within mainland China. The curators would have done well to recognize the rise of a contemporary Chinese art/fashion system as embodied in the fashion brand Shanghai Tang, collaborations between artists and fashion houses such as Liu Jianhua and Christian Dior, and hybrid fashion/design/art spaces such as *Xintiandi* and Three on the Bund. These art/fashion nexuses and spaces, which have sometimes fostered critical considerations of contemporary Chinese art or challenged the exploitative systems of globalization, comprise a multifaceted cultural terrain that should be acknowledged by exhibitions such as "China: Through the Looking Glass," positioned on the borders between art and fashion and Chinese and Western culture.

Had the organizers of "China: Through the Looking Glass" looked to include more current designers and artists from mainland China, they would have found many compelling figures, including the artists discussed throughout this book. In works by Yang Fudong, Zhou Tiehai, Xu Bing, and Cai Guo-Qiang, the dangers and disparities accompanying Shanghai's globalization and the globalization of the art world get critiqued, parodied, offset, or reframed in historic cross-cultural terms. In some cases, such as public projects by Ding Yi and installations made of ceramic objects or trash by Liu Jianhua, the revolutionary spirit of *haipai* returns, as artists represent Shanghai's harmful excesses and multivalent realities, hybridize media, reconfigure labor, or subvert the flows of monetary and cultural capital. Echoes of *old Shanghai* here serve as haunting reminders that the city's cosmopolitan facades mask fraught cultural histories that continue to resonate today, prompting re-imaginations of what a Chinese megacity, *above sea*, might have been and might yet be.

Notes

1 Ang Lee, Afterword to Zhang Ailing, 色,戒/*Se, jie/Lust,* Caution (1979), trans. Julia Lovell (New York: Anchor Books, 2007), 57. Lee directed the film version of Zhang Ailing's novella: *Lust, Caution,* directed by Ang Lee (United States: Focus Features, 2007), DVD.
2 Zhang Ailing, *Lust, Caution,* 25–26.

3 See Zhang Ailing's 1943 essay, "Chinese Art and Fashions," in which she defines Chinese modernity as operating on multiple levels—maintaining an insistence on the condition of the present, a stance against Chinese tradition (defined through the lens of Imperial China), and an entanglement with foreign influences. Zhang Ailing theorizes Chinese modernity in relationship to modern fashions that shed the past by removing the superfluous details that defined China's dynastic clothes. Zhang Ailing, "Chinese Life and Fashions" (1943), reprinted in *Lianhe wenxue (Unitas)* 3, no. 5 (1987) (Special issue on Eileen Chang): 65–71. See also postcolonial theorist Rey Chow's illuminating comments on this essay, in Chow, "Chapter Three: Modernity and Narration—in Feminine Detail," in *Woman and Chinese Modernity: The Politics of Reading Between West and East* (Minneapolis: University of Minnesota Press, 1991), 84–85.

4 See Thomas P. Campbell, Director's Forward, and Maxwell K. Hearn, "A Dialogue Between East and West," in Andrew Bolton et al., *China: Through the Looking Glass* (New York and New Haven: The Metropolitan Museum of Art and Yale University Press), 8, 13–14.

5 Thomas P. Campbell, Director's Forward, 8.

6 In this case, most guests wore loosely Chinese-themed gowns and accessories, such as models Jessica Hart, who wore a Chinese-seal-influenced gown by Valentino; Georgia May Jagger, who wore a dynastic robe-like dress by Gucci; and actress Sarah Jessica Parker, who wore a traditional Chinese imperial-style headdress by Cindy Chao.

7 Guo Pei is strikingly absent from the catalogue.

8 The curators did make efforts to move beyond simplistic binary oppositions, for example, in the inclusion of the cross-cultural origins of the Willow Pattern and the juxtaposition of Ming vases with Dutch and English knockoffs.

9 The exhibition's catalogue featured Yves Saint Laurent, Ralph Lauren, Oscar de la Renta, Christian Dior, Roberto Cavalli, Cristobal Balenciaga, Dries Van Noten, Vivienne Tam, Callot Soeurs, Jason Wu, Pierre-Louis Pierson, Main Bocher, Louis Vuitton, Coco Chanel, Jean Paul Gaultier, Alexander McQueen, Vivienne Westwood, Travis Banton, Vitaldi Babani, Anna Sui, Emilio Pucci, Paul Poiret, Missoni, Edward Molyneux, Rodarte, Mary Katrantzou, Maison Angès-Drécoll, Madeleine Vionnet, Giorgio Armani, Jeanne Lanvin, Valentino Garavani, Jean Patou, Charles James, Isabel Toledo, Martin Margiela, and Givenchy.

10 Introductory exhibition wall text, "China: Through the Looking Glass," Metropolitan Museum of Art, New York City, New York, United States, visited July 16, 2015.

11 As Rey Chow has convincingly argued, even seemingly appreciative cultural responses to the "Eastern other" can be loaded with biases. Chow quotes Italian director Bernardo Bertolucci's comments about his trip to China to make *The Last Emperor* (1987), a film that was projected onto a large gallery wall in "China: Through the Looking Glass": "I went to China because I was looking for fresh air. … It was love at first sight. … I thought the Chinese were fascinating. They have an innocence. They have a mixture of a people before consumerism, before something that happened in the West. Yet in the meantime they are incredibly sophisticated, elegant and subtle, because they are 4,000 years old," Bernardo

Bertolucci quoted in Rey Chow, "Seeing Modern China: Toward a Theory of Ethnic Spectatorship," in *Woman and Chinese Modernity*, 4. Here, Chow critiques Bertolucci's imposition of different registers of time onto Chinese people, observing "how positive, respectful, and admiring feelings for the 'other' can themselves be rooted in un-self-reflexive, culturally coded perspectives," Ibid.

12 Many of the films presented, including Bernardo Bertolucci's *The Last Emperor*, further enforce cultural stereotypes.

13 The exhibition catalogue includes important scholarly articles that tackled the problems of Orientialism and imagining China, such as Adam Geczy's "A Chamber of Whispers," Harold Koda's "Fashioning China," Mei Rado's "Imagery of Chinese Dress," and Homay King's "Cinema's Virtual Chinas," in *China: Through the Looking Glass*, 23–71.

14 For clips of related public relations discussions between curator Andrew Bolton, collaborator Anna Wintour, and members of the press in the PRC and the United States, see director Andrew Rossi's documentary, *The First Monday in May*.

Epilogue: Forgotten corners

A few years ago, my students and I organized an exhibition of contemporary photography from mainland China, presented in our small university-run gallery in Portland. The project began with a call for photographs, which we forwarded to Chinese art schools, museums, and cultural institutions; to individual artists, photographers, and photojournalists; and through Chinese social media channels such as Weibo and WeChat. We asked people to email photographs of contemporary life in the PRC and to consider, but not limit themselves to, themes such as urbanization versus developments in the rural countryside, the impact of foreign cultures on local identities, the environmental impacts of globalization, and gender issues amid societal shifts. We grew giddy at the abundant response. Hundreds of photographs streamed into our class's inbox. For the most part, the senders were previously unknown to me and my students. These strangers' submissions allowed us to see, through their eyes, a fuller representation of the PRC, a place whose modern and contemporary art we had been studying mainly through past exhibitions, scholarly articles, and survey texts.

We exhibited selections from all of those who answered the call—dozens of artists, filmmakers, photojournalists, students, professors, people from all walks of life—and later I published a bilingual catalogue. As signaled by its title, *Picturing Global China* (画说全球中国/*Hua shuo quanqiu zhongguo*), I myself was quick to adopt the *global China* buzz term. But the images generously submitted for the exhibition resisted any kind of universalizing globalism and created in its place a kaleidoscopic collage that began mapping the pluralistic dreams, realities, promises, and fissures of the PRC's radically altering landscapes amid globalization.

The photographs were shot all over mainland China—from the cosmopolitan capitals of Beijing and Shanghai to towns in the rural countryside in Henan Province, from ethnic minority villages in Yunnan and autonomous regions, such as Xinjiang, to fast-developing interior municipalities, like Chongqing. Taken from very personal, individual points of view and representing a wide variety of scenes, locales, people, and customs, these photographs unraveled the official nationalist rhetoric and foreign media hype surrounding global

China, showing the resounding ability of everyday images to debunk mythologies attached to a single nation's rise on an international stage. These surreal, mundane, experimental, and quixotic photographs tackled the ambitious goal of picturing global China but critically revealed that this lofty goal hovers constantly out of reach.

One of our exhibition's primary aims was to counter the male heteronormativity that dominated the field of contemporary Chinese art in the 1990s–2000s, and we were fortunate to be able to include many women artists and works that address sexuality, often vis-à-vis urban milieus. Numerous submissions came from Shanghai, such as artist Liu Tao's documentation of a private performance in the derelict muddy surrounds of Pudong International Airport, another symbol of the city's cosmopolitan status; film editor Liu Yuanyuan's images of a young woman's body photo-shopped over Shanghai's phallic skyscrapers; and scholar, photographer, and curator Gu Zheng's parodic photograph-of-a-photograph: the sparkling Liujiazui skyline hung over a shiny urinal. Liu Jiajia, a young female artist, sent in a set of photographs signaling how a new generation of Shanghai-based artists and intellectuals are critically responding to urban development while exploring alternative possibilities, past and future. The series, *The Forgotten Corner of the City was Quiet at Last*, comprises photographs of the streets of Shanghai, Liu Jiajia's hometown, as they have undergone rapid transformations (Plate 8). She sent in images of narrow *longtang* alleyways photographed in the mid-2000s and concrete high-rises in the same site shot six years later. She paired these images of impending demolition and disappearance with her own *cries of poetry*, which I translated as:

> As a city pursues rapid economic growth, it ignores ecology, environment, history, culture, and local architectural styles. … In the Moonlight I approached them. … Miss them. … Growing quietly near embrace them. Today gently touched by their sorrow I'm feeling their seclusions. My heart … feels the forgotten corners of the city that grow quiet at last.[1]

It is a widely held notion that translation inherently registers loss, encapsulated in the oft-cited Italian wordplay, *Traduttore, traditore* (*Translator, traitor*). Yet we continue to translate, because the alternative—to shut ourselves off from languages we don't readily understand—may result in nationalist isolationism and the halting of cross-cultural communication, generating losses far greater than the translator's betrayals. For the audience well versed in postmodern art theory, it seems naïve to think of art as capable of smoothly traversing national borders and cultural divides. Visual signifiers, like words, are deeply embedded in culture, with viewers evaluating images differently depending on their particular sociopolitical identities and experiences. As artist Yang Fudong remarked, images hold the power to delude.[2] Nonetheless, in artworks—as in photographs sent across seas, translated texts, cosmopolitan cities—there exists the potential for sharing diverse perspectives in and of our world.

Notes

1 Liu Jiajia, "The Forgotten Corner of the City was Quiet at Last," trans. by author and printed in *Picturing Global China* (Portland: University of Oregon and White Box, 2016), 47–48.
2 Yang Fudong, "Interview: The Power Behind," 175.

Bibliography

Archives

Asia Art Archive. Hong Kong, China.
Beijing Public Library, Special Collections. Beijing, China.
Cultural Revolution Archive of Private Collector Liu Debao. Shanghai, China.
Fudan University Archives, Special Collections. Shanghai, China.
Gu Wenda Studio Archives. Shanghai, China.
Hoover Institution Archives of Stanford University. Palo Alto, California, United States.
Liu Jianhua Studio Archives. Shanghai, China.
Lu Xun Museum Archives. Beijing, China.
Lu Xun Museum Archives. Shanghai, China.
Pang Xunqin Archives of Changhsu Museum. Changshu, Jiangsu, China.
Pang Xunqin Archives of Private Collector Pang Tao. Beijing, China.
Propaganda Poster Art Center Archives. Shanghai, China.
Shanghai Municipal Archives. Shanghai, China.
Shanghai Public Library, Special Collections. Shanghai, China.
ShanghART Gallery Archives. Shanghai, China.
Three Shadows Photography Art Centre and Archives. Beijing, China.
Xujiahui Library, Special Collections. Shanghai, China.

Sources

The names of Chinese authors who follow Chinese naming order are given with surname first and no comma. English titles designated in publications are listed after /. Titles that I have translated into English are enclosed in brackets. See chapter notes for Chinese characters of Chinese titles.

"A Vicious Motive, Despicable Tricks – A criticism of M. Antonioni's Anti-China Film 'China'." *Peking Review* 17, no. 5 (February 1, 1974): 8.
Adorno, Theodor, Walter Benjamin, Ernst Bloch, Bertolt Brecht, and Georg Lukács. *Aesthetics and Politics*. London: Verso, 1980.
Ai Weiwei, Feng Boyi, and Hua Tianxue. *Bu hezuo fangshi/Fuck Off*. Shanghai: East Link Gallery, 2000.
All About Shanghai: A Standard Guidebook. Hong Kong: Oxford University Press, 1935.

Andrews, Julia F. *Painters and Politics in the People's Republic of China, 1949–1979.* Berkeley and Los Angeles: University of California Press, 1994.

_____ "The Art of the Cultural Revolution," in Richard King (ed.), *Art in Turmoil: The Chinese Cultural Revolution, 1966–76.* Vancouver and Toronto: UBC Press, 2010, 27–57.

Andrews, Julia F. and Shen Kuiyi. *The Art of Modern China.* Berkeley: University of California Press, 2012.

Antoinette, Michelle. *Reworlding Art History: Encounters with Contemporary Southeast Asian Art after 1990.* Amsterdam and New York: Brill Academic Publishers, 2015.

Antoinette, Michelle and Caroline Turner, eds. *Contemporary Asian Art and Exhibitions: Connectivities and World Making.* Canberra: Australian National University Press, 2014.

Antonioni, Michelangelo. *Chung Kuo. Cina* [*China*], ed. Lorenzo Cuccu. Turin: Einaudi, 1974.

_____. *Michelangelo Antonioni: The Architecture of Vision: Writings and Interviews on Cinema*, ed. Marga Cottino-Jones, trans. Allison Cooper. Chicago: University of Chicago Press, 1991.

Art Research Center of the Literary and Arts Research Institute. "Pi heihua shi jia, Cuan dang qieguo shi zhen" ["Criticizing Black Painting Was False, Overthrowing the Party and Nation Was the True Intention"]. *Meishu* [*Fine Arts*], no. 2 (1977): 7.

Ballard, James Graham. *Miracles of Life: Shanghai to Shepperton, An Autobiography.* London: Fourth Estate, 2008.

Barboza, David. "Schooling the Artist's Republic of China." *New York Times* (March 30, 2008). http://www.nytimes.com/2008/03/30/arts/design/30barb.html.

Barthes, Roland. *The Fashion System.* New York: Hill and Wang, 1983.

Baudelaire, Charles. "The Painter of Modern Life," in Jonathan Mayne (ed.), *The Painter of Modern Life and Other Essays*, trans. Jonathan Mayne. New York: Da Capo Press, 1986, 1–40.

Benjamin, Walter. "Gespräch mit Anne May Wong: Eine Chinoiserie aus dem Alten Westen" ["Interview with Anna May Wong: A Chinoiserie from the Old West"]. *Die Literarische Welt* [*The Literary World*] 4, no. 27 (July 6, 1928): 213.

Bergère, Marie-Claire. *Shanghai: China's Gateway to Modernity*, trans. Janet Lloyd. Stanford, CA: Stanford University Press, 2009.

Beuys, Joseph. "An Appeal for an Alternative." in Kristine Stiles and Peter Selz (eds), *Documents of Contemporary Art: A Sourcebook of Artists' Writings and Theories.* Berkeley, CA: University of California Press, 1996, 636–638.

Bhabha, Homi. *The Location of Culture.* New York: Routledge, 1994.

Bolton, Andrew with John Galliano, Adam Geczy, Maxwell K. Hearn, Homay King, Harold Koda, Mei Mei Rado, and Wong Kar-wai. *China: Through the Looking Glass.* New York and New Haven: The Metropolitan Museum of Art and Yale University Press, 2015.

Brecht, Bertolt. "Fragen eines lesenden Arbeiters" ["Questions from a Worker Who Reads"], in Reinhold Grimm (ed.), *Bertolt Brecht, Poetry and Prose*, trans. Michael Hamburger. New York: Continuum, 2003, 63.

Caballero, David Rodriguez. "East-West-East: Interview with Cai Guo-Qiang," in *Cai Guo-Qiang: On Black Fireworks*. Valencia: Institut Valencia dArt Moderne, 2005: 104–131.

Cai Guo-Qiang. *Cai Guo-Qiang: Nongmin Dafenqi/Cai Guo-Qiang: Peasant Da Vincis*. Shanghai: Rockbund Art Museum, 2010.

_____. *Cai Guo-Qiang: Nongmin Dafenqi Cai Guo-Qiang: Peasant Da Vincis*. Guilin, China: Guangxi Normal University Press, 2010.

Chan, David, former director of Shanghai Gallery of Art. Interview by author, 3 June 2010, Shanghai. Audio recording. Osage Gallery, Shanghai, China.

Chen I-wan. "The Younger Group of Shanghai Artists." *T'ien Hsia Monthly* 5, no. 2 (September, 1937): 148.

Chen Sihe. "Gongren ticai shi haipai wenhua de yige chuantong" ["The Subject Matter of Workers is a Tradition of Shanghai Style"]. *Wenhui bao* [*Wenhui Newspaper*] (February 25, 2013): 10.

Cheng, Meiling. *Beijing Xingwei: Contemporary Chinese Time-Based Art*. London, New York, and Kolkata: Seagull Books, 2013.

Cheng Naishan. "Life in the Slow Lane." *Zing* (April 2008): 13.

Chiu, Melissa, ed. *Zhang Huan: Altered States*. New York: Asia Society, 2007.

Chiu, Melissa and Miwako Tezuka, eds. *Yang Fudong: Seven Intellectuals in a Bamboo Forest*. New York: Asia Society, 2009.

Chow, Rey. "China as Documentary: Some Basic Questions (inspired by Michelangelo Antonioni and Jia Zhangke)." *European Journal of Cultural Studies* (February 2014): 16–30.

_____. *Woman and Chinese Modernity: The Politics of Reading Between West and East*. Minneapolis: University of Minnesota Press, 1991.

Chung Kuo Cina. Directed by Michelangelo Antonioni. Milan: RAI Radiotelevisione Italiana, 1972.

Ciric, Biljana. *A History of Exhibitions: Shanghai 1979–2006*. Manchester: Centre for Contemporary Chinese Art, 2014.

Clark, David. "Contemporary Asian Art and Its Western Reception," in Melissa Chiu and Benjamin Genocchio (eds), *Contemporary Art in Asia: A Critical Reader*. Cambridge, MA and London: MIT Press, 2011, 154–162.

Clark, Timothy J. *The Painting of Modern Life: Paris in the Art of Manet and his Followers*. Princeton, NJ: Princeton University Press, 1984.

Cochran, Sherman. *Big Business in China: Sino-Foreign Rivalry in the Cigarette Industry 1890–1930*. Cambridge, MA: Harvard University Press, 1980.

Colmey, John. "Everything You Wanted to Know About the Handover (But Were Afraid to Ask)." *TIME* (Special Issue: Hong Kong, 1997): 115.

Crimp, Douglas, Lynne Cooke, and Kristin Poor, eds. *Mixed Use Manhattan: Photography and Related Practices, 1970s-Present*. Cambridge, MA: MIT Press, 2010.

Croizier, Ralph. "Post-Impressionists in Pre-War Shanghai: The Juelanshe (Storm Society) and the Fate of Modernism in Republican China," in John Clark (ed.), *Modernity in Asian Art*. Sydney, Australia: Wild Peony, 1993, 135–154.

Dal Lago, Francesca. "Crossed Legs in 1930s Shanghai: How 'Modern' the Modern Woman?." *East Asian History* 19 (June 2000): 103–144.

Danzker, Jo-Anne Birnie, Ken Lum, and Zheng Shengtian, eds. *Shanghai Modern, 1919–1945*. Munich: Museum Villa Stuck and Hatje Cantz, 2005.

de Certeau, Michel. *The Practice of Everyday Life*, trans. Steven Rendall. Berkeley: University of California Press, 1984.

Description of 2006 Shanghai Biennial. "World Events." Asia Art Archive. http://www.aaa.org.hk/WorldEvents/Details/5983.

Ding Yi, artist. Interview by author, 29 April 2010, Shanghai. Audio recording. Ding Yi's Studio, Shanghai, China.

Ding Yi. "Interview with Hans Ulrich Obrist," in *Hans Ulrich Obrist: The China Interviews*. Hong Kong and Beijing: Office for Discourse Engineering, 2009, 144–153.

Dirlik, Arif. "Global South: Predicament and Promise." *The Global South* 1, no. 1 (Winter 2007): 12–23.

Dirlik, Arif and Xudong Zhang. *Postmodernism & China*. Durham and London: Duke University Press, 2000.

Doran, Valerie C., ed. *China's New Art, Post-1989*. Hong Kong: Hanart TZ Gallery, 1993.

Dushi Fengguang/Cityscape. Directed by Yuan Muzhi. 1935. Shanghai: Mingxing Film Company.

Eco, Umberto. "De Interpretatione, Or the Difficulty of Being Marco Polo (On the occasion of Antonioni's "China" film)." *Film Quarterly* 30, no. 4 (Summer 1977): 8–12.

Elkins, James, ed. *Is Art History Global?*. New York and London: Routledge, 2006.

Enwezor, Okwui, Terry Smith, and Nancy Condee, eds. *Antinomies of Art and Culture*. Durham and London: Duke University Press, 2008.

Er Dongqiang, documentary photographer and cultural historian. Interview by author, 29 December 2009, Shanghai. Audio recording. Deke Erh Centre, Shanghai, China.

Fang Zengxian. "Preface to *2000 Shanghai Bienniale*," in Chen Long (ed.), *Shanghai shuangnian/Shanghai Biennial 2000*. Shanghai: Shanghai Art Museum, 2000, n.p.

Fei Xiaotong. *China's Gentry* (1948), ed. Margaret Park Redfield. Chicago and London: University of Chicago Press, 1953.

The First Monday in May. Directed by Andrew Rossi. New York: Relativity Studios, 2016.

Fong, Wen C. *Between Two Cultures: Late-Nineteenth-and Twentieth-Century Chinese Paintings from the Robert H. Ellsworth Collection in the Metropolitan Museum of Art*. New York: Metropolitan Museum of Art, 2001.

Foster, Hal, Rosalind Krauss, Yves-Alain Bois, and Benjamin Buchloh. *Art Since 1900: Modernism, Antimodernism, Postmodernism, Volume 2: 1945-Present*, 2nd edn. New York: Thames and Hudson, 2011.

Fu Lei. "Xunqin de Meng" ["Xunqin's Dream"]. *Yishu xunkan/L'Art* 1, no. 3 (September 1932): 12–13.

Gao Minglu. *The Wall: Reshaping Contemporary Chinese Art*. Beijing and Buffalo, NY: Millenium Art Museum and University of Buffalo, 2005.

____. *Total Modernity and the Avant-Garde in Twentieth Century Chinese Art*. Cambridge, MA: MIT Press, 2011.

____. "'Particular Time, Specific Space, My Truth': Total Modernity in Chinese Contemporary Art," in Terry Smith, Okwui Enwezor, and Nancy Condee (eds), *Antinomies of Art and Culture: Modernity, Postmodernity, Contemporaneity*. Durham, NC: Duke University Press, 2008, 133–164.

Garrett, Valery. *Chinese Dress: From the Qing Dynasty to the Present*. Rutland, VT: Tuttle Publishing, 2008.

Gladstone, Paul. *Contemporary Art in Shanghai: Conversations with Seven Chinese Artists*. Hong Kong: Blue Kingfisher, 2012.

Glissant, Édouard. *Poetics of Relation*, trans. Betsy Wing. Ann Abor: The University of Michigan Press, 2010.

Goldberger, Paul. "Shanghai Surprise: The Radical Quaintness of the Xintiandi District." *The New Yorker* (December 26, 2005). https://www.newyorker.com/magazine/2005/12/26/shanghai-surprise.

Gomorrah. Directed by Matteo Garrone. Italy: Fandango and RAI Cinema, 2008.

Goodman, Bryna. *Native Place, City, and Nation: Regional Networks and Identities in Shanghai, 1853–1937*. Berkeley, CA: University of California Press, 1995.

Gu Wenda, artist. Interview by author, 22 August 2008, Shanghai. Audio recording. Gu Wenda's Studio, Shanghai, China.

____. *Tiantang hongdeng (Jinmao dasha, Shanghai)/Heavenly Lantern (Jinmao Tower Shanghai)*, trans. David Mao. Shanghai: Gu Wenda Studio, 2005.

Gu Zheng, artist, curator, cultural critic, and cultural historian. Interview by author. 15 May 2010, Shanghai. Audio recording. Shanghai, China.

____. *Chengshi biaoqing/Expressions of the City*. Shenyang: Volumes Publishing Company, 2009.

"Guided by Mao Tse-tung's Thought: Red Guards Destroy the Old and Establish the New." *Peking Review* 9, no. 36 (September 2, 1966): 18.

Guo Xiaohong. "Shanghai APEC 2001: Its Significance," 2001 in China." October 22, 2001, http://www.china.org.cn/english/20989.htm.

Haishang chuanqi/I Wish I Knew. Directed by Jia Zhangke. 2010. Shanghai: Shanghai Film Group Corporation.

Hay, Jonathan. "Double Modernity, Para-Modernity," in Terry Smith, Okwui Enwezor, and Nancy Condee (eds), *Antinomies of Art and Culture: Modernity, Postmodernity, Contemporaneity*. Durham, NC: Duke University Press, 2008, 113–132.

Hou Hanru. "Shanghai Spirit: A Special Modernity," in Chen Long (ed.), *Shanghai shuangnian/Shanghai Bienniale 2000*. Shanghai: Shanghai Art Museum, 2000, n.p.

Hou Hanru and Hans-Ulrich Obrist. *Cities on the Move: Urban Chaos and Global Change – East Asian Art, Architecture, and Film Now*. London: Hayward Gallery, 1999.

Introductory Exhibition Wall Text. "China: Through the Looking Glass." Metropolitan Museum of Art, New York, 2015.

Introductory Wall Plaque. Shikumen Museum. *Xintiandi*, Shanghai, China, 2010.

Jameson, Fredric. *The Cultural Turn: Selected Writings on the Postmodern, 1983–1998*. London: Verso, 1998, 1–20.

____. *Postmodernism, or, the Cultural Logic of Late Capitalism*. Durham, NC: Duke University Press, 1991.

Jervis, John. "Sunflower Seeds: Ai Weiwei." *ArtAsiaPacific* 72 (March/April 2011), http://artasiapacific.com/Magazine/72/SunflowerSeedsAiWeiwei.

Jiang Qing. "Summary of the Forum on the Work in Literature and Art in the Armed Forces with Which Comrade Lin Piao Entrusted Comrade Chiang Ching." *Peking Review* 10, no. 23 (June 2, 1967): 10–16.

Joselit, David. *After Art*. Princeton, NJ: Princeton University Press, 2013.

Khullar, Sonal. *Worldly Affiliations: Artistic Practice, National Identity, and Modernism in India, 1930–1990*. Oakland: University of California Press, 2015.

King, Homay. *Lost in Translation: Orientalism, Cinema, and the Enigmatic Signifier*. Durham, NC: Duke University Press, 2010.

Knight, Michael and Dany Chan, eds. *Shanghai: Art of the City*. San Francisco: Asian Art Museum of San Francisco, 2010.

Kokas, Aynne. *Hollywood Made in China*. Berkeley and Los Angeles: University of California Press, 2017.

Krens, Thomas and Alexandra Munroe, eds. *Cai Guo-Qiang: I Want to Believe*. New York: Guggenheim Museum, 2008.

Kuo, Jason, ed. *Visual Culture in Shanghai, 1850s–1930s*. Washington, D.C.: New Academia Publishing, 2007.

Kwon, Miwon. "Is it a Small World After All?." *Empire/Globe: Art in International Networks*, 10 April 2004, Yale University, Whitney Humanities Center. Conference Presentation.

Lady Blue Shanghai. Directed by David Lynch. Shanghai: Christian Dior, 2010.

Laing, Ellen Johnston. *The Winking Owl: Art in the People's Republic of China*. Berkeley and Los Angeles: University of California Press, 1998.

Lee, Ang. "Afterword," in Zhang Ailing (ed.), *Lust, Caution*, trans. Julia Lovell. New York: Anchor Books, 2007, 59–61.

Lee, Leo Ou-fan. *Shanghai Modern: The Flowering of a New Urban Culture in China: 1930–1945*. Cambridge and London: Harvard University Press, 1999.

Lee, Pamela M. *Forgetting the Art World*. Cambridge, MA: MIT Press, 2012.

Leung, Simon, Janet A. Kaplan, Wenda Gu, Xu Bing, and Jonathan Hay. "Pseudo Languages: A Conversation with Wenda Gu, Xu Bing, and Jonathan Hay." *Art Journal* 58, no. 3 (Autumn, 1999): 86–99.

Li Baoquan. "Hongshui fan le" ["A Great Flood Rises"]. *Yishu Xunkan/L'Art* 1, no. 5 (October 11, 1932): 9.

Li, Jie. *Shanghai Homes: Palimpsests of Private Life*. New York: Columbia University Press, 2015.

Li Lei, artist and director of Shanghai Art Museum. Interview by author. 15 June 2010, Shanghai. Audio recording. Li Lei's Studio, Shanghai, China.

Li Xin, ed. *Shanghai Glamour*. Shanghai: Shanghai People's Fine Art Publishing House, 2010.

Liang, Samuel. "Amnesiac Monument, Nostalgic Fashion: Shanghai's New Heaven and Earth." *Wasafiri* 23, no. 3 (September 2008): 47–55.

____. *Mapping Modernity in Shanghai: Space, Gender, and Visual Culture in the Sojourners' City 1853–98*. New York: Routledge, 2012.

____. "Where the Courtyard Meets the Street: Spatial Culture of the Li Neighborhoods, Shanghai, 1870–1900." *Journal of the Society of Architectural Historians* 67, no. 4 (December 2008): 482–503.

Liu Debao, cultural producer and collector. Interview by author, 9 May 2010, Shanghai. Video recording. Private residence and archival warehouse of Liu Debao, Shanghai, China.

Liu Jianhua, artist. Interview by author. 17 August 2011, Shanghai. Audio recording. Liu Jianhua's Studio, Shanghai, China.

_____. *Dialectical Views on Social Spectacle*. Beijing and Seoul: Arario Gallery and Beijing Jinge Printing Co., 2007.

_____. *Export – Cargo Transit*. Shanghai: Shanghai Gallery of Art, 2008.

Liu Jiajia. "The Forgotten Corner of the City was Quiet at Last," in Jenny Lin (ed.), *Picturing Global China*, trans. Jenny Lin, 47–48. Portland: University of Oregon and White Box, 2016.

Lu, Hanchao. *Beyond the Neon Lights: Everyday Shanghai in the Early Twentieth Century*. Berkeley and Los Angeles: University of California Press, 2004.

Lu, Victoria, curator and former director of Shanghai MOCA. Interview by author. 8 June 2010, Shanghai. Audio recording. Shanghai MOCA, Shanghai, China.

Lu Xun. "Jingpai yu Haipai" ["Beijing Style and Shanghai Style"]. *Shenbao ziyou tan [Shenbao Free Talks]* (January 17, 1934): 15.

_____. *Selected Works of Lu Hsun*, trans. Yang Hsien-yi and Gladys Yang. Beijing: Foreign Language Press, 1956.

Maharaj, Sarat. "Counter Creed: Quizzing the Guangzhou Triennial 2008 according to James Joyce's 'Catechetical Interrogation.'" *Printed Project: 'Farewell to Post-Colonialism,' Querying the Guangzhou Triennial* 11 (2008): 8.

Malu Tianshi/Street Angel. Directed by Yuan Muzhi. 1937. Shanghai: Mingxing Film Company.

Mao, Zedong. *Quotations from Mao Tsetung*. Beijing: Foreign Language Press, 1972.

_____. *Mao Zedong's Talks at the Yan'an Conference on Literature and Art: A Translation of the 1943 Text with Commentary*, ed. Bonnie S. McDougall, trans. Bonnie S. McDougall. Ann Arbor: Center for Chinese Studies, University of Michigan, 1980.

Martin, Jean-Hubert. *Magiciens de la Terre*. Paris: Centre Pompidou, 1989.

Mathur, Saloni. "Museums and Globalization." *Anthropological Quarterly* 78, no. 3 (Summer 2005): 697–708.

Morton, Patricia. *Hybrid Modernities: Architecture and Representation at the 1931 Colonial Exposition, Paris*. Cambridge, MA: MIT Press, 2000.

Murphey, Rhoads. *Shanghai: Key to Modern China*. Cambridge, MA: Harvard University Press, 1953.

Ni Yide. "Juelanshe Xuanyan" ["Storm Society Manifesto"]. *Yishu Xunkan/L'Art* 1, no. 5 (October 11, 1932): 8.

_____. "Yishujia de Chun Meng" ["Artist's Spring Dream"]. *Yishu Suibi [Art Essay]*. Shanghai: Wenyi Chufangshi, 1999, 21–23.

Niu Ruchen. *Zhongguo diming youlai cidian/Chinese Placenames Original Dictionary*. Beijing: Central People's University Press, 1999.

Ong, Aihwa. *Flexible Citizenship: The Cultural Logics of Transnationality*. Durham, NC: Duke University Press, 1999.

_____. "What Marco Polo Forgot: Contemporary Chinese Art Reconfigures the Global." *Current Anthropology* 53, no. 4 (August 2012): 471–483.

Ong, Aihwa and Ananya Roy, eds. *Worlding Cities: Asian Experiments and the Art of Being Global*. Malden, MA: Wiley-Blackwell, 2011.

Pang Jun. "Illuminator of Modern Chinese Design: Pang Xunqin," in Wu Wenxiong (ed.), *Pang Xunqin: Zhongguo Chuangtong Tuan (China Decoration Figure Pang Xunqin)*, 56–62. Shanghai: Renmin Meishu Chubanshi and Changshu Fine Art Museum, 2009.

Pang, Laikwan. *The Art of Cloning: Creative Production during China's Cultural Revolution*. New York: Verso, 2017.

Pang Tao, artist and daughter of Pang Xunqin. Interview by author. 6 September 2011, Beijing. Audio recording. Private residence and studio of Pang Tao, Beijing, China.

Pang Xunqin. *Gongyi meishu sheji* [*Industrial and Fine Art Design*]. Beijing: People's Fine Arts Publishing Company, 1981.

_____. *Jiushi zheyang zou guolai de* [*This is the way it happened/This is the path I traveled down*]. Beijing: Shenghua, douxin, xin he sanlian shudian, 2005.

_____. *Pang Xunqin wenxuan: lun yishu sheji meiyu* [*Pang Xunqin's essays: on art, design, fine arts education*]. Jiangsu: Jiangsu Jiaoyu Chu Ban Shi/Jiangsu Education Publishing House, 2007.

Pann, Lynn. *Shanghai Style: Art and Design Between the Wars*. Hong Kong: Joint Publishing Co., 2008.

Perlez, Jane. "Where the Wild Things Are: China's Art Dreamers at the Guggenheim." *New York Times* (September 20, 2017). https://www.nytimes.com/2017/09/20/arts/design/guggenheim-art-and-china-after-1989.html?mcubz=0.

Pickowicz, Paul, Kuiyi Shen, and Yingjin Zhang. *Liangyou, Kaleidoscopic Modernity and the Shanghai Global Metropolis, 1926–1945*. Leiden: Brill, 2014.

Pollard, David E. *The True Story of Lu Xun*. Hong Kong: The Chinese University Press, 2002.

Proser, Adriana. "Seven Sages of the Bamboo Grove: Chinese Models of the Unconventional," in *Yang Fudong: Seven Intellectuals in a Bamboo Forest*, Melissa Chiu and Miwako Tezuka (eds). New York: Asia Society, 2009, 25–27.

Qiu, Ruimin, artist and director of Shanghai Oil Painting and Sculpture Institute. Interview by author. 3 September 2011. Audio recording. Private residence and studio of Qiu Ruimin, Shanghai, China.

_____. ed. *40 Years of Shanghai Youhua Diaosu Yuan (Shanghai Oil Painting and Sculpture Institute): 1964–2005*. Shanghai: Shanghai Jiaoyu Chubanshe, 2005.

Rent Collection Courtyard: Sculptures of Oppression and Revolt. Beijing: Foreign Language Press, 1968.

"Repudiating Antonioni's Anti-China Film." *Peking Review* 17, no. 8 (February 22, 1974): 13.

Rowe, Peter G. and Seng Kuan. *Shanghai: Architecture and Urbanism for Modern China*. New York: Prestel, 2004.

Sassen, Saskia. *The Global City: New York, London, Tokyo*. Princeton, NJ: Princeton University Press, 2001.

Saviano, Roberto. *Gomorrah: A Personal Journey into the Violent International Empire of Naples' Organized Crime System*, trans. Virginia Jewiss. New York: Picador and Farrar, Straus and Giroux, 2006.

Sejie/Lust, Caution. Directed by Ang Lee. 2007. United States: Focus Features.

"Shanghai, Tianjin xianxi xinde geming re" ["Shanghai and Tianjin stir up new revolutionary heat"]. *Bo er ta la bao* [*Bortala Newspaper*] (August 26, 1966): n.p.

Shanghai Tang. http://www.shanghaitang.com/en/shanghai-tang.

Shi Dawei, ed. *Shanghai Zhongguo huayuan/Shanghai Chinese Painting Academy: 1956–2004*. Shanghai: Shanghai Renmin Meishu Chuban Shi, 2005.

Shih, Shu-mei. *The Lure of the Modern: Writing Modernism in Semicolonial China, 1917–1937*. Berkeley and Los Angeles: University of California Press, 2001.

Silbergeld, Jerome. "Photography Goes to the Movies: On the Boundaries of Cinematography, Photography, and Videography in China," in Jerome Silbergeld, Dora C. Y. Ching, Judith G. Smith, and Alfreda Murck (eds), *Bridges to Heaven: Essays on East Asian Art in Honor of Professor Wen C. Fong*. Princeton, NJ: P.Y. and Kinmay W. Tang Center for East Asian Art and Department of Art and Archaeology, Princeton University, 2011, 875–906.

Siu, Helen F. "Retuning a Provincialized Middle Class in Asia's Urban Postmodern: The Case of Hong Kong," in Aihwa Ong and Ananya Roy (eds), *Worlding Cities: Asian Experiments and the Art of Being Global*. Malden, MA: Wiley-Blackwell, 2011, 129–159.

Sky Ladder: The Art of Cai Guo-Qiang. Directed by Kevin Macdonald. 2016. New York: Netflix.

Smith, Terry. *Contemporary Art: World Currents*. Upper Saddle River, New Jersey, and Hong Kong: Prentice Hall, 2011.

Song Tao, artist. Interview by author. 27 December 2009, Shanghai. Audio recording. Private residence and studio of Song Tao, Shanghai, China.

Sontag, Susan. *On Photography*. New York: Farrar, Straus and Giroux, 1977.

Spivak, Gayatri Chakravorty. "Can the Subaltern Speak?," in Patrick Williams and Laura Chrisman (eds), *Colonial Discourse and Postcolonial Theory*. New York: Columbia University Press, 1994, 66–112.

_____. *A Critique of Postcolonial Reason: Toward a History of the Vanishing Present*. Cambridge, MA: Harvard University, 1999.

Stallabrass, Julian. *Art Incorporated: The Story of Contemporary Art*. Oxford: Oxford University Press, 2004.

Stella. "Shanghai Tang Café, Modern Chinese Cuisine." *Zing* (February 2010): 5.

Stranahan, Patricia. *Underground: The Shanghai Communist Party and the Politics of Survival, 1927–1937*. Lanham, MD: Rowman & Littlefield Publishers, 1998.

Sullivan, Michael. *The Meeting of Chinese Eastern and Western Art*. Berkeley: University of California Press, 1973.

Summers, David. *Real Spaces: World Art History and the Rise of Western Modernism*. London: Phaidon, 2003.

Tai, Hung-chao. "The Oriental Alternative: An Hypothesis on Culture and Economy," in *Confucianism and Economic Development: An Oriental Alternative?*. Washington, D.C.: The Washington Institute Press, 1989, 6–37.

Tang, David. *Chink in the Armour*. Hong Kong: Enrich Publishing, 2010.

Tang, Xiaobing. *Origins of the Chinese Avant-Garde: The Modern Woodcut Movement*. Berkeley: University of California Press, 2007.

The True Cost. Directed by Andrew Morgan. United States: Life is My Movie Entertainment Company, 2015.

Tung, Lily. "Arts Abroad; Spreading Opennness With a 3rd Shanghai Biennale." *New York Times* (May 30, 2001), http://www.nytimes.com/2001/05/30/arts/arts-abroad-spreading-openness-with-a-3rd-shanghai-biennale.html.

Turner, Matthew. "Early Modern Design in Hong Kong." *Design Issues* 6, no. 1 (Autumn 1989): 79–91.

Visser, Robin. *Cities Surround the Countryside: Urban Aesthetics in Postsocialist China.* Durham, NC: Duke University Press, 2010.

Wakeman Jr., Frederic and Wen-hsin Yeh, eds. *Shanghai Soujourners.* Berkeley: Institute of East Studies, University of California at Berkeley, 1992.

Wang Dongling, artist. Interview by author. 17 April 2010, Hangzhou. Wang Dongling's studio, Hangzhou, China.

Wang, Edward. "Air Pollution Linked to 1.2 Million Premature Deaths in China." *New York Times* (April 1, 2013). http://www.nytimes.com/2013/04/02/world/asia/air-pollution-linked-to-1-2-million-deaths-in-china.html.

Wang Huangsheng. "Preface to the Third Guangzhou Triennial," in Johnson Chang Tsong-Zung, Gao Shiming, and Sarat Maharaj (eds), *Farewell to Post-Colonialism: The Third Guangzhou Triennial.* Guangzhou: Guangdong Museum of Art, 2008, 30–31.

Wang Hui. *China's New Order: Society, Politics, and Economy in Transition*, trans. Theodore Huters and Rebecca Karl. Cambridge, MA: Harvard University Press, 2003.

_____. "The Dialectics of Art and the Event," in Thomas Krens and Alexandra Munroe (eds), *Cai Guo-Qiang: I Want to Believe*, trans. Rebecca Karl. New York: Guggenheim Museum, 2008, 42–49.

_____. "Imagining Asia: A Genealogical Analysis," in Melissa Chiu and Benjamin Genocchio (eds), *Contemporary Art in Asia: A Critical Reader.* Cambridge, MA and London: MIT Press, 2011, 87–106.

Wang Jun, curator and former director of Epson Gallery, Shanghai. Interview by author. 17 May 2010, Shanghai. Audio recording. Shanghai, China.

Wang Nanming. "The Shanghai Art Museum Should Not Become a Market Stall in China for Western Hegemony – A Paper Delivered at the 2000 Shanghai Biennale," in Wu Hung (ed.) with Peggy Wang, *Contemporary Chinese Art: Primary Documents.* New York: The Museum of Modern Art, 2010, 353.

Wasserstrom, Jeffery. *Global Shanghai, 1850–2010: A History in Fragments.* New York: Routledge, 2009.

Weber, Max. *The Protestant Ethic and the Spirit of Capitalism*, ed. Peter Baehr and Gordon C. Wells, trans. Peter Baehr and Gordon C. Wells. New York: Penguin Books, 2002.

Wolf, Charles, Brian G. Chow, Gregory S. Jones, and Scott Harold. *China's Expanding Role in Global Mergers and Acquisitions Markets.* Santa Monica, CA: RAND Corporation, 2011.

Wong, Edward. "Chinese Authorities Raze an Artist's Studio." *New York Times* (January 12, 2011), http://www.nytimes.com/2011/01/13/world/asia/13china.html.

Wong, Winnie. *Van Gogh on Demand: China and the Readymade.* Chicago: University of Chicago Press, 2013.

Wood, Benjamin, architect. Interview by author. 1 April 2010, Shanghai. Audio recording. Benjamin Wood's Studio, Xintiandi, Shanghai, China.

_____. "Xintiandi in Shanghai." *Zing* (April 2006): 20.

Wu, Chin-tao. "Biennials without Borders," in Simon Leung and Zoya Kocur, *Theory in Contemporary Art since 1985*, 2nd edn. Oxford: Blackwell Publishing, 2012, 56–63.

_____. "Missing in Action: Women Artists and Biennials." National Taiwan Normal University Graduate Institute of Art History, May 26, 2017. Conference Paper.

Wu Hung, ed. *Xu Bing – Yancao jihua* [Xu Bing – *Tobacco Project*]. Beijing: Zhongguo Renmin Daxue Chubanshe, 2006.

_____. *Zhang Huan gongzuo shi* [*Zhang Huan's Studio*]. Guangdong: Guangxi Normal University Press, 2009.

_____. "A Case of Being 'Contemporary': Conditions, Spheres, and Narratives of Contemporary Chinese Art," in Terry Smith, Okwui Enwezor, and Nancy Condee (eds), *Antinomies of Art and Culture: Modernity, Postmodernity, Contemporaneity*. Durham, NC: Duke University Press, 2008, 290–360.

_____. *Wu Hung on Contemporary Chinese Artists*. Hong Kong: Timezone 8, 2009.

_____. "Xu Bing's Tobacco Project and its Context," in John B. Ravenal (ed.), *Xu Bing: Tobacco Project*. Richmond, VA: Virginia Museum of Fine Arts, 2011, 37–40.

_____. *Contemporary Chinese Art*. New York: Thames and Hudson, 2014.

Wu Hung and Huang Rui, eds. *Beijing 798: Reflections on Art, Architecture and Society in China*. Beijing: Timezone 8, 2008.

Wu Qington. *Zhou Enali zai wenhua dageming zhong: huiyi Zhou Enlai tong Lin Biao Jiang Qing liang ge fangeming jituan de douzheng* [*Zhou Enlai in the "Cultural Revolution": Recalling Zhou's Struggle against Jiang Qing and Lin Biao, Two Counter-revolutionary Figures*]. Beijing: Chinese Communist Party History Publishing House, 2002.

Wue, Roberta. *Art Worlds: Artists, Images and Audiences in Late Nineteenth-Century Shanghai*. Hong Kong: Hong Kong University Press, 2014.

Xiao, Jiwei. "A Traveller's Glance: Antonioni in China." *New Left Review* 79 (January–February 2013): 103–120.

Xu Bing, artist. Interview by author. 13 May 2010, Beijing. Audio recording. Beijing, China.

Yang Fudong, artist. Interview by author. 13 September, 2008, Shanghai. Audio recording. Shanghai, China.

Yang Peiming, collector. Interview by author. 21 February 2010, Shanghai. Propaganda Poster Art Center, Shanghai, China.

Ye, Annie, marketer for Shui-On Group. Interview by author. 1 March 2010, Shanghai. Shui-On Headquarters, Shanghai, China.

Yeh, Catherine. *Shanghai Love: Courtesans, Intellectuals, and Entertainment Culture, 1850–1911*. Seattle: University of Washington Press, 2006.

Yoshihisa Higasa. "We Follow Chairman Mao's Revolutionary Line on Art and Literature," *China Reconstructs* XVII, no. 4 (April 19, 1968): 32–33.

Yue, Meng. *Shanghai and the Edges of Empire*. Minneapolis: University of Minnesota Press, 2006.

Zhang Ailing. "Chinese Life and Fashions" (1943). *Lianhe wenxue (Unitas)* 3, no. 5 (1987) (Special issue on Eileen Chang): 65–71.

Zhang Huan. http://www.zhanghuan.com/.

Zhang Qing. "Beyond Left and Right: Transformation of the Shanghai Biennial," in Chen Long (ed.), *Shanghai shuangnian/Shanghai Biennial 2000*, Shanghai: Shanghai Art Museum, 2000, n.p.

Zhang Xudong, *Whither China? Intellectual Politics in Contemporary China*. Durham and London: Duke University Press, 2001.

Zhang Yaxuan and Molly Nisbet. *Yang Fudong: Seven Intellectuals in a Bamboo Forest*, ed. Angie Baecker. Beijing: Office for Discourse Engineering, 2008.

Zhang, Yingjin. *Cinema and Urban Culture in Shanghai, 1922–1943*. Stanford, CA: Stanford University Press, 1999.

Zhang Zhen. *An Amorous History of the Silver Screen: Shanghai Cinema, 1896–1937*. Chicago and London: University of Chicago Press, 2005.

Zheng Shengtian and Melissa Chiu, eds. *Art and China's Revolution*. New York and New Haven: Asia Society in association with Yale University Press, 2008.

Zhou Tiehai, artist. Interview by author. 18 August 2008, Shanghai. Audio recording. Zhou Tiehai's Studio, Shanghai, China.

_____. *The Art of Zhou Tiehai*. Shanghai: Shanghai Art Museum, 2006.

Zhu Boxiong and Chen Ruilin, eds. *Zhongguo xihua wushi nian, 1898–1949* [*Fifty Years of Western Painting in China*]. Beijing: People's Art Publishing House, 1989.

Zhuang, Jiayun. "Left Hand and Right Hand—Waving from the Past in the Post-Socialist Factory." *Bad Hauntings: Contemporary Asian Art in the Post-Era*, Association for Asian Studies (AAS) annual conference, 2011, Honolulu, Hawaii. Conference Presentation.

Zukin, Sharon. *Loft Living: Culture and Capital in Urban Change*. Baltimore: Johns Hopkins University Press, 1982.

Index

Page numbers in italics indicate an illustration.